T. S. ELIOT AN

All of Eliot's poetry, from 'The [...] to 'Little Gidding', is alive to [...] political problems of prejudice. [...] the great poet of an age when the siege of contraries is unprecedentedly fierce: never has the accusation of prejudice been more inflamed and yet never has there been so wide an agreement that no understanding of anything is possible without preconceptions. *T. S. Eliot and Prejudice* considers each phase of Eliot's poetic career in the light of these vital difficulties and challenges.

Christopher Ricks is at Boston University, having taught previously in Oxford, Bristol and Cambridge. He is the author of *Milton's Grand Style* (1963), *Tennyson* (1972, revised 1987), *Keats and Embarassment* (1974), *The Force of Poetry* (1984), and *T S Eliot and Prejudice* (1988). He edited *The Poems of Tennyson* (revised 1987) and *The New Oxford Book of Victorian Verse* (1987), and co-edited *The State of the Language* (1980 and 1990, Faber) and *The Faber Book of America* (1992).

T. S. ELIOT
AND PREJUDICE

Christopher Ricks

faber and faber

LONDON · BOSTON

First published in 1988
by Faber and Faber Limited
3 Queen Square London WC1N 3AU
This paperback edition first published in 1994

Photoset by Wilmaset, Birkenhead, Wirral
Printed in Great Britain by Clays Ltd, St Ives plc

Christopher Ricks is hereby identified as author of this work in
accordance with Section 77 of the Copyright, Designs and
Patents Act 1988

A CIP record for this book
is available from the British Library
ISBN 0-571-17035-8

CONTENTS

CONTENTS

It is easy indeed, to call names, or to separate the word *prejudice* from the word *reason*; but not so easy to separate the two things.

The best way to prevent our running into the wildest excesses of prejudice and the most dangerous aberrations from reason, is, not to represent the two things as having a great gulph between them, which it is impossible to pass without a violent effort, but to show that we are constantly (even when we think ourselves most secure) treading on the brink of a precipice; that custom, passion, imagination, insinuate themselves into and influence almost every judgment we pass or sentiment we indulge, and are a necessary help (as well as hindrance) to the human understanding; and that, to attempt to refer every question to abstract truth and precise definition, without allowing for the frailty of prejudice, which is the unavoidable consequence of the frailty and imperfection of reason, would be to unravel the whole web and texture of human understanding and society.

> William Hazlitt, *The Atlas*,
> 18 April 1830

This week we are printing two articles presenting the opposite sides of an ancient controversy – that between the sport and the grind. The discussion, though never final, is always interesting, when it is the attempt of each to justify himself without injustice to the opponent. No one need hope to settle the dispute. But if all prejudice and misunderstanding are cleared away, it is possible for each partisan, while retaining his own opinions, to see that there is much reason in the other man's contention and after all that's the best excuse for most arguments; for each side to acknowledge sympathetically the right of the other to his own point of view. And in this case the divergence – in ideals – may not be so great as is thought.

> 'The Point of View', unsigned editorial by
> T. S. Eliot (Class of 1910) in the *Harvard Advocate*,
> 20 May 1909

and the sea at morning like a presumption of the mind.

> from *Anabasis*, the translation by T. S. Eliot of
> *Anabase*, a poem by St.-John Perse

I

PRUFROCK AND OTHER OBSERVATIONS

J. Alfred Prufrock

PRUFROCK

THE EGOIST, Ltd., is publishing in May a small book of Poems

Prufrock and other Observations

by Mr. T. S. ELIOT.   Price 1s.; postage 2d.

The month is May 1917. Think what it is then, to wonder whether to cough up a shilling. The title gives little away. Yet Eliot, as he said two years later of Hawthorne, has even the minor token of literary genius, the genius for titles.[1] The unobtrusive word 'Observations' has its felicity, in perfectly balancing – as a poem itself should – the claims of the perceptive eye against those of the wise mind, observations being both the remarkings and the remarks. But it is 'Prufrock' which famously, enduringly, did the trick.

It was shrewd of *The Egoist* to have at the head of the advertisement the ineffaceable surname alone, and only subsequently to mount the full title. It was more than shrewd of Mr T. S. Eliot not to muster the full title of the poem for the volume's title.[2] Eliot's achievement has since been such that all

1 – *The Athenaeum*, 25 April 1919.
2 – Lyndall Gordon twice gives the volume's title as *The Love Song of J. Alfred Prufrock and Other Observations*, in *Eliot's Early Years* (1977), pp. 68, 85.

I

the world has come to know not only what *Prufrock* means but who Prufrock is. Ezra Pound misreported at the time, in the *Little Review*,[1] that *The Egoist* was 'in the act of publishing Mr. Eliot's poems, under the title *Mr. Prufrock and Observations*'. Fortunately not, for the success of the title of the 'small book of Poems' was partly in not letting on. Nor is it an ordinary thing to do, to pluck a name from within the title of a poem and to let it speak volumes.

It is a measure of the distance between a great poet and his imaginative patron (John Quinn) or his acute publisher (Alfred Knopf), that the patron and the publisher should have concurred in believing that the title *Prufrock and Other Observations* would damage sales and should have settled for the later publication in the USA of *Poems* by T. S. Eliot.[2]

Then, back in 1917, before ever you entered upon reading a line of poetry by Mr T. S. Eliot, you would have been met by the title of the first poem in this, his first book of poems: 'The Love Song of J. Alfred Prufrock'. At once the crystalline air is thick with incitements to prejudice. For we are immediately invited, or incited, to think and to feel our way through a prejudicial sequence. First, as often with prejudice, comes a concession: that of course a man cannot be blamed for being called Prufrock. Second, that nevertheless the name does have comical possibilities, given not only the play of 'frock' against 'pru' – prudent, prudish, prurient – but also the suggestive contrariety between splitting the name there, at *pru* and *frock*, as against splitting it as *proof* and *rock*. And, third, that therefore a man in these circumstances might be well advised to call himself John A. Prufrock or J. A. Prufrock, rather than to risk the roll, the rise, the carol, the creation of 'J. Alfred Prufrock'. Maugham is a name that could countenance W. Somerset as its herald; W. Somerset Prufrock would have been another story-teller. And then we are further invited to think and to feel that should Mr Prufrock, as is his right, plump for J. Alfred Prufrock, he must not then expect the words 'The Love Song of' to sit happily

1 – May 1917.
2 – *The Waste Land: A Facsimile and Transcript of the Original Drafts*, edited by Valerie Eliot (1971), p. xvii.

in his immediate vicinity. The tax returns of J. Alfred Prufrock, fine, but a love song does not harmonize with the rotund name, with how he has chosen to think of himself, to sound himself. He has, after all, chosen to issue his name in a form which is not only formal but unspeakable: no one, not even the most pompous self-regarder, could ever introduce himself as, or be addressed as, J. Alfred Prufrock. He has adopted a form for his name which is powerfully appropriate to a certain kind of page but not to the voice, and which is therefore for ever inimical to the thought of love's intimacy. 'I'm in love.' 'Who's the lucky man?' 'J. Alfred Prufrock.' Inconceivable.

But then life often involves these choices and these sacrifices; if you want to cut a public figure and to wax ceremonious and to live on the business page or the title page, you may have to relinquish the more intimate happinesses. And all of this is unobtrusively at work before ever we have arrived at a word of the poem.

Unjust, of course, these incitements. What's in a name? Yet even with something like a name, which is usually given and not chosen, we manage to exercise choices, to adopt a style which becomes our man, or, if we are Prufrock, to wear our name with a difference. Then a name starts to become so mingled with its owner as to call in question which is doing the owning.

'The Love Song of J. Alfred Prufrock': even while the title tempts us – not necessarily improperly – to suspect things about the man, it raises the question of whether we are entitled to do so. Can we deduce much from so localized a thing as how a man chooses to cast his name? Can we deduce anything? But then can we imagine that one either could or should refrain from doing any deducing? Straws in the wind are often all that we have to go on. 'And should I have the right to smile?': the question ends the succeeding poem, 'Portrait of a Lady',[1] but it is a question that haunts the whole book.

As so often with prejudice, one kind of categorizing melts into another. For the teasing speculation as to what sort of man

1 – Quotations from Eliot's poems, by kind permission of Faber and Faber and Mrs Eliot, are from *Collected Poems 1909–1962* (1963); on the text of Eliot, see A. D. Moody, *Thomas Stearns Eliot: Poet* (1979), Appendix A.

names himself in such a way, especially given 'Prufrock' as his climax, merges itself in the class question, not just what class of man but what social class. Calling oneself J. Alfred Prufrock has an air of prerogative and privilege. The class presumption in turn brings a whole culture and society with it.

Eliot, praising Kipling, said that he would probably never have given his poem the title 'The Love Song of J. Alfred Prufrock' 'but for a title of Kipling's that stuck obstinately in my head, "The Love Song of Har Dyal"'.[1]

> Alone upon the housetops to the North
> I turn and watch the lightnings in the sky –
> The glamour of thy footsteps in the North.
> *Come back to me, Beloved, or I die!*
>
> Below my feet the still bazar is laid –
> Far, far below the weary camels lie –
> The camels and the captives of thy raid.
> *Come back to me, Beloved, or I die!*
>
> My father's wife is old and harsh with years,
> And drudge of all my father's house am I –
> My bread is sorrow and my drink is tears.
> *Come back to me, Beloved, or I die!*

How gratifyingly the words 'The Love Song of' accommodate themselves to such a name as Har Dyal; and yet how disconcerting is this accommodation, since it is so largely the product of prejudice, of plangent acquiescence in the erotic-exotic. The poem may speak, more than once, of the North, but in the East its pleasure lies. It is the East of glamour and camels, of raids and languor, and of Tennyson's Fatima, likewise longing for the beloved, and rotating the word 'below', and threatening or promising to die (while rhyming this with the vistas of the sky). Kipling then ends by matching Fatima to Tennyson's Ulysses ('Matched with an aged wife'), as if a touch of the harsh would

1 – *Kipling Journal*, March 1959. The poem is included by Eliot in *A Choice of Kipling's Verse* (1941).

stave off sentimentality. But the cadences and the refrain stretch out upon their comfortable easternry, and though Har Dyal may be being condescended to, the name does not disturb the movement of the title or of the poem. Yet when Eliot took the titular phrasing from Kipling and then disconcerted it with a name that feels so out of keeping, he was not intent that we should merely recline upon the incongruity. He was not substituting for an easy transit of romantic sentiment an easy transit of romantic cynicism. Rather, the invitation was not only to an acknowledgement of how promptly we let ourselves be moved to inference (perhaps not ill-founded) but also to some uneasy reflection upon how deferentially we do so. It is Eliot's genius to bring home not only how inescapably available are the incitements to and of prejudice, but also how precarious they are; he understands how so little information controls so much behaviour; and how this fact of life must itself therefore be controlled.

The impulse in the title 'The Love Song of J. Alfred Prufrock', and then in the title's relation to the poem, is not single, is not solely a skilled ministering to prejudice. And what can be a sharper focus for prejudice than a name? The poet in these years 1916–18 used to sign some of his philosophical prose 'T. Stearns Eliot'.[1] No, the impulse is dual, a ministering to prejudice, but also an alerting to the fact that this, perilous yet not necessarily wrong, is what is working. If the impulse in the poem's title were only the prejudicial incitement, then Eliot would be what in 1920 he denied that he was: 'I am considered by the ordinary newspaper critic as a wit or satirist.'[2] The effect would be to minister not only to prejudice but to prejudice's complacency. But if the impulse were only to unsettle with second thoughts the first thoughts of prejudice, this would minister not only to irony but to irony's complacency, its assurance that it alone need never dirty its gloves with anything as low as categorizing. Eliot remained suspicious of irony's other-directed suspicion:

1 – All who study Eliot are indebted to Donald Gallup for his great work of scholarship, *T. S. Eliot: A Bibliography* (second edition, 1969).
2 – *The Waste Land: A Facsimile and Transcript*, p. xviii.

What we rebel against is neither the use of irony against definite men, institutions or abuses, nor is it the use (as by Jules Laforgue) to express a *dédoublement* of the personality against which the subject struggles. It is the use of irony to give the appearance of a philosophy of life, as something final and not instrumental, that leaves us now indifferent; it seems to us an evasion of the difficulty of living, where it pretends to be a kind of solution of it.[1]

For what, in the case of 'The Love Song of J. Alfred Prufrock', could be less struggled against than prejudicial amenability?

It is such a principled artistic doubleness in Eliot's poem, matching a psychological *dédoublement* and yet sane with it, which necessitates dissenting even from Hugh Kenner's formulations, which catch not the title fully but one half of its energies:

How much of the grotesque melancholy of *Prufrock* radiates from the protagonist's name would be difficult to estimate. It was surgical economy that used the marvellous name once only, in the title, and compounded it with a fatuous 'J. Alfred'. It was a talent already finely schooled that with nice audacity weighed in a single phrase the implications of this name against those of 'Love Song'. It was genius that separated the speaker of the monologue from the writer of the poem by the solitary device of affixing an unforgettable title.[2]

An unforgettable title, yes, and Kenner does it a small wrong when he curtails it to *Prufrock* there; cumbrous or fatiguing as it may be to have to keep reciting 'The Love Song of J. Alfred Prufrock', the poem is entitled to it. For to say that 'it was surgical economy that used the marvellous name once only, in the title' asks that Prufrock not be offered *as* the title. 'One begins', Eliot said of a talk, 'by choosing a title, in order to assure oneself that one has a subject: for a title is a kind of substitute or shadow of a subject.'[3] The title 'The Love Song of J. Alfred Prufrock' shadows the subject.

Yet if Eliot concocted 'J. Alfred' only so that this might be flatly 'fatuous', his creation would be less than great because it

---

1 – *The Criterion*, xii (1933), 469. On the larger significance of the *dédoublement*, in Laforgue and in Bergson and Janet, see Piers Gray, *T. S. Eliot's Intellectual and Poetic Development 1909–1922* (1982), pp. 68–72.
2 – *The Invisible Poet: T. S. Eliot* (1960), p. 4.
3 – 'Scylla and Charybdis' (1952); *Agenda*, xxiii (1985), 5.

would minister to effortless superiority. But Eliot's poems have what he called (in Blake) the unpleasantness of great poetry just because they do not exempt from their stringencies either themselves or their reader,[1] who may after all be a *hypocrite lecteur*. Their enterprise is not only a matter of making us feel certain things – or of making us admit to feeling them – but also of making us contemplate how it is that we have been made to feel so.

> She and the lady in the cape
> Are suspect, thought to be in league;
> Therefore the man with heavy eyes
> Declines the gambit, shows fatigue,
> > ('Sweeney Among the Nightingales')

Eliot's art declines the suspect gambit of collusion. 'Thought to be in league': readers may like to think that they are in league with Eliot, since this would be such a relaxation from the fatigue of thinking out exactly what one feels. There was no way of Eliot's precluding this gambit, short of writing not poems in their vigilance but bills of lading.

Whatever else Eliot effected by these early poems, he ruffled people, and there is something missing from any criticism which comes across as entirely unruffled, as if rufflement were for other people. It was to be Eliot's profoundest stricture upon Pound that under Pound's auspices the depths of Hell had become socially secure. There is after all a social class of the non-torturable, or so its would-be members think. The six-line epigraph to 'The Love Song of J. Alfred Prufrock' comes from the depths of Dante's Hell; whereas 'Mr. Pound's Hell, for all its horrors, is a perfectly comfortable one for the modern mind to contemplate, and disturbing to no one's complacency: it is a Hell for the *other people*, the people we read about in the newspapers, not for oneself and one's friends.'[2] Eliot was to incorporate this turn of phrase within 'The Church's Message to the World':

1 – 'William Blake', *Selected Essays* (1932; third edition, 1951), p. 317.
2 – *After Strange Gods* (1934), p. 43.

One reason why the lot of the secular reformer or revolutionist seems to me to be the easier is this: that for the most part he conceives of the evils of the world as something external to himself. They are thought of either as completely impersonal, so that there is nothing to alter but machinery; or if there is evil *incarnate*, it is always incarnate in the *other people* – a class, a race, the politicians, the bankers, the armament makers, and so forth – never in oneself.[1]

'Something external to himself': Yeats averred that 'We make out of the quarrel with others, rhetoric, but of the quarrel with ourselves, poetry'.[2] For the distinction between rhetoric and art, a distinction which is central to the adjudication of these responses to 'The Love Song of J. Alfred Prufrock', is clearly not a matter of rhetoric's being either less or more persuasive than art. The distinction is the further responsibility undertaken by art, as to how it achieves its persuasions and suasions. Rhetoric, being entirely instrumental, asks no questions. This is not irresponsible of it, but is a consequence of its being a-responsible. Art, though, does not exempt from its 'suspicious and interrogating eye' its own procedures; art has eyes not only in the back of its head but also into the back of its head. The evil to which rhetoric may be put is not conceived of by the artist as something external to himself. Eliot in 1909 had admired 'a conversational quality' in James Huneker: 'not conversational in admitting the slipshod and maladroit, or a meagre vocabulary, but by a certain informality, abandoning all the ordinary rhetorical hoaxes for securing attention'.[3] This is beautifully adroit, not least in the way it brings out that though in one sense rhetorical hoaxes are indeed designed to secure attention, they are also designed to secure inattention, inattention to their own procedures, their being perhaps hoaxes.

Eliot was to find in his religious faith a consummation of his faith in art, and the religious scepticism which he valued (quite other than free-thinking) will parallel the artistic self-scepticism which distinguishes art from rhetoric.

---

1 – *Listener*, 17 February 1937.
2 – *Per Amica Silentia Lunae*: *'Anima Hominis'* (1917), *Mythologies* (1959; 1969 edition), p. 331.
3 – *Harvard Advocate*, 5 October 1909.

The Church offers today [1935] the last asylum for one type of mind which the Middle Ages would hardly have expected to find among the faithful: that of the sceptic.

Obviously, I mean by the sceptic, the man who suspects the origins of his own beliefs, as well as those of others; who is most suspicious of those which are most passionately held; who is still more relentless towards his own beliefs than towards those of others; who suspects other people's motives because he has learned the deceitfulness of his own. According to this outline of the sceptic, Voltaire was a very imperfect sceptic: for, although he questioned the Christian Faith, which in itself, and at that time, was perhaps a worthy thing to do, he did not sufficiently question his own motives for questioning the Christian Faith.[1]

To apply this so as to distinguish rhetoric from art is to bring within sceptical vigilance not only beliefs but means; not only one's motive — what has moved oneself — but how one moves others. Even the greatest writers may fail here.

Catiline fails, not because it is too laboured and conscious, but because it is not conscious enough; because Jonson in this play was not alert to his own idiom, not clear in his mind as to what his temperament wanted him to do.[2]

Being alert to one's own idiom is being clear about the relation of one's mind to one's temperament: such is the nexus of rhetoric and prejudicial possibility.

An artist may sin, and this sin may be a matter of failing to detect something; yet Eliot gets the priority wrong when, deploring James's relationship to his character Rowland Mallet in *Roderick Hudson*, he says:

He too much identifies himself with Rowland, does not see through the solemnity he has created in that character, commits the cardinal sin of failing to 'detect' one of his own characters.[3]

Eliot's Jamesian pincers around 'detect' are a fine touch, but Eliot does not see through his own rhetoric. For to say that it is not just a sin, and is not just the sin, but is 'the cardinal sin', to fail to detect one of one's own characters, is to melodramatize; it would be even more grave in a novelist to fail to animate a

---

1 – *Time and Tide*, 5 January 1935.
2 – 'Ben Jonson', *Selected Essays*, p. 149.
3 – *Little Review*, August 1918.

character, or to fail to be at all interested in a character. But in any case the prior obligation of a writer is not the detection of what one's character is being but of what one's words are doing. Otherwise, sin (artistic or religious) becomes – like Pound's Hell – something for the other people, not for oneself and one's friends. Eliot in 1918 was tart about Clive Bell's owning the franchise of Civilization: 'He loves Truth, certainly, and according to his own admission, but his task is the dispensing of it to an audience of whose approval he is sure beforehand.'[1] The audience, consequently, of whose approval Bell was most sure beforehand was Bell.

It is internal vigilance, and its achieved balance, with which art challenges not only others but itself; Eliot was able to forgive but not to condone those who so yielded to the external pressures of the day as to fail to maintain the equilibrium:

Nowadays [1921] we find occasionally good irony, or satire, which lacks wit's internal equilibrium, because their voices are essentially protests against some outside sentimentality or stupidity.[2]

Wit can be assisted by rhetoric but only if it also resists rhetoric. You might detect a failure of internal equilibrium in a sentence of Eliot's about pressures. The sentence is at once a wisdom and a lapse:

It is human, when we do not understand another human being, and cannot ignore him, to exert an unconscious pressure on that person to turn him into something that we *can* understand: many husbands and wives exert this pressure on each other.[3]

This is a profoundly true reflection, except only that – despite its conscious intention to be fair-minded – it then turns out to reflect more upon women than upon men. For even if one doesn't believe that it is necessary on every occasion to get worked up about the gender-prejudicing that is inherent in saying 'he' when one means someone, this particular occasion is such that it is an important failure of vigilance in Eliot to say 'him' and 'him' (for 'another human being') as the preamble to

1 – *The Egoist*, June–July 1918.
2 – 'Andrew Marvell', *Selected Essays*, p. 304.
3 – *Notes towards the Definition of Culture* (1948; new edition, 1962), p. 64.

remarking that 'many husbands and wives exert this pressure on each other'. For the effect of the 'unconscious pressure' exerted by that repeated 'him' is to foster the unconscious accord of a reader that though it may abstractly be granted that 'husbands and wives exert this pressure on each other', it is usually or naturally wives who exert this pressure on husbands. Internal equilibrium would here have entailed being truly even-handed in the very wording.

The account, then, that is given by Hugh Kenner of the title 'The Love Song of J. Alfred Prufrock' is not interested enough in any distinction between rhetoric and art, art suspecting other people's motives and means because it has learned the deceitfulness of its own. Kenner is altogether undisconcerted by the way in which he would be allowing Eliot's words to work their will; Kenner is content to accept as art of genius what would be, if his were the sufficient terms for it, only rhetoric of genius. So it is that he over-securely speaks of the 'implications' of the name J. Alfred Prufrock: 'It was a talent already finely schooled that with nice audacity weighed in a single phrase the implications of this name against those of "Love Song".' *Implications* claims too much, and, in so doing, makes the poem minister to complacency. Implications is the word that is important as exactly not the claim made by the title and by the poem. For implications may be secure of their ground, where intimations, say, or suggestions, had better not be. A 'suggestion' used to be a temptation and still may be. Eliot is not in the easy business of manipulative incitements to prejudiced superiority, but in the challenging double enterprise of inciting both shrewd suspicion and a suspicion of such shrewd suspicions. To narrow one's eyes is to see more but of less. Eliot means suspicion exactly. The suspect might, just might, be acquitted. Prejudice is a shrewd suspicion, and while half of its shrewdness consists in its being likely to be right, the other half consists in its not going out on the limb of insisting that it will be proved right.[1] Suspicion needs to issue

---

1 – 'In order correctly to appraise a man of action we must meet him: or we must at least have known enough men of similar pursuits to be able to draw a shrewd guess about one whom we have not met' (*Notes towards the Definition of Culture*, p. 85).

in responsible interrogation. Eliot was suspicious of Pater and of Sir Thomas Browne, and of how they achieved their eloquent effects:

I only wish to take the precaution of looking upon the Monna Lisas of prose, the drums and tramplings of three conquests, the eloquent just and mightie deaths, with a suspicious and interrogating eye, and making quite certain what, if any, solid and genuine bit of life they have pounced upon and raised to the dignity of poetry.[1]

Talking of Michelangelo

Like all of Eliot's poems, 'The Love Song of J. Alfred Prufrock' is occupied with the power of names. Within the poem proper, the first name stamped itself as unmistakably a power of Eliot's.

> In the room the women come and go
> Talking of Michelangelo.

Strikingly, given that critics delight to bark and bite ('these days of dog-eat-dog in the criticism of literature and life')[2], critics concur in sensing that the women are mouthing art-speak. Grover Smith talks with confidence: 'And the women meanwhile are talking, no doubt tediously and ignorantly, of Michelangelo.'[3] John Crowe Ransom, who is more than a critic because a true poet, speaks of the women 'about whom with some contempt he makes the refrain'.[4] Yet those two lines never do become a refrain, contrary to the expectations which Eliot creates when, having furnished the thirteenth and fourteenth lines of the poem, they duly recur as the thirty-fifth and thirty-sixth lines – only to recur no more; they had indeed seemed set to be the poem's refrain, and then the poem refrains from them, most unexpectedly; the two lines themselves come

1 – *The Chapbook*, April 1921.
2 – *English Review*, liii (1931), 118.
3 – *T. S. Eliot's Poetry and Plays* (1956), p. 18.
4 – In *T. S. Eliot: The Man and His Work*, edited by Allen Tate (1966; 1971 edition), p. 139.

and go, and then come and go, to come no more in all the further
ninety-five lines.

Ransom stakes himself upon a rhetorical question: 'How
could they have had any inkling of that glory which Michelangelo had put into his marbles and his paintings?'

Helen Gardner does not as a woman have any different sense
of the women: 'The absurdity of discussing his giant art, in high-
pitched feminine voices, drifting through a drawing-room, adds
merely extra irony to the underlying sense of the lines.'[1] And
Hugh Kenner unfolds the rhetoric which fosters such feelings:

The closed and open o's, the assonances of *room*, *women*, and *come*, the
pointed caesura before the polysyllabic burst of 'Michelangelo', weave a
context of grandeur within which our feeling about these trivial women
determines itself.[2]

It is not to be credited that 'room', 'women' and 'come' ever
were *assonances* for Eliot's ear, but the nub is that Kenner is
again too unmisgiving about rhetoric; he understands its effec-
tiveness but not what is to be understood by this.

For Eliot was preternaturally alert both to rhetoric's indispen-
sability and to rhetoric's eagerness to dispense with moral and
spiritual considerations; Eliot was fascinated by what he called
the pathology of rhetoric. In 1919 he stressed 'the cardinal point
in criticizing the Elizabethans: we cannot grasp them, understand them, without some understanding of the pathology of
rhetoric. Rhetoric, a particular form of rhetoric, was endemic, it
pervaded the whole organism; the healthy as well as the morbid
tissues were built up on it'.[3] Rhetoric is intimate with the
prejudicial; both are endemic; the healthy as well as the morbid
tissues are built upon both; but the great poem is one which is
discriminatingly revelatory of this, being doubly apprehensive.

1 – *The Art of T. S. Eliot* (1949; 1968 edition), p. 84.
2 – *The Invisible Poet*, p. 6.
3 – 'A Romantic Aristocrat', *The Sacred Wood* (1920; second edition 1928), p. 30.
For an anthology-cum-taxonomy of Eliot's own rhetorical skills in his criticism, see
Edward Lobb, *T. S. Eliot and the Romantic Critical Tradition* (1981), Chapter 3,
'Eliot as Rhetorician'; and for an acute study of 'the pathology of rhetoric' in
relation to romantic self-deception, Chapter 2 of Ronald Bush, *T. S. Eliot: A Study
in Character and Style* (1984).

'A feeling of apprehensiveness, conducive to attention, is aroused in the reader.'[1]

For the critics miss a cardinal point of Eliot's when they fail to interrogate their chafing. They miss one of the things which is salutary in the lines:

> In the room the women come and go
> Talking of Michelangelo.

What none of the critics will own is how much their sense of the lines is incited by prejudice – not therefore to be discounted but not to be counted upon. You can hear the stilling of a stirring conscience when Grover Smith reaches for a dubious 'no doubt': 'And the women meanwhile are talking, no doubt tediously and ignorantly, of Michelangelo.' For all we *know*, as against suspect (perhaps justifiably, but still), the women could be talking as invaluably as Kenneth Clark. We'd of course be willing to bet that the women were talking odious art-talk, but we'd better not bet our bottom dollar on it. 'The race is not always to the swift,' said Damon Runyon, 'nor the battle to the strong, but that's the way to bet.' True, and a good poem – like a gentleman – does not bet on a certainty.

This is not at all to deny the incitements, rather to stress how frail each of them is and how even the plaiting of them does not create a rope. Eliot repeatedly refuses the satisfactions, the complacencies, of the secure or indubitable. Agreed, this could be because he was content to elicit from others his own mere prejudices without caring whether such were licit. But it is at least possible that the poems engage the difference between the healthy and the morbid tissues.

Eliot declined to give the world a novel about Prufrock, while at the same time persistently invoking the novel, especially the Jamesian novel. In 1935 he wrote:

What the help and encouragement of men of an older generation may be like, what it feels like, what useful stimulus or perhaps misdirection it may give, I do not know. At a time which may be symbolised by the figures 1910, there was literally no one to whom one would have dreamt of

1 – 'Charles Whibley', *Selected Essays*, p. 498.

14

applying. One learnt something, no doubt, from Henry James, and might have learnt more. But Henry James was a novelist, and one who gave the most formidable appearance of exclusive concentration on his own kind of work.[1]

A great part of Eliot's enterprise was to resist 'exclusive concentration on his own kind of work', though in this sense only, and to bring over into poetry the truths and satisfactions of James's kind of work, while not yielding to what he considered a novelist's propensity to forgive too much. Eliot esteemed novels which rose to the particular challenge, as did *Bubu of Montparnasse*, of being 'both compassionate and dispassionate',[2] a challenge which the novel's antecedent liberalism seemed to him always in danger of ducking.

Yet there is then an oddly unforgiving, an inappropriately illiberal, aspect to the behaviour of the critics, who are cheated – as it apparently feels to them – by Eliot of the novel's assurances in 'The Love Song of J. Alfred Prufrock', cheated of the fuller context of evidence which allows a reader to give high-minded vent to mercy and to justice. Robbed of their prey, or rather, robbed of the assurance that certain of the people put before them may unmisgivingly be considered prey, the critics write the recriminatory novel which Eliot succeeded in not providing. 'And the women meanwhile are talking, no doubt tediously and ignorantly, of Michelangelo'; 'The absurdity of discussing his giant art, in high-pitched feminine voices, drifting through a drawing-room': what are these commentaries but the scratching of an itch? Given a poem, write a novel about it. Most critics of poetry are poets *manqués*, but many critics of Eliot are novelists *manqués*.

Robbed of the satisfactions of judicial or judgemental indubitability, the critics are impelled to fashion these for themselves. Yet, in the suasions of rhythm for instance, Eliot declines to provide either of the two likely rhythmical ways of pairing the lines. He does not give the heroic couplet of satirical disparagement which might have seemed set in motion by the first line; say:

[1] – *New English Weekly*, 12 September 1935.
[2] – By Charles-Louis Philippe; preface by Eliot (1932; 1945 edition), p. 14.

> In the room the women come and go
> Talking of manly Michelangelo.

Nor does he give the namby-pamby swaying which might have been authorized by the second line:

> The women come, the women go,
> Talking of Michelangelo.

A rhythm can pass an unmistakable judgement. Eliot does not avail himself of this. So can an adjective, and here too Eliot declines the gambit. There is no adjective to damn the women; it is the critic, not the poem, that says 'these trivial women'. Again, there is no adverb to damn the women; it is the critic, not the poem, that says 'talking, no doubt tediously and ignorantly'. Nothing is voiced about the women's voices; it is the critic, not the poem, that hears 'high-pitched feminine voices' when the voices, for all we hear, could be as honourably gruff as those of the stereotyped woman don. Nor will the poem's verb categorically indict the women, for 'talking' is simply – and disturbingly for any scrupulous relation with the complacencies of prejudice – the most neutral such word in the language; nothing about 'Prating of Michelangelo' or 'Prattling of Michelangelo'. 'Talking of' is indeed mildly fastidious, but then 'talking about' would be mildly vulgar. It is the critic who musters a verb which disparages, so that the women are 'drifting through a drawing-room'.

True, the women are called 'the women', and there is something disturbing about that, a whiff of the prejudicial all right. *Stanley and the Women*: Kingsley Amis knew what he was doing. Yet once more the question of prejudice has its habit of rounding on the questioner. If this is not the right way of putting it, what is? 'In the room women come and go': this would be out of the frying pan into the fire. And to insist in advance that the fact that the talkers about Michelangelo are women could not possibly have anything to do with it (whatever 'it' might turn out to be) is simply to prejudice the whole matter.

The women come and go, certainly, and people narrow their eyes at that (people who themselves are inevitably involved like all of us in coming and going), but what would we prefer the women to do? Our hearts would hardly go out to them if they were described as rooted to the spot talking of Michelangelo. Even the rhyme of 'go' and 'Michelangelo', with its many disparities, cannot be taken as unmistakably, groundedly, derogatory, since for one thing it must be heard after its immediate predecessor:

> Oh, do not ask, 'What is it?'
> Let us go and make our visit.

After the prissy pursedness of that rhyme, the rhyme of 'go' and 'Michelangelo' might even feel generous; and the stress or pitch of the word 'go' within the lines about the women is affected by the 'Let us go' (itself a reprise from the opening of the poem) just before, so that the intonation within the couplet is not what might be the level simper of

> In the room the women come and go

but rather

> In the room the women *come and* 'go'

'The heroic sound', says Kenner, 'and especially the carefully dramatized sound of the painter's name, is what muffles these women.' But what exactly *is* the carefully dramatized sound of the painter's name? For there is a compacted potency in even the small question of how to pronounce Michelangelo.

Foreign names, whether of persons or of places, always lay you open to the charge of prejudice, for to pronounce them as if you were a native of their habitat may be to claim too much, may be to 'appropriate' them. It is also to court affectation. But to anglicize them is to run upon the other horn of the same dilemma. It used to be a mark at once of respect for the international, and of national self-respect, to anglicize, especially as this was a tribute to great names. 'My buried life, and Paris in the Spring': the mark of a world city was bestowed upon Paris as it is not upon Paree, which is merely a flick of the tourist. It is not for Englishmen to say Roma, and it is in its way handsome of us to say Rome; why, we even say Naples, those of us who would die rather than say Napoli. 'Are these ideas right or wrong?'

Michelangelo, then? Eliot has cunningly criss-crossed the matter, spelling the name as if it were not English (which was not, for instance, the poet Whitehall's way with it) but pronouncing it – the recording of Eliot is clear as a bell – in the English manner. I once heard Charles Tomlinson in a lecture pronounce the name in the Italian manner; it was extraordinary how sharply this point of pronunciation could puncture J. Alfred Prufrock, 'pinned and wriggling', and yet how unjust this might be, for perhaps it would not have been affectation but a proper respect for the immitigable foreignness of Michelangelo which would have moved Prufrock – or Charles Tomlinson – to say the name so.

Needless to say, the critics are not imagining things, though they are not then being imaginative about this. They are right to pick up a smell from the lines (Eliot's poems engage the fascination of smells as prejudicial), but they are wrong to write as if what were before them were not an impalpable smell but a palpable dossier. There are great writers who prepare dossiers; one of them learnt from Eliot the conjunction of women and of Michelangelo (and of nationalistic prejudice), while permitting his character to indulge an unEliot unmistakability of misogyny:

He clenched his hands in a fury against the enormous impertinence of women, their noisy intrusive curious enthusiasm, like the spontaneous expression of admiration bursting from American hearts before Michelangiolo's tomb in Santa Croce.[1]

Samuel Beckett did not reprint 'Assumption' (1929); later he wrote a poignant dramaticule for three women, *Come and Go*.

Dryden knew how to mount a dossier:

> But how shou'd any Sign-post-dawber know
> The worth of *Titian*, or of *Angelo*?
> ('To Mr. Lee, on his *Alexander*')

[1] – *transition*, Number 16–17, June 1929.

Dryden called upon, and wished directly to promulgate, the scornful assurance which can be heard in 'any Sign-post-dawber' and in the rhetorical question 'But how shou'd . . .?' – which indeed was to be Ransom's rhetorical question: 'How could they have had any inkling . . . ?' Dryden's satirical imperiousness is founded upon the heroic couplet's being the medium for panegyric as well as (so therefore) for disdain. Robert Whitehall praised Robert Streeter's painting, his *Allegory of Truth*:

> That future ages must confess they owe
> To Streeter more than Michael Angelo.[1]

A ringing conclusion, but not the end of the matter, for time has called the bluff not only of the painter Streeter but of his poet Whitehall. But Whitehall was right to judge that there was nothing inherently mocking about such a rhyme as 'owe' and 'Michael Angelo'. Dryden's mockery is rendered unmistakable only by the broad strokes of 'Sign-post-dawber' and 'But how shou'd . . . ?'

Nor would 'women come and go' have to mock. Christina Rossetti made those four words the climax of a thrillingly positive vision:

> You looking earthward, what see you?
> Milk-white, wine-flushed among the vines,
> Up and down leaping, to and fro,
> Most glad, most full, made strong with wines,
> Blooming as peaches pearled with dew,
> Their golden windy hair afloat,
> Love-music warbling in their throat
> Young men and women come and go.
>
> ('The Convent Threshold')

She was imagining a world where it was gladdening for women to come and go – except, indeed, that here the women are complemented by men: 'Young men and women come and go.'

1 – I owe my knowledge of these lines to E. H. Gombrich, *Ideals and Idols* (1979).

'Love-music' here is not the love song of J. Alfred Prufrock. But Eliot set himself a different duty from that of either Dryden or Christina Rossetti; it was a double duty, and when Kenner limits his feeling to a singular on our behalf ('our feeling about these trivial women'), I wish to urge the claims not only of a plural (our feelings about these women) but also of a further range of feeling: our feelings about what we have been moved to feel, by Eliot's profound insinuations, about these women; not only about what we have been moved to feel, but about how we have been moved.

It is this further range, in relation to the initial (initiating and not conclusive) incitements, which raises the poem above rhetoric to art; raises it as many a great romantic poem has been raised. Eliot is as much a romantic poet as a classical one, and he found new forms for romanticism's creative propensity to be moved by the sense of how the mind had been moved. Geoffrey Hartman contemplated 'The Solitary Reaper' with awe: 'Thus Wordsworth, under the impress of a powerful feeling, turns round both it and its apparent cause, respecting both and never reducing the one to the other'.[1]

Clough was suspicious of this:

This sentimentalising over sentiment; this sensibility about sensibility, has been carried, I grant, by the Wordsworthians to a far more than Wordsworthian excess. But he has something of it surely. He is apt to wind up his short pieces with reflections upon the way in which, hereafter, he expects to reflect upon his present reflections.[2]

Eliot too was suspicious of romanticism's tendency to thrill to vistas; what made it possible for him to profit from romanticism's example was his conviction of both a religious (that of the faithful sceptic) and a philosophical worth in such a way of proceeding. A romantic poet such as Valéry has recesses unentered by Gray. Comparing Gray's 'Elegy Written in a Country Churchyard' with Valéry's 'Le Cimetière Marin', Eliot wrote in 'Scylla and Charybdis':

1 – Wordsworth's Poetry 1787–1814 (1964), p. 8.
2 – Poems and Prose Remains (1869), i, 319.

The content of Gray's poem, as I have said, consists chiefly of ideas which have occurred to all men in all languages at all times. Hence its structure is merely the plausible sequence by which one such thought leads to another. Valéry's poem has what I call the philosophic structure: an organisation, not merely of successive responses to the situation, but of further responses to his own responses.[1]

At the time of 'The Love Song of J. Alfred Prufrock', Eliot was a philosopher. But (or, with a different prejudice, So) he was aware that philosophy, like romanticism, was tempted by narcissistic regression. The social world, for all its faults, can mount one form of resistance to narcissism, and to narcissism's extremity, solipsism. When Eliot, in 'The Love Song of J. Alfred Prufrock', provokes further responses to his own responses, or suggests the price of admission to the poem's invitations, the poem is both threatened and protected, both enslaved and freed – like Prufrock himself and like all of us – by the social world.

What is it that makes so feeble Peter Viereck's 'Love Song of Prufrock Junior'? The fatigued parasitism of its title, for a start, as if there were any hope of competing with Eliot here of all places; and then the poem's lax recourse to the comfortably prejudicial, or prejudice without tears of any kind.

> Must all successful rebels grow
> From toreador to Sacred Cow?
> What cults he slew, his cult begot.
> 'In my beginning', said his Scot,
> 'My end'; and aging eagles know
> That 1912 was long ago.
> Today the women come and go
> Talking of T. S. Eliot.

How technically mindless – given that five of the eight lines are to rhyme with 'grow' – to begin with the non-rhyme of grow and cow; how flaccid the tissue of allusion to Eliot in comparison with Eliot's own genius in allusion; and how vacant the collusively predictable rhythms where Eliot's had been so expertly unsure.

1 – *Agenda*, xxiii (1985), 19–20.

In 1916, the year between printing 'The Love Song of J. Alfred Prufrock' in *Poetry* and printing it in *Prufrock and Other Observations*, Eliot expressed quiet desperation in contemplating his own and his wife's hopes: 'I often feel that *J.A.P.* is a swan-song, but I never mention the fact because Vivien is so exceedingly anxious that I shall equal it, and would be bitterly disappointed if I do not.'[1] The poem was certainly not to be the swan-song of T. Stearns Eliot. One reason is the continuity of the poem with Eliot's creative sense of not only the perils of prejudice but the indispensabilities of what will be called prejudice.

Such, though with too little fear of prejudice's dangers, had been the preoccupation of the dialogue (1683) by Fontenelle which Ezra Pound translated in the May 1917 issue of *The Egoist*. Here Strato and Raphael of Urbino argue about prejudice, Strato taking the liberal position of repudiating prejudice, and Raphael the conservative one of welcoming it. Raphael announces: 'I assure you that my defence of prejudice is disinterested, and that by taking prejudice's part I laid myself open to no small ridicule.' But Fontenelle and Pound are not themselves disinterested, and they make sure that Raphael has the better of it. Strato is the one who is genially ridiculed, for his gullibility about reason, her powers and her ways. The dialogue itself becomes increasingly prejudiced, so that by the end Raphael is being furnished not only with the stronger arguments but with more than twice as many words in which to mount them. Raphael makes good points, but it is not good that there is so little even-handedness in the dialogue. The one thing that a serious discussion of prejudice does not need is a prejudicial rigging. Fontenelle and Pound have hired Strato the straightman; this demeans not only Strato but Raphael and the dialogue. The end permits Raphael to be too securely conclusive:

Strato: Thus one should preserve the prejudices of custom in order to act like the next man but destroy the habits of thought in order to think like the sage.

Raphael: Better preserve them all. You seem to forget the old Samnite's

1 – *The Waste Land: A Facsimile and Transcript*, p. xi.

answer when his compatriots sent to ask him what should be done with the Roman army which they had caught in the Caudine forks. The old man replied that they should put them all to the sword. The Samnites thought this too cruel; he then said they should let them go free and unscathed, and in the end they did neither, and reaped the evil result. It is the same with prejudices, we must either keep the whole lot or crush them out altogether, otherwise those you have eliminated will make you mistrust those which remain. The unhappiness of being deceived in many things will not be balanced by the pleasure of its being an unconscious deceit, and you will have neither the illumination of truth nor yet the comfort of error.

Strato: If there were no means of escaping your alternative, one should not long hesitate about taking a side. We should root out all prejudice.

Raphael: But reason would hunt out all our old notions and leave nothing else in their place. She would create a species of vacuum. And how could one bear this? No, no, considering how slight an amount of reason inheres in all men, we must leave them the prejudices to which they are so well acclimatized. These prejudices are reason's supplement. All that is lacking on one side can be got out of the other.

It was imprudent to end so one-sided a dialogue with 'All that is lacking on one side . . .'. Nor is it only hindsight, the knowledge of what became of the anti-Semite Ezra Pound broadcasting from Rome during the war, that gives a chill to the movement here from a philosophical discussion of prejudice to a cruel *realpolitik*, an unperturbed acceptance of the wisdom of putting a captured Roman army to the sword. It was Milton, whom Pound detested for 'his asinine bigotry, his beastly hebraism, the coarseness of his mentality',[1] who exposed the rhetoric of a self-justifying cruelty, compelled

> To do what else though damnd I should abhorre.
>> So spake the Fiend, and with necessitie,
> The Tyrants plea, excus'd his devilish deeds.
>
> (*Paradise Lost*, IV 392–4)

Unlike Pound, Eliot never rested content with taking a side here, not even the side of Raphael. That Strato's tender liberalism is to be suspected of credulity does not mean that Raphael's tough conservatism is not to be suspected of it. Watery Charybdis is no more dangerous than craggy Scylla, and Eliot

1 – *Literary Essays*, edited by T. S. Eliot (1954), p. 238.

knew that 'the danger of freedom is deliquescence; the danger of strict order is petrifaction'.[1]

'These prejudices are reason's supplement. All that is lacking on one side can be got out of the other.' Immediately below those final categorical words of the dialogue in *The Egoist* of May 1917, there appeared the intriguing advertisement.

PRUFROCK

THE EGOIST, Ltd., is publishing in May a small book of Poems

Prufrock and other Observations

by Mr. T. S. ELIOT.   Price 1s.; postage 2d.

---

1 – *Notes towards the Definition of Culture*, p. 81.

II

ANTI-SEMITISM

Uglier touches

With his title 'The Love Song of Har Dyal', Kipling provided a hint for 'The Love Song of J. Alfred Prufrock'. He did the same with 'The Broken Men', which Eliot acknowledged combining with Morris's 'The Hollow Land' to create 'The Hollow Men'.[1] It is nevertheless unlikely that Kipling was returning a compliment to the author of The Waste Land when in 1930 he entitled a poem 'The Waster'.

> From the date that the doors of his prep-school close
>   On the lonely little son
> He is taught by precept, insult, and blows
>   The Things that Are Never Done.
> Year after year, without favour or fear,
>   From seven to twenty-two,
> His keepers insist he shall learn the list
>   Of the things no fellow can do.
> (They are not so strict with the average Pict
>   And it isn't set to, etc.)
>
> For this and not for the profit it brings
>   Or the good of his fellow-kind
> He is and suffers unspeakable things
>   In body and soul and mind.
> But the net result of that Primitive Cult,

---

1 – *Times Literary Supplement*, 10 January 1935. Robert Crawford has shown the diverse importance to *The Waste Land* of Kipling's 'The Finest Story in the World' in *The Savage and the City in the Work of T. S. Eliot* (1987), pp. 132–6.

> Whatever else may be won,
> Is definite knowledge ere leaving College
>   Of the Things that Are Never Done.
> (An interdict which is strange to the Pict
>   And was never revealed to, etc.)
>
> Slack by training and slow by birth,
>   Only quick to despise,
> Largely assessing his neighbour's worth
>   By the hue of his socks or ties,
> A loafer-in-grain, his foes maintain,
>   And how shall we combat their view
> When, atop of his natural sloth, he holds
>   There are Things no Fellow can do?
> (Which is why he is licked from the first by the Pict
>   And left at the post by, etc.)

Lionel Trilling had a notable public exchange with T. S. Eliot on the matter of prejudice: specifically, on Rudyard Kipling and the Jews. Trilling had reviewed in *The Nation* Eliot's selection of Kipling's verse,[1] and had discriminatingly deplored it: 'Mr. Eliot, it is true, would not descend to the snippy, *persecuted* anti-Semitism of ironic good manners which, in "The Waster", leads Kipling to write "etc." when the rhyme requires "Jew".' Within his letter of reply (published 15 January 1944), Eliot demurred:

I would observe that in one stanza, at least, the rhyme required is not to *do* but to *done*: and the obvious rhyme for *done* is not *Jew* but *Hun*. Kipling made several opportunities for expressing his dislike of Germans; I am not aware that he cherished any particularly anti-Semitic feelings. In any case, the interest of the poem lies rather in his criticism of the English than in any aversion to Jews, Germans, or Scotsmen that may be imputed to him.

The subjoined reply by Trilling was characteristic and exemplary. First, he apologized for having been in error: he had said, prejudicially, that Eliot 'must have been at some trouble to procure the poem for his selection, for it is not included in the Inclusive Edition'. Eliot's letter had shown that this was not so:

1 – 16 October 1943.

the poem was readily accessible in the Definitive Edition. The apology was exemplary, first, because the honour of simple apology by a reviewer on a point of fact was not ordinary then and is not ordinary now. But what was no less fine in Trilling was his not being unnerved by having had to apologize; his not being deflected from engaging with Eliot's defence of Kipling and of the crucial rhymes; and his not being dissuaded from substantiating that Kipling could not be exculpated by Eliot's defence.

But I cannot admit Mr. Eliot's second objection. The gist of 'The Waster' is that the English, because of their public-school code, are always being beaten by certain unscrupulous racial groups. In the first and last stanzas they are beaten by the etc.-Jew because they believe that 'There are Things no Fellow can do'; in the second stanza they are beaten by the etc.-Hun because they think that there are 'Things that Are Never Done'; and in all three stanzas they are beaten by the Pict . . . It is of course true that the poem criticizes the English for being the victims of their own code; but the criticism, because of the nature of the comparisons by which it is made, is so ambiguous as to be almost a kind of praise.

Then, with a felicitous infusion of Eliot's own dryness of manner, Trilling ended:

As anti-Semitism goes these days, I suppose Kipling is not – to use Mr. Eliot's phrase – particularly anti-Semitic. I certainly should not think of isolating for discussion what anti-Semitism he has, but only of mentioning, as one aspect of a complex xenophobia, his queasy, resentful feelings about Jews.

Not particularly anti-Semitic: these were incautious words of Eliot's, not least in their measured air of caution; even Nicholas Mosley, in his very honourable life of his father Sir Oswald Mosley,[1] lapses into the oblivious when he says of Mosley's fore-marchers, the British Fascisti, that they were 'not particularly anti-semitic'. It is not only that the phrase suggests an

---

1 – Eliot admired much in Charles Maurras, and repudiated some things; for Oswald Mosley he showed his contempt. 'I have at hand a book containing statements by Sir Oswald Mosley, which anyone with the merest smattering of theology can recognize to be not only puerile but anathema. So far as I know, the Church has given no direction to the Faithful in response to these statements' (*New English Weekly*, 21 March 1935).

equanimity on the point of scarcely caring; it is also that there is a small crucial ambiguity in it. For 'not particularly' may mean either 'not very' or 'not specifically'. Eliot's use (as Trilling shrewdly intimates) hovers conveniently for him between the two, with the suggestion both that Kipling was not *very* anti-Semitic, and that he was not anti-Semitic *in particular* since he had harsh things to say here of Germans, too, and Picts, and even perhaps of the English. But Eliot should never have descended to these shifts on behalf of such a poem. 'The Waster' is not less appalling for being so dextrous.

As with Kipling, there can be no isolating for discussion what anti-Semitism Eliot had or did not have, though he, like Kipling, had his queasy resentful feelings about Jews. The question of anti-Semitism in Eliot is important exactly because it cannot be isolated for discussion; it entails the larger, though admittedly not more intense, question of prejudice in general.[1]

George Steiner wrote a letter to the *Listener*,[2] about, summarily, 'Eliot's anti-semitism':

The obstinate puzzle is that Eliot's uglier touches tend to occur at the heart of very good poetry (which is *not* the case of Pound). One thinks of the notorious 'the Jew squats on the window-sill . . . Spawned in some estaminet of Antwerp' in 'Gerontion'; of

> The rats are underneath the piles.
> The Jew is underneath the lot.

in 'Burbank with a Baedeker: Bleistein with a Cigar'; of

> Rachel *née* Rabinovitch
> Tears at the grapes with murderous paws

in 'Sweeney among the Nightingales'.

---

1 – This is to agree with Graham Martin that 'anti-semitism is *not* a marginal issue in Eliot's work (revealed only in unfortunate asides, and discernible only to the paranoia of Jewish critics)'; but I dissent from the tone and substance of Martin's further remark that 'when he was still struggling to attach himself to an acceptable version of English society (in the deepest sense), the uncultured Jew functioned as a fictional whipping-boy for his own suppressed subversive self' (*Eliot in Perspective*, edited by Graham Martin, 1970, pp. 24–5). See also J. Mitchell Morse, *Prejudice and Literature* (1976), of which pp. 168–73 are on Eliot; Morse's anger has dignity but it does not, in my judgement, move him to any sufficient analysis, either of Eliot in particular or of prejudice in essence.

2 – 29 April 1971. The ellipsis in the quotation is Steiner's.

Steiner shows courage in this insistence that the uglier touches are not only continuous with Eliot's greatness as a poet but are sometimes intimate with it, whereas if you dropped the anti-Semitic passages from Pound's *Cantos* you would lose no poetry for which Pound deserves gratitude. Yet Steiner's word 'puzzle' – 'The obstinate puzzle . . .' – is not quite it, since this suggests the possibility of a solution.

Then again, the instances from Eliot's poems are much more diverse and elusive than Steiner's summary (in a letter only) could unfold. The consciousness in 'Gerontion' after all is not offered as healthy, sane and wise; who would wish to be he, and what endorsement then is being asked for the thoughts of his dry brain in its dry season?[1] Some of the queasy resentful feelings are bent upon a different Jew who may indeed be the owner, Christ.

> My house is a decayed house,
> And the Jew squats on the window sill, the owner,
> Spawned in some estaminet of Antwerp,
> Blistered in Brussels, patched and peeled in London.

It is like some appalling *curriculum vitae* and *cursus honorum*. But is this *curriculum mortis* and *cursus dishonorum* to be held against Gerontion or against 'Gerontion'? Is it an earnest that the Jew is socially and spiritually rotten or that the dry brain which savours such sour gusto has rotted? Gabriel Pearson has written stirringly about these lines, exulting in their vituperative energy in a way which is then braced against his deploring their substance:

The Jew 'squats' (an undoubted filament to 'merds' here), is 'spawned', 'blistered', 'patched' and 'peeled' in a swift aggressive flurry of strong verbs. One can scarcely avoid an impression of inflicted retaliations. Here is the 'jew'[2] placarded, as owner, on an appositional sill, being spattered,

---

1 – Piers Gray describes the poem as 'the meditation of a soul contemplating its own disintegration, disintegration both physical and ideal', and he shows that 'the structure of the poem's meditation is intimately but subversively related to the metaphorical structure of Paul's teaching' (*T. S. Eliot's Intellectual and Poetic Development 1909–1922*, p. 211).

2 – Lower-case j in Eliot's text until 1963.

degraded and mutilated. Like a veritable Elder of Zion he is made to exemplify the squalor he is accused of causing. Yet the attack is at the same time deftly distanced. The indefiniteness of 'some' is furthered by the allusive knowingness of 'estaminet'. The reader finds himself divided between levels of aggression and disdain which may turn out to be an attack on him.[1]

To Pearson's vivid exploration of the animus within the poem (not necessarily the same as the animus of the poem) should be added that the reader and the Jew do not exhaust the imaginable objects of attack: Gerontion, embittered and wily, is not immune from attack, ours or his. What his history gives may be 'What's not believed in'.

Nor will the instance from 'Sweeney among the Nightingales' settle exactly where a confident repudiation would have it. The Jewish immigration into the United States brought many Jews who changed their names, and perhaps some, in changing their names, wished to conceal the Jewish name which might invite yet more prejudice. But the immigration also brought many who were simply allotted names upon entry, either as anglicizings of their foreign Jewish names or arbitrarily. And then there is the question, the one manifested in the form 'Rachel *née* Rabinovitch', of a change of name by marriage. Clearly this invites or incites the possibility of a prejudiced disapproval of such marriages as cross the Christian/Jewish divide – a disapproval that it would itself be an act of prejudice to suppose was limited to the Christian side of the divide. 'Rachel *née* Rabinovitch' invites the further suspicion that one devious motive for, or aspect of, such a marriage is that in changing one's name one will disguise one's Jewishness. Some such thoughts as these must swirl in with the line.

Yet any simple confidence that Eliot's line is merely riding upon the prejudice has to acknowledge that such confidence would itself prejudice the matter. For the line does not say that Rachel's married name is not Jewish; does not say that she has been metamorphosed into, for instance, Rachel Winthrop or Rachel Lowell or Rachel Eliot. 'Rachel *née* Rabinovitch': for all

1 – *Eliot in Perspective*, ed. Martin, p. 87.

that the line explicitly vouchsafes, she might be Rachel Bleistein *née* Rabinovitch. This is not to deny that it is natural to suspect otherwise, or even that it is right to suspect otherwise; but it is wrong to put it to oneself that one knows rather than suspects, and this matters because of the relation of prejudice – of which Eliot stands accused – to suspicion.

> The silent vertebrate in brown
> Contracts and concentrates, withdraws;
> Rachel *née* Rabinovitch
> Tears at the grapes with murderous paws;
>
> She and the lady in the cape
> Are suspect, thought to be in league;

For the line 'Rachel *née* Rabinovitch' gets its especially disconcerting power from the fact that you can't in English say 'Rachel *née* Rabinovitch', and not just in the sense – relevant though this is too – that *née* is not an English word. It is odd to say '*née*' without supplying the name which has supplanted the maiden name; it is more than odd to supply the sequence of the first name and the maiden name, linked by *née*, while withholding the married name. The *Oxford English Dictionary* did not include *née*, though it could have done since the earliest citation (1758) now given in the Supplement so much antedates the *OED*; what the citations show is that if you use *née*, you give too the married name: 'The interview between Rebecca Crawley, *née* Sharp, and her Imperial Master' (*Vanity Fair*).[1] But in Eliot's line the surname which is now Rachel's is remarkably – just because unremarkedly – withheld in a way that is sinisterly inconceivable in any world of social remark; what is sinister is such a dark way of speaking, much more than any darkness possessed by Rachel. The effect is dramatic, in both senses of dramatic, and the line – like so much else in 'Sweeney among the Nightingales' – is beaded with the sweat of two equally horrible opposite fears: the fear that the terrors, here in this sleazy dive, may be paranoid, and the fear that they may not be. The line, the

---

1 – Likewise *Webster's Dictionary*: 'used in introducing the maiden family name of a married woman, as Madame de Stael, *née* Necker'.

very notion – 'Rachel *née* Rabinovitch' – is tense with a dramatized (terrorized) dementia unaware apparently that this is no way to speak. 'An idea which may appear to an outsider a pure imagination, possesses fatality for one crazed by fear or passion.'[1] The same goes for the imagination of a reader, who is both insider and outsider. Piers Gray has urged that 'the connotations of animality are suggested in the name Rachel: a "rache" is "A hunting-dog which pursues its prey by scent", *Shorter Oxford English Dictionary*'.[2] But the nature of this unsettling poem is not such as to assure us whether, for instance, this suggestion is a warranted deducing or a pure imagination crazed by fear or passion.

A robustly demotic account of the dramatization of the narrator in 'Sweeney among the Nightingales' has been given by Malcolm Pittock: 'He does not know what the hell is going on: it is merely his prejudices (as in the case of "Rachel *née* Rabinovitch"), cultural associations, and the occasional prideful reaching after the illusion of omnipotence which allow him to bluff himself into thinking that he has everything taped.'[3] But Pittock has no way of commenting on 'the evidence of unreasonable prejudice' without himself having recourse to a further prejudice, albeit a benignly credulous one: 'It is certain, however' (pre-emptively prejudicing any open consideration of the matter), 'It is certain, however, that Flora *née* Macdiarmid would not have done at all; for we have no prejudices against a woman merely because she is of Scottish origin, be she who she may, and wherever on the globe she is to be found.' Don't we, now? Has no one picked on the Picts? It was his anti-Scottish prejudice that Hopkins made the occasion for floating the matter of prejudice:

You say 'prejudices are *ipso facto weak* and foolish'. You say this *apropos* of my Anti-Scottish prejudice. Now whether this is '*weak* and foolish' is

---

1 – Eliot, *Knowledge and Experience in the Philosophy of F. H. Bradley* (1964), p. 54.

2 – *T. S. Eliot's Intellectual and Poetic Development 1909–1922*, p. 210.

3 – *Essays in Criticism*, xxx (1980), 34–5. Pittock says that the poem is 'using a well-known formula for the giving of a woman's unmarried name (Rachel *née* Rabinovitch)', but those three words precisely do not fit the usual formula.

not the question; disabuse me of it if you reasonably can; but you are quite wrong about prejudices themselves. I cannot now enter into the discussion of the subject. I will only mention that my opinions on it, expressed some time ago in a school essay, were confirmed by a late article in *The Saturday*, which of course I was glad to see, on Prejudice and Prejudices. Read it if you can, but at all events ask yourselves in a thorough and unconventional manner whether Prejudices are what you say – or whether they are not, on the contrary, often a passive, and sometimes almost an active wisdom. I dare assert virtue has few greater supports than what you think so necessarily bad, prejudices.[1]

Postpone for now Hopkins's challenge. Prejudices against the Scottish, *pace* Pittock, are found all over the globe, and moreover there is a substantial overlap of one prejudice against the Scottish with one against the Jews: tightfistedness; so that when Pittock reaches for what he believes will be a clinching neutral instance, his cooperative subconscious thwarts him. And what deeply prejudicial stroke, down there, was it which actually came up with the name MacDiarmid as the one which could not but be a prejudice-free zone? MacDiarmid, the man who was proud to list as his recreation in *Who's Who* 'Anglophobia'.

Granted, any instance of any effect at all in a great poet asks a more patient adherence and investigation than these caveats of mine about George Steiner's summary justice. But the prior point is that the instances themselves must be discriminated the one from the other. The more so, since Eliot himself, conscious of the intertwinings of these poems of 1918–19, did not – certainly at the time – estimate the difference between the dramatized hallucinatory clarity of 'Sweeney among the Nightingales' and the melodramatized (that is, irresponsibly diffused) animus of 'Burbank with a Baedeker: Bleistein with a Cigar'. For that which can save melodrama from irresponsibility is just what is missing from the latter poem, being that which Eliot pinpointed in praise of a Wilkie Collins novella, *The Haunted Hotel*: 'Fatality in this story is no longer merely a wire jerking the figures. The principal character, the fatal woman, is herself obsessed by the idea of fatality; her motives are melodramatic;

1 – To Baillie, 6 September 1863; *Further Letters*, edited by Claude Colleer Abbott (second edition, 1956), p. 205; referring to *The Saturday*, 4 July 1863.

she therefore compels the coincidences to occur, feeling that she is compelled to compel them. In this story, as the chief character is internally melodramatic, the story itself ceases to be merely melodramatic, and partakes of true drama'.[1]

For Eliot has so written 'Burbank with a Baedeker: Bleistein with a Cigar' as to ensure that there can be no true drama, no drama available to scrutiny as truth and thereby 'placed', to apply James's word to a poem which alludes to James's writing. For there is no 'chief character' (this is one reason for insisting on the poem's full title, especially as the first draft had as title only 'Bleistein with a Cigar'), and so there is no position from which to gain purchase upon whether anyone is 'internally melodramatic', while at the same time there is an obdurate emphasis on fatality and on the fatal woman:

> Burbank crossed a little bridge
>   Descending at a small hotel;
> Princess Volupine arrived,
>   They were together, and he fell.

Tennyson's line exactly in his poem of revenge, 'The Sisters' — except of course for the switched pronoun: 'They were together, and she fell'. For Eliot's story is not of a man fatally and fatedly attractive (murdered by the sister of his victim) but of a *femme fatale*. Eliot's poem, like Collins's novella for Eliot, is 'obsessed by the idea of fatality'; is steeped in melodramatic motives; and is the work of a poet here compelling coincidences to occur. For the poem is compulsively allusive, itself an ostentatious coinciding, 'a wire jerking the figures' of Tennyson and Henry James and Shakespeare and Browning and and and; all this, with Eliot himself feeling that he is compelled to compel the coincidences, just as he compels the coinciding of Burbank and the Princess. 'Descending at a small hotel': The Haunted Hotel.

For the subtitle of Collins's tale of fatality and murder exactly fits Eliot's Venetian poem: 'A Mystery of Modern Venice'. Collins's anguished *femme fatale* is the Countess Narona (kin to 'the countess' of Eliot's epigraph and to the poem's Princess

1 – 'Wilkie Collins and Dickens' (1927), *Selected Essays*, p. 467.

Volupine); a cigar is bizarrely important to Collins's plot; so is the Countess's concealment as 'Mrs James' (the poem is a Jamesian story); and the central blackmail in the story is the threat by the Countess's brother to sell himself: ' "The woman who will buy me", he says, "is in the next room to us at this moment. She is the wealthy widow of a Jewish usurer." '

Collins mounts a plot which is no mystery once it is plumbed. Eliot thickens the plot of his poem to render it unplumbable. This is what makes the Jewish instance from 'Burbank with a Baedeker: Bleistein with a Cigar' different in kind from that in 'Gerontion' or from 'Rachel *née* Rabinovitch', quite differently objectionable. 'Burbank with a Baedeker: Bleistein with a Cigar' is irresponsibly cunning in its combination of the overt and the covert. On the one hand, there is its flatly oppressive opprobious parallelism:

> The rats are underneath the piles.
> The Jew is underneath the lot.

Yet even this does not come clean, since the effect of the article, 'The Jew', is to disparage all Jews ('The heathen Chinee is peculiar') while nevertheless leaving open a bolt-hole for the disingenuous reply that a particular Jew only is meant – some merchant of Venice. But then the indubitable parallelism of the rats and the Jew is masqued by the poem's being Eliot's most dubious, not only as to its worth but as to its deep obfuscation, at once obsessed and calculated. It is the only one of Eliot's collected poems penned with the ink of the cuttle-fish;[1] it uses its energies of ink (its own, and those of the coinciding previous writers) at once to announce and to conceal its whereabouts. Of Grover Smith's remarking in an aside that the poem 'is in execrable taste', Gabriel Pearson observed:

It is pointless merely to execrate because execration is precisely what the poem seeks to provoke. It is a hate poem, and when this is grasped its allusiveness – not to mention that of the epigraph whose six lines are made up of as many quotations – is understood as part of its central emotion, the

1 – To exempt 'Ode', which was published by Eliot in 1920 but not collected by him; it too muddies its pool.

wadding and buffering of raw places, disguises worn by the violence and despair enacted by stanza and syntax. This wadding becomes in turn an element of over-control or repression, which in turn generates further verbal violence.[1]

This is the murky equivocal form of the concealing by exposure which deeply preoccupied Eliot. In this same year, 1919, Eliot found it estimable in Pound: 'He must hide to reveal himself'.[2] Later he was even to find a form of it unexpectedly estimable in G. K. Chesterton:

Behind the Johnsonian fancy-dress, so reassuring to the British public, he concealed the most serious and revolutionary designs – concealing them by exposure, as his anarchist conspirators chose to hold their meetings on a balcony in Leicester Square.[3]

And in 1920 (the year after publishing 'Burbank with a Bae-deker: Bleistein with a Cigar'), it was an application of the same thought, this time necessitating a condoling reservation about a fellow-writer, which animated Eliot's exploration of a particu-lar congeries which is crucial to his understanding of prejudice. In pondering a verse-play by J. Middleton Murry, Eliot brought together the following considerations, all crucial to his art, to his imagination, and to the nature of prejudice. First, the needed predisposition of an audience, what he calls here 'a prepared-ness, a habit, on the part of the public, to respond in a predictable way, however crudely, to certain stimuli'.[4] Second, a suspicion. Third, an instinct. Fourth, a protection. Fifth, prejudicial names. Sixth, language's aspiration, in the

1 – *Eliot in Perspective*, ed. Martin, p. 90. Robert Crawford has a sympathetic analysis of the poem in terms of Eliot's understanding of anthropology, ritual, and cultural values (*The Savage and the City in the Work of T. S. Eliot*, pp. 110–16). But Crawford makes light of the poem's relation to its Jews, and, when he concludes his five pages with, 'The poem is funny, but at everyone's expense', it should be retorted that the groups, races and classes in the poem cannot equally afford the expense.
2 – *The Athenaeum*, 24 October 1919.
3 – *The Tablet*, 20 June 1936.
4 – *The Athenaeum*, 14 May 1920. Eliot attenuated this when he refined away 'however crudely', for *The Sacred Wood* (p. 64): 'a preparedness, a habit on the part of the public, to respond to particular stimuli'.

highest poetry, to silence.[1] Seventh, a pressure. Eighth, the relation of poetry to drama. And ninth, the concealment which reveals, though in Murry's case not happily:

Mr. Murry cannot escape an audience – comparatively small and comparatively cultivated – which has no dramatic habits, but desires to share, to destroy his solitude. We may suspect that Mr. Murry is aware of this audience, and that he instinctively protects himself from its intrusion by the titles which he gives his characters:

> I thought I heard the spinning of the wheel
> Of Destiny, and this is what she span:
> Such close-knit intertexture of two hearts . . .
> That even the hungry Fates must hold their shears
> From so divine a pattern.

The adjective 'hungry' may be questioned as irrelevant to the figure; but it is a fine passage. And I quote it to ask why the author should place such language in the mouths of personages to whom he gives names like Cinnamon, Angelica, Caraway, and Vanilla Bean. The key of the music is a lovers' melancholy with many under- and over-tones; the third act is pitched at that intensity at which language strives to become silence, and the end is definitely tragic. Why these grocery names? It is a movement of protection against the cultivated audience. Whoever is acutely sensitive of the pressure of this intruder will have his own grimace or buffoonery, to avoid sentiment or to decorate sentiment so that it will no longer appear personal, but at most – safely fashionable. This concealment is a 'give-away'; but we cannot say that Mr. Murry has given himself away either, for his 'close-knit intertexture' is a maze of such subtilized and elusive feelings as will hardly be threaded by any but those whom he would be willing to admit.

But 'Burbank with a Baedeker: Bleistein with a Cigar', too, has its protections, instincts, suspicions, and prejudicial names. It too becomes 'a maze of such subtilized and elusive feelings as will hardly be threaded by any but those whom he would be

---

1 – 'Burnt Norton': 'Words, after speech, reach / Into the silence.' In an unpublished lecture on 'English Letter Writers' (1933), Eliot said of Lawrence's remarking 'this stark, bare, rocky directness of statement' which 'alone makes poetry, today': 'This speaks to me of that at which I have long aimed, in writing poetry . . . To get *beyond poetry*, as Beethoven, in his later works, strove to get *beyond music*.' (Quoted by F. O. Matthiessen, *The Achievement of T. S. Eliot*, second edition 1947, p. 90.)

willing to admit'. This concealment is a give-away; but we cannot say that Mr Eliot has given himself away either.

The poem's multiplicity of partial dramatizations furnishes a licence which Eliot seldom claimed and which is here licentious in allowing him to vent the pent without taking the rap. The poem permits Eliot too easy an application of his remark, not in itself unprincipled, that a poet's 'lines may be for him only a means of talking about himself without giving himself away'.[1] For about this particular form of not giving himself away 'there hangs the shadow of the impure motive' (Eliot on Donne);[2] hence the back-rush of aggressiveness. Eliot wrote of Pound, the year before this poem:

In the longer 'contemporanea' the majority of readers will probably find signs of dessication. I do not think that this is right; but I am not sure that there has not been in some instances a self-consciousness which has induced reserve, with a back-rush of aggressiveness.[3]

The ugliest touch of anti-Semitism in Eliot's poetry, in my judgement, is the 'Dirge' (sibling to 'Burbank with a Baedeker: Bleistein with a Cigar') which was posthumously published with the manuscript of The Waste Land.[4] The first of the two stanzas is this:

> Full fathom five your Bleistein lies
> Under the flatfish and the squids.
> Graves' Disease in a dead jew's eyes!
> When the crabs have eat the lids.
> Lower than the wharf rats dive
> Though he suffer a sea-change
> Still expensive rich and strange

Pound himself jotted on the manuscript: '?? doubtful'. Eliot wrote as the first draft 'dead jew's eyes'; he then added 'man's'

1 – 'Virgil and the Christian World', On Poetry and Poets, p. 122.
2 – 'Lancelot Andrewes', For Lancelot Andrewes (1928), p. 20.
3 – To-Day, iv (1918), 8–9.
4 – Grover Smith's judgement arrives at the closing reflection that 'A more purely literary effect can hardly be imagined'. But his fifteen lines on 'Dirge' make no mention whatsoever of either Bleistein or Jew; a more purifying critical effect can hardly be imagined (The Waste Land, 1983, p. 72).

above 'jew's', bracketing the two words; and in the fair copy he had 'dead jew's eyes'. Yet even here, in confronting what is probably the darkest variant reading in Eliot – a dead jew's eyes/ a dead man's eyes – it is crucial that resistance to an injustice perpetrated by Eliot should not issue in an injustice to Eliot. It is all too easy to make disingenuous use of a convenient fact about manuscript material: that it may with equal plausibility, in principle though not in instance, be cited as evidence of what the writer really did or really did not think and feel. For any superseded words – say, Tennyson's cry to the spirit of Arthur Hallam, there in the manuscripts of *In Memoriam* XCIII, 'wed me' – may have been rescinded by the writer as false or may have been censored as too true. 'Dirge' doubles the stakes, in that not only is there a variant reading added and then withdrawn, but the whole poem was written and then withdrawn, or rather never sent forth. The unavoidable doubleness of the principle lends itself to a critic's duplicity of *parti pris*; no critical insistence should be trusted which does not acknowledge the doubleness and say why on any particular occasion the pressure is running this way and not the opposite.

Eliot did not publish this 'Dirge'; it does not become us to claim assuredly to know why not, especially as one thing at issue in questions of prejudice is the sufficiency of evidence. To determine that the poem was suppressed because Eliot so much believed it (not disbelieved it) is to succumb to just such a prompt prejudice as is reprehended in Eliot.

Moreover, Eliot – who believed in redemption and whose art is redemptive – came to contemplate the painful admission

> Of things ill done and done to others' harm
> Which once you took for exercise of virtue.
> ('Little Gidding')[1]

The unpublished 'Dirge' about a drowned Jew might then be seen to count for less, even to matter exactly as the impulse

---

1 – The lines are more lacerating once they are revised from 'ill done then done in all assurance' and from 'Which once you thought were exercise of virtue'; see Helen Gardner's indispensable study of *The Composition of Four Quartets* (1978), p. 192.

triumphed over, an ugliness of spirit the contemplation of which could precipitate beauty and justice, crystallizing in the due limpid indifference within 'Death by Water':

> Gentile or Jew
> O you who turn the wheel and look to windward,
> Consider Phlebas, who was once handsome and tall as you.

Excessive tolerance

Usually in considering Eliot's 'uglier touches' of anti-Semitism, the immediate matter is to judge how gravely the anti-Semitism is to be deplored. But the emphasis in this present consideration is rather upon two prior points: what exactly in Eliot's words is to be deplored, and why exactly it is to be deplored. Such an emphasis is in danger of being altogether too patient with impatient injustice, but the neglect of these attentions is in danger of visiting upon a great injustice an injustice which though lesser is pernicious.

Eliot did not publish 'Dirge'; he did publish (in 1934) *After Strange Gods*, his Virginia lectures of 1933, though he never permitted a second edition – which, for a professional publisher and a writer whose works did not lack readers, amounts to a substantial withdrawing. It is necessary to take offence at some things in *After Strange Gods*; it is necessary, too, to give Eliot credit for at least some rescinding of the book. One flash is notorious. Eliot has been invoking the necessity for tradition:

Tradition is not solely, or even primarily, the maintenance of certain dogmatic beliefs; these beliefs have come to take their living form in the course of the formation of a tradition. What I mean by tradition involves all those habitual actions, habits and customs, from the most significant religious rite to our conventional way of greeting a stranger, which represent the blood kinship of 'the same people living in the same place'.

Eliot then speaks of the need for stability; the development of tradition asks that the bulk of the population have 'no incentive or pressure to move about'. Then this:

The population should be homogeneous; where two or more cultures exist in the same place they are likely either to be fiercely self-conscious or both to become adulterate. What is still more important is unity of religious background; and reasons of race and religion combine to make any large number of free-thinking Jews undesirable. There must be a proper balance between urban and rural, industrial and agricultural development. And a spirit of excessive tolerance is to be deprecated.[1]

Often the sentence about free-thinking Jews (or the second half of it) is quoted, with anger, on its own. The sentence is insensitive and worse. Yet it is importantly less objectionable than the sequence of sentences within which it is deployed. First, because the sequence is disingenuous. Second, because the sequence is a more insidious incitement to prejudice than any single sentence, since prejudice is most powerfully itself when sequential, being characterized not by sudden outcroppings (as aphorism or outburst) but by plausible processes of corrupted reasoning, by the disguising of a *non sequitur*. And third, because the sentence about free-thinking Jews, in and of itself, is more defensible, less indefensible, than it will seem if one does not scrutinize one's indignation at it.

Clearly the understanding of what it is to be a Jew is something to which learned sensitive scholars have devoted lifetimes; the matter is complicated far beyond the possibilities of these present pages. Yet, if it is held that Eliot refused to recognize the intricacy of the matter, it must not then be insisted at the same time that the matter is perfectly simple and that it was crass of Eliot to get it wrong. Is the entwining of 'race and religion' in Jewishness of Eliot's making? We wince now, with good cause, from almost any use of the word 'race', and yet to preclude the word, or some variant upon it, from all discussion of what it is to be Jewish, and of how this was or is conceived of by Jews themselves, would be an elision too easily making against Eliot. What in 1933 constituted Jewishness for Jews themselves? If Eliot's speaking of 'race and religion' is badly wrong, what is the right way to conceive of the matter, from within Judaism and Jewish tradition itself? J. Mitchell Morse says, apropos of Eliot and anti-Semitism, 'we Jews are not a

1 – *After Strange Gods*, pp. 18–20.

race';[1] Philip Roth, more perplexedly truthful, has written in *The Counterlife* (1986) a novel which, among other things, is a dramatized body of arguments about why the relation of Jewishness to the racial is not that simple.

To turn for help to an encyclopaedia of the Jewish religion is to find that the entry under Jew becomes all but unfathomable in its intricacy (full of honourable dubiety and of caveats, as well as of acknowledged differences of learned judgement and of traditions within Judaism, Orthodox and Reform) just as soon as the elucidation touches upon the tender questions of birth and parentage, and upon the difference between a Jewish mother and a Jewish father, and upon conversion. It is apparently agreed that conversion, let alone a missionary enterprise, plays a quite other and much smaller part within Judaism than it does within Christianity; this fact itself bears upon the difficult intertexture of race and religion. *The Encyclopaedia of the Jewish Religion* speaks of 'the non-Jew who wishes to become a Jew';[2] describes what is entailed; and adds:

Such a convert is in every respect a Jew and is considered to be on a par with a natural born Jew. He suffers from practically no disabilities, except that the female convert cannot marry a priest.

This clarifies, but what it clarifies is that the encyclopaedia is unable to make the matter entirely clear. There is an inconsistency between saying that a convert 'is in every respect a Jew' and then continuing 'and is considered on a par with a natural born Jew'; 'is considered' is something less than 'is', and one can be 'on a par' only with that with which one is not 'in every respect' identified. 'He suffers from practically no disabilities': this is tonally too close to *not particularly* for comfort. There is then more than an awkwardness in saying that 'He suffers from practically no disabilities' and at once following this with 'except that the female convert cannot marry a priest', where (first) the move from 'he' to the woman is insensitive; where (second) it is odd to say 'practically no disabilities' and then name only one as if that were the only one (why not in that case

1 – *Prejudice and Literature*, p. 172.
2 – Edited by R. J. Zwi Werblowsky and Geoffrey Wigoder (1966).

say simply 'suffers from one, and only one, disability'?); and where (third) it is not clear why this last withholding of this right from the (female) convert is not a very serious one. It apparently does not even need to be said that the male convert cannot be a priest, since a priest here (not a rabbi but a *kohen* or of the tribe of Levi) is a family decendant and therefore an embodiment of parentage and race. The point is not that the encyclopaedia's account should be repudiated, but that it brings out the difficulties and even intractabilities attending the question, and which are not merely willed into existence by those unsympathetic to the Jewish religion. The convert 'is considered on a par with a natural born Jew': possibly those last words would not have to entail race, but it is reasonable to inquire why not exactly.

Presumably a rabbi does not believe that any large number of free-thinking Jews is desirable, though he would find it offensive to word the point so; he could concur with Eliot's point while arguing that this does not mean that Eliot has the right to concur with him, since it might not, for a believer in Judaism, be 'reasons of race and religion' that would make any large number of free-thinking Jews undesirable, only reasons of religion. Nevertheless, a man of religious belief, whether Christian or not, not only might but should deprecate free-thinkers. Not just 'free-thinking Jews', admittedly, but then Eliot never spared free-thinking Christians, and someone of Eliot's beliefs might legitimately contend that the idea of free-thinking Christians is self-contradictory in a way that the idea of free-thinking Jews is not, since being a Jew does not necessarily stand to belief exactly as being a Christian does.

Admittedly, Christianity has in practice repeatedly fallen short of its ideals in a way that does not surprise non-Christians (or Christians, for that matter), but the ideal itself is of a community or communion based entirely upon subscription or conversion to a creed, not at all upon any considerations of race or parentage. Not that Eliot would have mollified away all difficulties for Christianity in its relation to race; *After Strange Gods*[1] itself expresses about Hopkins's conversion within

1 – p. 47.

Christianity a reservation such as could be bent upon conversion to Christianity:

> To be converted, in any case, while it is sufficient for entertaining the hope of individual salvation, is not going to do for a man, as a writer, what his ancestry and his country for some generations have failed to do.

That such considerations were among those in Eliot's head, even if he must now be judged to have closed his mind in 1933 to their dangerous difficulties, is clear from the self-defence he conducted in correspondence in 1940 when he was accused of tendencies towards anti-Semitism and when the sentence about free-thinking Jews was cited.[1] Eliot replied:

> As to the question of my supposed anti-Semitism, I had imagined that your impression was founded on the particular sentence you quote. I hope, however, that on another reading you will give me the credit for meaning exactly what I said. By free-thinking Jews I mean Jews who have given up the practice and belief of their own religion, without having become Christians or attached themselves to any other dogmatic religion. It should be obvious that I think a large number of free-thinkers of any race to be undesirable, and the free-thinking Jews are only a special case. The Jewish religion is unfortunately not a very portable one, and shorn of its traditional practices, observances and Messianism, it tends to become a mild and colourless form of Unitarianism. The free-thinking European, or American of European race, retains for the most part a good many of the moral habits and conventions of Christianity. If he does not retain them individually, still these habits survive to some extent in the community. The Jew who is separated from his religious faith is much more deracinated thereby than the descendant of Christians, and it is this deracination that I think dangerous and tending to irresponsibility. But my view does not imply any prejudice on the ground of race, but merely a recognition of what seems to me an historical social situation. It is quite possible, of course, that all people of Christian descent will become so emancipated from Christianity in the course of time that this sentence of mine will cease to have any meaning.

This is not corroded with ill will, but it is not persuasive. It has a tone of pleading, partly of special pleading ('the free-thinking Jews are only a special case'), and as argument it is under-

1 – 10 May 1940. This correspondence with J. V. Healy is now at the Harry Ransom Humanities Research Center, University of Texas at Austin.

described and undersubstantiated to the point of being perverse. For one can easily imagine the exactly opposite case being maintained: not that the Jewish religion is 'unfortunately not a very portable one', but that unfortunately it has been a very portable one – has had to be, because of those misfortunes to which Eliot is not compassionate enough; and not that the moral habits and conventions of Judaism are not retained by free-thinking Jews, but that they strongly and even disconcertingly are.

It is not that Eliot liked or respected the fact (as it seemed to him) that lapsed Christians retain 'for the most part a good many of the moral habits and conventions of Christianity'; he thought this a bad form of free-thinking free-loading, insidious and corrupt, a self-deception such as came between the soul and its recognition of truth. There would be more hope of salvation if a lapsed Christian would face the extent to which his life was indeed intolerable to him without the moral habits and conventions of that Christianity which he is refusing to give its due or his dues. Self-protection should be painfully peeled, and Eliot's admiration for Djuna Barnes's *Nightwood* as a religious vision of life is at one with his valuing it for its seeing a cruel paradox of the suffering that supposes itself to be post-Christian:

The miseries that people suffer through their particular abnormalities of temperament are visible on the surface: the deeper design is that of the human misery and bondage which is universal. In normal lives this misery is mostly concealed; often, what is most wretched of all, concealed from the sufferer more effectively than from the observer. The sick man does not know what is wrong with him; he partly wants to know, and mostly wants to conceal the knowledge from himself.[1]

There was then for Eliot a distinction between Judaism and Christianity here, as to falling away from the religion, which he persistently worried at, and not only because of any queasy and resentful feelings about Jews. It was a central belief of his that ceasing to be a Christian was not as easy as it might seem when all you really did was continue to live on unearned Christian

---

1 – Introduction (1937) to Djuna Barnes, *Nightwood* (second edition 1950), pp. 5–6.

capital. Sharply critical in 1927 of Bertrand Russell's *Why I Am Not a Christian*, Eliot gave reasons for believing that 'Mr. Russell is essentially a low Churchman, and only by caprice can call himself an Atheist': 'For one only ceases to be a Christian by being something else definite – a Buddhist, a Mohammedan, a Brahmin.'[1] Eliot may well have been wrong to believe this, or differently wrong to suppose that such a thing could not be said likewise of someone who lapses from Judaism, but this would not necessarily be because Eliot had himself here lapsed into anti-Semitism.

Yet the point about 'free-thinking Jews' is instinct with animus, and if the animus is directed more upon free-thinkers than upon Jews (who, it is claimed, 'are only a special case'), why was Eliot moved to the inflammatory reference to Jews at all? Because the Jewish religion, shorn and liberalized, 'tends to become a mild and colourless form of Unitarianism': Eliot's way of putting it in the letter of 1940 brings home the extent to which his uneasiness in these matters is compounded, and even prompted, by his hostility towards the Unitarianism from which he had escaped with lacerations, Unitarianism which he was prepared to characterize categorically as 'outside the Christian Fold'.[2]

The intersection of the Jewish and the Unitarian in this letter of Eliot's corroborates William Empson's inspired interpretation of the anti-Semitic impulses in the *Waste Land* manuscript (which harbours 'Dirge') as intimate with Eliot's repudiation of his father and of his father's religion. Empson says of Eliot's anti-Semitism, 'A writer had better rise above the ideas of his time, but one should not take offence if he doesn't'; Empson takes less offence not only because 'Dirge' was not published in *The Waste Land* or elsewhere, but also because for Empson the Jews were standing in for the Unitarian father. Not that this means they would find themselves any the less pilloried, but it constitutes a reminder that for Eliot there were pseudo-Christians any large number of whom he found undesirable. In Empson's words:

1 – *The Criterion*, vi (1927), 179.
2 – *The Criterion*, x (1931), 771.

Eliot wanted to grouse about his father, and lambasted some imaginary Jews instead (as a backroom boy at Lloyd's, doing rather technical work, and living very quietly, he was not of course regularly meeting the millionaires). But we have also to reckon with the very odd habits of Symbolist poetry. What is happening to the Jews is what was happening in *The Tempest* to the prince's father; have they then something in common? Eliot's grandfather went to St Louis as a missionary preaching Unitarianism, and incidentally founded a university there; Eliot's father continued to be a staunch Unitarian while going into business. Eliot himself at Harvard read Sanskrit, a thoroughly Boston-Brahmin thing to do, and remarked soon after that it was almost impossible to be a Christian after studying the Far Eastern religions. Unitarians describe themselves as Christians but deny that Jesus was God, whereas Eliot was beginning to feel a strong drag towards a return to the worship of the tortured victim. Now if you are hating a purse-proud business man who denies that Jesus is God, into what stereotype does he best fit? He is a Jew, of course; and yet this would be a terrible blasphemy against his family and its racial pride, so much so that I doubt whether Eliot ever allowed himself to realise what he was doing. But he knows, in the poem, that everything has gone wrong with the eerie world to which the son is condemned.[1]

Eliot's correspondence with J. V. Healy did not end amicably, for what was being asked of Eliot was a retraction more ample than any that he was prepared to make; the most he could offer on 19 June 1940 was this: 'The whole tone of *After Strange Gods* is of a violence which I now deprecate' (that word again, it has a dying fall), 'and I am sure that it contains many statements or assertions which I should now wish to qualify: but I do not think that the sentence which was in question is one of them. At least, having given the explanation which I have given you, I can only express regret at the possibilities of mis-interpretation.'

Yet that sentence of Eliot's is greatly to be regretted. But more sharply to be deplored is the relation of the sequence of the sentences to their substance:

. . . reasons of race and religion combine to make any large number of free-thinking Jews undesirable. There must be a proper balance between urban and rural, industrial and agricultural development. And a spirit of excessive tolerance is to be deprecated.

1 – *Using Biography* (1984), pp. 196–7.

What is discreditable, because it is not sincerely meant to be credited, is the claim that the third sentence, with its leading 'And' ('And a spirit of excessive tolerance is to be deprecated'), is to be understood in relation to the 'urban and rural, industrial and agricultural development' of the preceding sentence, where it makes no sense whatever, while in fact it is being winged not towards urban and agricultural development but towards the Jews of the first sentence.

The point is not the wisdom of Eliot's belief in a proper balance of urban and rural, industrial and agricultural development; he is not fabricating this, and on later occasions he gave valuable expression to the same thought within contexts which were in no way disingenuous. It is necessary to quote at some length to show how different from that in *After Strange Gods* these contexts are.

The civil and religious elements cannot be isolated from each other. It is not simply a problem of altering a part of the whole system to fit in with modern developments: if that were so, we might, as ecclesiastical reformers, be busy in trying to adapt church organization to a world which, as civil reformers, we were trying to change in such a way that the church would not need to be altered, or, more likely, would need to be altered on very different lines. We have the problem of trying to strike the right balance between urban and rural, between agricultural and industrial life, and the problem of the future system of the Church is bound up with that. The ignoring of the integral religious-social problem, by defenders of Christian faith, has led, I think, in the past generation to our stressing the conscious element in the lapse away from Christianity, to the neglect of what I believe to have been a more powerful cause, the social changes, the mobility, the insecurity, the mechanization of minds and the atomization of individuals in an industrial age, which have operated unconsciously upon the mass of human beings. (1940)[1]

The man of letters should know that uniformity means the obliteration of culture, and that self-sufficiency means its death by starvation.

The man of letters should see also, that within any cultural unit, a proper balance of rural and urban life is essential. Without great cities – great, not necessarily in the modern material sense, but great by being the meeting-place of a society of superior mind and more polished manners – the

1 – *Christendom*, x (1940), 228–9.

culture of a nation will never rise above a rustic level; without the life of the soil from which to draw its strength, the urban culture must lose its source of strength and rejuvenescence. (1944)[1]

These two sequences about a right balance and a proper balance do themselves possess a proper balance. But it is very different with the sequence from *After Strange Gods*, for the barb about 'excessive tolerance' has nowhere to strike home but to those Jews, and the syntactical prophylaxis which manufactures the *cordon sanitaire* of an intermediate sentence – to guard against what would not be a misunderstanding at all – is disingenuous. That Eliot is being irresponsibly mastered by the impulsion of his rhetoric is clear from the circularity or vacancy with which 'excessive' is exploited: 'a spirit of excessive tolerance is to be deprecated.' For this allows him to promise a dishonourable pardon to those who act out their intolerance, while not himself being openly inflammatory since his way of putting it maintains nothing. After all, a spirit of excessive tolerance is indeed to be deprecated – the only trouble being that this is not a judgement about tolerance but a consequence of what the word 'excessive' everywhere means. How could there be a spirit of excessive anything which was not to be deprecated? The sentence is destructively self-fulfilling in a way which is itself a rhetorical prejudicing of the issue. Such rhetoric seeks to use nullity; its nemesis is that the free-thinking Jews are not the ones who are annulled by it.

The disingenuousness of the sequence there in *After Strange Gods* is a matter not only of animus but of self-deception. For to look back at the sequence not only of syntax but of thinking is to see that Eliot had become ensnared in the consequences of his having wrenched aside his dangerous line of thought.

The population should be homogeneous; where two or more cultures exist in the same place they are likely either to be fiercely self-conscious or both to become adulterate. What is still more important is unity of religious background; and reasons of race and religion combine to make any large number of free-thinking Jews undesirable.

1 – *Horizon*, x (1944), 384.

Cultural unity, we are told, is important; what is still more important is unity of religious background; and from these propositions it should therefore follow that in a predominantly Christian society reasons of race and religion combine to make any large number of Jews undesirable: Jews, whether free-thinking or not. Not Jews alone, of course, but in 1933 the religious unity of the USA in general or of Virginia in particular was not threatened by an influx of Buddhists or Mohammed-ans.[1] Yet Eliot, for reasons which (as flinching always com-plicatedly is) are very slightly to his credit but more to his discredit, could not quite bring himself to say that reasons of race and religion combine to make any large number of Jews undesirable. That outcome of the thinking is at once suppressed and betrayed. The punctuation ('background; and rea-sons . . .') does not have the disingenuous candour of a colon, which would dare you to deny that the next thought was a true consummation ('What is still more important is unity of religious background: reasons of race and religion com-bine . . .'); but nor does Eliot separate off the further stage by making it openly a new sentence; he relies on the semi-colon and the 'and'. He might, if he had not winced, have advanced the full dangerous sequence: that, in a predominantly Christian society, unity of religious background makes any large number of Jews undesirable, and that moreover there are reasons why free-thinking Jews are especially undesirable. Instead, he collapsed his thoughts, and made himself responsible for a paragraph which at once appals and palters.

Never does that side of Eliot which manifests itself in *hauteur* seem so betraying, such a self-betrayal too, than when a horror is played down. In 1933, the word 'undesirable', bent upon free-

---

1 – William M. Chace adduces pertinent facts: 'Let us remember the date of this extraordinary statement: 1933. The great years of American immigration were over. The exclusionary Immigration Act of 1924, drafted by Senators Albert Johnson and David A. Reed, had had its effect. But from 1820 to 1930, no less than thirty-eight million people had immigrated. Two and one-half million Jews had entered the country between 1880 and 1913 alone. In 1933, one hundred and twenty million people, fourteen million of them foreign-born, were living in the United States. It is in this context that Eliot's praise of a homogeneous citizenry must be seen' (*The Political Identities of Ezra Pound and T. S. Eliot*, 1973, p. 160).

thinking Jews, already lacked compassion. By 1936, even more too late, Eliot was prepared to print in *The Criterion* an unsigned review which was armoured in fastidious unimagination and which – whether or not the review was by Eliot – had the stamp of his approval and the stamp of his tone.

The Yellow Spot: The Outlawing of Half a Million Human Beings: A Collection of Facts and Documents Relating to Three Years' Persecution of German Jews, Derived chiefly from Nationalist Socialist Sources, very carefully assembled by a Group of Investigators. With an introduction by the Bishop of Durham. (Gollancz, 1936.) 8s. 6d. cloth; 5s. paper.

There should be somebody to point out that this book, although enjoying a cathedratic blessing, is an attempt to rouse moral indignation by means of sensationalism. Needless to say, it does not touch on how we might alleviate the situation of those whose misfortunes it describes, still less on why they, among all the unfortunates of the world, have a first claim on our compassion and help. Certainly no English man or woman would wish to be a German Jew in Germany to-day; but not only is our title to the moral dictatorship of the world open to question, there is not the least prospect of our being able to exercise it. More particularly, it is noticeable that the jacket of the book speaks of the 'extermination' of the Jews in Germany, whereas the title-page refers only to their 'persecution'; and as the title-page is to the jacket, so are the contents to the title-page, especially in the chapter devoted to the ill-treatment of Jews in German concentration camps.[1]

This is shameful. It is to be hoped that such cruelly self-righteous impercipience as this was later recognized by Eliot to be among the things ill done and done to others' harm which once he took for exercise of virtue.

'And a spirit of excessive tolerance is to be deprecated': to be great it was not essential that Eliot should always speak roundly but the great Eliot never speaks so circularly. He writes far more creditably of tolerance when he makes real two related convictions: that much of what passes for tolerance is merely indifference, and that Christians might not only have to endure but to welcome intolerance. In 1932, the year previous to the delivery

1 – *The Criterion*, xv (1936), 759–60. Ronald Bush contrasts this notice with the book and its reception elsewhere, in *T. S. Eliot: A Study in Character and Style*, pp. 226, 274.

of *After Strange Gods* he had hit this better note in ending his 'little piece of parenthetical oratory' about Middleton Murry's condescension towards the Church, with the tart reflection that apparently the Church

is to be tolerated, as the persons of retarded development who will continue to patronise the Church will be tolerated. But for my part, I prefer to hope that I shall be untolerated, intolerant and intolerable.[1]

When it came to his own faith at least (at most, perhaps), he could understand something of the cruel paradoxes of persecution. It was in 1933 that he wrote:

In the last three or four hundred years we have passed through successive stages of schism, heresy, and toleration. Possibly the age of toleration is coming to an end, and we may be again approaching a period in which Christians in Western Europe and America will be persecuted. I hardly expect so much as that.[2]

Six years later:

When the Christian is treated as an enemy of the State, his course is very much harder, but it is simpler. I am concerned with the dangers to the tolerated minority; and in the modern world, it may turn out that the most intolerable thing for Christians is to be tolerated.[3]

It is evidence of how deep such a thought goes in Eliot that there is an echo of what will not for him have been a 'merely' literary critical remark: 'A form, when it is merely tolerated, becomes an abuse. Tolerate the stage aside and the soliloquy, and they are intolerable; make them a strict rule of the game, and they are a support'.[4]

A discrimination might be made between one of the sayings of 1933 ('And a spirit of excessive tolerance is to be deprecated') and another of the same year, no less disconcerting but much more salutary:

Perhaps these misunderstandings cancel out: we [Catholics, and especially Anglo-Catholics] are qualified as bigoted reactionaries, or as reckless

1 – *Listener*, 6 April 1932.
2 – *Christian Register*, 19 October 1933.
3 – *The Idea of a Christian Society* (1939), p. 23.
4 – *The Dial*, lxxi (1921), 215.

socialists, according to the disposition of the hostile critic and the tendencies of some individual Catholic whom he has in mind. I think that the
virtue of tolerance is greatly overestimated, and I have no objection to
being called a bigot myself; but that is an individual concern.[1]

This means exactly what it says. For Eliot was warning of the
dangers not of valuing but of overvaluing tolerance.

The value itself had first to be distinguished from the mas-
querader, indifference. In 'What is a Classic?', Eliot deplored a
new kind of provincialism: 'It is a provincialism, not of space,
but of time; one for which history is merely the chronicle of
human devices which have served their turn and been scrapped,
one for which the world is the property solely of the living, a
property in which the dead hold no shares.'

If this kind of provincialism led to greater tolerance, in the sense of
forbearance, there might be more to be said for it; but it seems more likely
to lead to our becoming indifferent, in matters where we ought to maintain
a distinctive dogma or standard, and to our becoming intolerant, in
matters which might be left to local or personal preference.[2]

When he praised Kipling for his 'attitude of comprehensive
tolerance', he pounced to a footnote: 'Not the tolerance of
ignorance or indifference'.[3]

Eliot was sometimes too prompt to protest against the overvaluing of tolerance, and tardy about protesting against intolerance; but at least he had a substantial sense of what tolerance
was. He energized the need to distinguish it from indifference.
Anti-liberal rather than illiberal, he would not have colluded
with the present evisceration of tolerance, an evisceration of
which liberals ought to be the first to disapprove. For tolerance
has come to mean *not disapproving*, whereas the indispensa-
bility of tolerance, its unique social and human triumph, consists in its disapproving yet permitting; there is no particular
virtue in – or even a meaning to – permitting or tolerating that
of which you in any case approve. Tolerance itself then is
reduced to being a human device which has served its turn and

1 – *Christendom*, iii (1933), 180–1.
2 – 'What is a Classic?', *On Poetry and Poets* (1957), p. 69.
3 – 'Rudyard Kipling', *On Poetry and Poets*, p. 242.

been scrapped. A conservative such as Eliot is less of an enemy to tolerance or toleration than is the impugner of disapproval as in itself a failure of tolerance. Or say rather that Eliot is the right enemy. 'Fortunate the man who, at the right moment, meets the right friend; fortunate also the man who at the right moment meets the right enemy.'[1]

Suburban prejudice

'As for Mr. Pound, I have already made it clear that I do not associate myself with any of his opinions about Jews':[2] Eliot in 1940. In 1933 Oswald Mosley said that 'Hitler has made his greatest mistake in his attitude to the Jews'; but this did not stop Mosley from taking a leaf out of Hitler's black book. 'His greatest mistake': this rings a cracked bell. For Ezra Pound was there at Mosley's Black House, along with his pamphlet for the British Union of Fascists, *What is Money For?* Pound, who eventually came to contrition's lockjaw, spoke too of a mistake.

Ezra Pound is often credited these days with remorse or even repentance. Donald Davie has asked, or pleaded: 'To take only the most blatant and damaging of the charges, his anti-Semitism, should we not respect him for admitting, however belatedly, "the worst mistake I made was that stupid, suburban prejudice of anti-Semitism"? It appears not. On the contrary one gets the clear impression that for Pound to confess his faults is almost worse than having committed them.'[3]

It will sound churlishly unforgiving to treat Davie's rhetorical question ('should we not respect him . . .') as if it were a real question, and then to answer it with 'Well, not altogether, no'. Yet it is not only that the word 'mistake' is scarcely commensurate with the political and spiritual monstrosity of Pound's anti-Semitism. (It is Davie who speaks of Pound's confessing his

1 – *Notes towards the Definition of Culture*, p. 59.
2 – To J. V. Healy, 19 June 1940.
3 – *Pound* (1975), p. 12. Pound made his remark in conversation with Allen Ginsberg in 1967 (*Evergreen Review*, June 1968).

faults; Pound here speaks only of making a mistake.) What must be further faced is that in the very moment which we are asked to respect for its rising above an old prejudice Pound sinks back into one: 'that stupid, suburban prejudice of anti-Semitism'. The word 'suburban' can be so counted on to do its prejudicial work as not even to be visible (apparently) as prejudice. There is something in Pound's linking of anti-Semitism with the suburbs, given the snobbish enclaves and the real-estate clauses or 'understandings'; but anti-Semitism has virulently flourished in the cities too, and in the East End of London as much as in the West End. That Pound's remark is massively inaccurate (would that it were exclusively the suburbs which had housed the prejudice that is anti-Semitism) is important, but less important than the incorrigible habit of mind which had recourse to the prejudicial thought and word 'suburban'.

Pound's unforgiving repudiation of the suburb (which permits him the malign reciprocity of using the suburb as a scapegoat for the Jews, and then the Jews as a scapegoat for the suburb) lethally animates him whenever he winces from the deracination which had damaged him. In a letter of 31 March 1921 to Thomas Hardy (the man of gnarled roots), Pound brought home that he could not avail himself of a single un-English usage (having recourse to a French turn instead) without the American suburb's being to blame; there is something at once impressively continuous and dementedly escalatory about the way in which Pound moves from his title *Homage to Sextus Propertius* to the deepest rootlessness.

I ought – precisely – to have written 'Propertius soliloquizes' – turning the reader's attention to the reality of Propertius – but no – what I do is to borrow a term – aesthetic – a term of aesthetic *attitude* from a French musician, Debussy – who uses 'Homage à Rameau' for a title to a piece of music recalling Rameau's manner. My 'Homage' is not an English word at all.

There are plenty of excuses – and no justification. I come from an American suburb -- where I was not born – where both parents are really foreigners, i.e. one from New York and one from Wisconsin. The suburb has no roots, no centre of life.[1]

1 – 31 March 1921; quoted by Davie, *Pound*, p. 49.

This writhes. 'I come from an American suburb – where I was not born': this at once claims a changeling's credulous dignity (at least I wasn't born in a suburb) and laments a further indignity (and I didn't have any roots even in such rootlessness). That to come from somewhere else in the United States (United?) is to be a foreigner: this intensely underlies all the apprehensions of foreignness in Pound, and many of them in Eliot. For Pound in 1913, the account of *Patria Mia* had to begin with the words: 'America, my country, is almost a continent and hardly yet a nation';[1] and by 'America' there, he importantly did not mean either of the sub-continents, let alone the pair of them, but the United States of America. There is a poignant comedy, inadvertent, in Pound's saying that in Philadelphia both his parents were 'really foreigners, i.e. one from New York and one from Wisconsin'.

Eliot in 1919 regretted, of an article on American literature, that it 'is not supplemented elsewhere in the book by any coherent study of the society of which Hawthorne did not quite form a part': 'Such a supplement would be as useful to most Americans as to foreigners, inasmuch as in this context "foreigners" includes all Americans who are not New Englanders.'[2] This way of speaking, in Eliot or in Pound, makes one think of the grimly ludicrous moment in the film *Dog Day Afternoon* when the Brooklyn bank-robbers, bristling at their hostages, bespeak a 'plane to fly them to safety. What country do they want to fly to? 'Wyoming.'

Pound's last sentence is one of death: 'The suburb has no roots, no centre of life.' But these agonies, these energies, live on, and precipitate the cancerous vitality which will later speak unmisgivingly of 'that stupid, suburban prejudice of anti-Semitism'. 'There are plenty of excuses – and no justification', and this must severely limit our Homage to Ezra Pound.

1 – *Patria Mia* (1950; 1962 edition), p. 9.
2 – *The Athenaeum*, 25 April 1919. Eliot later wrote: 'The American intellectual of to-day has almost no chance of continuous development upon his own soil and in the environment which his ancestors, however humble, helped to form. He must be an expatriate: either to languish in a provincial university, or abroad, or, the most complete expatriation of all, in New York. And he is merely a more manifest example of what *tends* to happen in all countries' (*The Criterion*, x, 1931, 484–5).

The double scapegoating has something of a parallel in Eliot's damning the liberalized Jews by means of Unitarianism (again the unforgettable and unforgiven early years) and then Unitarianism by means of the Jews. But Pound's is the worse state, by far. He stands in need of his own styptic maxim: Pity for the infected, but preserve antisepsis. So that when Lincoln Kirstein can say, 'Towards the end of his long life he recognized his septic anti-Semitism as "a suburban prejudice" ',[1] some scepticism should be visited upon the word 'recognized'. Again, Davie speaks of the 'horrific examples' of Poundian anti--Semitism which sickened and enraged Charles Olson; but being keen not to minister to English complacency, Davie moves within brackets to remind us that there is more than one style of anti-Semitism: these things sickened and enraged Olson, '(though as much in Mrs. Pound's genteel English version as in Pound's red-necked American)'.[2] Yet 'red-necked' there is thick-skinned, since it manifests exactly the same kind of prejudice as it is deploring, while itself being invisible as prejudice because it is so perfectly in collusion with the reigning prejudices.[3]

Corruptions within an allegiance always involve double standards. One present-day corruption within liberalism (this is not an indictment of liberalism but an indictment of a failure of vigilance) is manifest in the way in which people who would blench or blanch at anything resembling an ethnic slur are now happy to collude with the ethnic slur which preposterously reserves the word 'ethnic' itself for certain privileged (dis-privileged) ethnicities or even restaurants. Complacent enlightenment is notable too for permitting itself just the one indispensable ethnic slur: WASP or Wasp.

[Acronym f. the initial letters of White Anglo-Saxon Protestant.] A member of the American white Protestant middle or upper class descended from early European settlers in the U.S. Freq. *derog.*

It is unhelpful of the Supplement to the *OED* to say merely 'early European' there, as if Anglo-Saxonry were irrelevant.

1 – *New York Review of Books*, 30 April 1981.
2 – *Trying to Explain* (1980), p. 146.
3 – On the redneck slur, see Russell Davies on a life of Elvis Presley, *London Review of Books*, 21 January – 3 February 1982.

The first citation is 1962. The willingness to stereotype and to use derogatory labels, provided that you do so from the vantage-point of the correct political allegiance, is clear from the *Times Literary Supplement* in 1968 (the 1960s sometimes exchanging one set of prejudicial stereotypes for another): 'The Jew can choose to leave his ghetto by "passing" or by breaking the more and more flimsy barriers put up by Wasp (and non-Wasp) anti-Semitism, but the Negro cannot.'

This elegantly ugly appeal to ethnic prejudice suggests, whether you are conscious of it or not, that the White Anglo-Saxon Protestant is a pest that stings, that doesn't even make honey, and that should be crushed. Moreover, the location within wealth, privilege, and power grotesquely misrepresents or masks some important political realities, such as that there are a great many very poor white Anglo-Saxon Protestants in the USA, and such as that there are some very wealthy, privileged and powerful Catholic and Jewish dynasties. This creates the slovenly comedy that, as long as a public figure has enough of these perquisites, he can be dubbed a Wasp even if he is famously and familially not a Protestant at all – a posthumous conversion visited upon John F. Kennedy for one. The insinuation that any white Anglo-Saxon Protestant is stylishly moneyed is false and politically pernicious. That by no means all white Anglo-Saxon Protestants are Wasps is an awkward fact, to be in some sense known and in no sense recognized, the point of the prejudicial ethnic acronym being to help ensure that what is known should not be acknowledged. Someone might retort that the word has come to *mean* the affluently exclusive middle- and upper-class ones, and might appeal to the *Random House Dictionary* (1987), which moves from the expansion of the acronym (acknowledged there as derogatory and offensive) as White Anglo-Saxon Protestant to this: 'a member of the privileged established white upper middle class in the United States'. But the trouble is that these ethnic and religious slurs have a way of being incontinent. Perhaps (the etymology is uncertain) a wog was originally no more than a particular stratum, a Westernized Oriental Gentleman; but the word was offensive even so, and it did not stay put if that was where it was meant to be, and people are right now to find the word crudely prejudicial. Such people would do well to find Wasp crudely prejudicial too. My own belief is that society at present has worked itself into an exacerbated hypertrophy of solicitude about labels (only some of which are libels), so it is not so much that I am shocked by Wasp as that I am shocked by the conniving blindness of those who, all eyes for such slights in the ordinary way, see nothing shocking in this particular one, it being visited upon those who had injustice coming to them.

What the literary world does is hire suave hit-men like Gore Vidal to enunciate for it. Take a characteristic prejudicial move such as this of Vidal's, with its pre-emptive strike against Eliot and his 'prejudices':

Incidentally, I have never quite understood Eliot's wisecrack that James had a mind so fine that no idea could violate it. In James one is always aware of a highly subtle intelligence with all its (changing) biases and viewpoints as it considers everything from communism to D. H. Lawrence. I, on the other hand, have never detected much in the way of 'ideas', as opposed to moods or prejudices, in Eliot's curious neurotic commentaries. But then, Eliot ended a mere Christian; James ended an artist.[1]

But Eliot, who consummated his gratitude to James here with the words 'He is the most intelligent man of his generation', was not indulging a wisecrack, he was engaged upon a Jamesian exactitude of praise:

James's critical genius comes out most tellingly in his mastery over, his baffling escape from, Ideas; a mastery and an escape which are perhaps the last test of a superior intelligence. He had a mind so fine that no idea could violate it.[2]

When a correspondent in the *New York Review of Books*,[3] Eleanor Cook, pointed out that Eliot's remark about James, though exquisitely silky, was in context a praise and not a dispraise (for who other than Vidal would want to have his or her mind *violated* by an idea?), Vidal, at a loss except for words, fell back upon this: 'I am in Cook's debt not only for quoting

1 – *New York Review of Books*, 6 November 1986.
2 – *Little Review*, v (1918), 46; previously in *The Egoist*, January 1918.
3 – 18 December 1986.

Eliot in full but for omitting, out of tact, the occasion for his remarks: a review of that all-time neo-conservative black hole, Henry Adams.' But this is not a fact which Cook had omitted out of tact, but a fabrication of Vidal's: Eliot's words occur not within his (hostile) review of *The Education of Henry Adams* at all, but within 'In Memory of Henry James', one of the two essays in which Eliot in 1918 contemplated what this recent death meant to life, to the life of art and the life of the mind. 'In Memory of Henry James' contains not one word about Henry Adams. No *NYR* correspondent then thought that it was worth the candle (since Vidal does not pay these gambling debts) to expose the lie of this prejudicial slur upon Eliot. This, from someone who is pleased to detect in Eliot no ideas, only 'moods and prejudices'.

As for 'Eliot ended a mere Christian': giving soft-spoken offence (to a purring audience) is Vidal's forte; but ought liberal readers of the *New York Review* to acquiesce so happily in a crass prejudice against Christianity such as they would never countenance against any other religion?

Language itself, in ways that are both good and bad, has a habit of not acquiescing. It puts up its resistance not only to the best-laid plans but to the best-intentioned ones, so it will not do to pretend, for instance, that now we have settled upon the excellently neutral terms 'blacks' and 'whites' for those pigmentations (no more not only of the rancour of 'nigger' but also of the condescension of the capital N for Negro or of B for Black, and no more of the evasiveness of 'coloured' with its different cruel nuance elsewhere), we have settled the matter. For, whatever the emancipated guardians of the language may say, you cannot speak of Chinese and Japanese as 'yellows' or of Indians as 'browns'; the concordat about blacks and whites represents a political settlement that this is the racial distinction which really matters. The latest *bien-pensant* portmanteau, 'people of colour', licensed by the Modern Language Association, does not begin to meet the problem of there being many pigmentations but only two that are currently granted their linguistic differentiation as nouns; and in any case the term 'people of colour' introduces its own newly offensive prejudicialities. The point is not, in this honourable search for terms which will escape prejudice and achieve a simple descriptive neutrality, that all is lost; merely that not all is won.

A terrible slander

There are four ways of considering the matter of Eliot and anti-Semitism, and these next sections address them. First, there is the biographical, which would attend to Eliot the man. Second, the historical, which would attend to the times, the very different times in which Eliot lived – different not only from our day or from days previous to his, but differing in themselves, decade from decade. Third, there is the dissociated, which claims that whatever Eliot's personal or political doings and sayings may have been, the poems are quite another matter. And last there is the continuous, which believes that the matter of anti-Semitism has a particular importance because it cannot be isolated from the larger issues of categorizing and prejudice in Eliot's poetry, issues which are as responsible for his greatness as for his rare lapses from greatness.

'I am not an anti-Semite and never have been,' Eliot insisted. 'It is a terrible slander on a man.'[1] In due time, there will be enough known of Eliot's friendships and of his behaviour for there to be some confidence of humane judgement. In his biography of Eliot, Peter Ackroyd (who was not assisted by the Eliot estate) reports his findings.

In his unpublished correspondence there are four references. On two occasions he used the word 'Jew' as a perjorative [sic] adjective – once in a letter to John Quinn, dated 12 March 1923, and once in a letter to Ezra Pound, dated 31 October 1917. In a letter to Herbert Read, dated '16 February' (probably written in 1925) he described a racial prejudice from which he was not immune – although he did not specify that prejudice, its nature is clear from the context, in which he offered Disraeli as an example of what he meant. Finally in a letter to Bonamy Dobrée – dated by Dobrée 'about March 1929' – he made a number of supercilious remarks about the

1 – Quoted in William Turner Levy and Victor Scherle, *Affectionately, T. S. Eliot* (1968), p. 81.

Jews. All the available evidence suggests, then, that on occasions he made what were then fashionably anti-semitic remarks to his close friends. Leonard Woolf, himself a Jew, has said, 'I think T. S. Eliot was slightly anti-semitic in the sort of vague way which is not uncommon. He would have denied it quite genuinely.'[1]

'Slightly anti-semitic', or 'not particularly anti-Semitic'. This makes dispiriting reading, and perhaps biographically Eliot will not be able to hope for better than this measured distaste for his failings in what were for him the disturbed 1920s. The only occasion when Eliot felt able to mount a substantial critique of anti-Semitism came when he was in a sense convenienced (hugely though not dishonourably) by its being Soviet Russia, the left and not the right, whose anti-Semitism was the occasion for reprimand. Eliot was replying in 1954 to an invitation to comment on the Soviet persecution of dissident Jewish intellectuals:

> As one of the poets who has enjoyed the generosity of the Poetry Center and the kind attention of its audience, I am glad for the opportunity to respond to your letter of the 12th instant. But a mere statement of my approval of the need to take a public stand against the present anti-Semitic policy of the Soviet government is far short of what I feel writers should do – for what humane person could refuse to lend force to such a protest? I think we should go on record with sentiments much deeper than that.
>
> The one notable distinction between the current anti-Semitism in the Soviet Union, and the anti-Semitism of Nazi Germany is, I think, this: that the Soviets have 'benefited' from the errors of the Nazis, and are much more clever propagandists. The Nazis persecuted Jews for being Jews, and so brought down on themselves the antipathy and censure of all the civilized world. The Soviets hold back from any open doctrine of racial superiority because this would too egregiously countermand their published principles, and confuse the workings of their foreign policy. Just as they have denigrated and silenced their more important Christian victims – not on the basis of their being Christians, but always on some trumped-up notion of incivility or treason – so the Jews who are condemned to death, or worse, are always accused on some other pretext, than that of being Jews. But in the end there is no difference.
>
> In all anti-Semitic drives by governments there is a discernible pattern of *policy* and *hysteria*. The hysteria of the masses is whipped up by cold deliberation. Yet there is a quotient of hysteria even in the deliberation

1 – *T. S. Eliot* (1984), pp. 303–4.

itself. True anti-Semitism – as distinct from anti-Semitism in Moslem areas, which tends to carry with it the old burdens of familiar racial, nationalistic and religious opposition – is a force wholly inside of one country, or of a ruling clique against the Jews who happen to be its own citizens. It is a symptom of the deepest dilemma, chaos and of the malfunctioning of the economy and in the religious pretensions of that nation; and is used to the point of exploitation by rulers as a radical remedy which, in the end, only aggravates the disease of which it is a symptom. These remarks provide a more reasonable ground for the conviction which I have long held, that any country which denies the rights of its own citizens or makes pariahs of any body of its own nationals – and most especially the Jews – will sooner or later have to pay the full price for so doing; and even the 'uninvolved' people whom it governs will have to expiate the crime of having allowed such a government to lead them.[1]

This raises as many questions, and as many heckles, as it settles. There is, for instance, the claim that the one notable distinction between Soviet and Nazi anti-Semitism is that Soviet Russia has learned disguise, as if the Nazi death-camps did not constitute a notable distinction of a monstrous kind. And there is the discrimination, not unreal but seriously underdescribed and tendentious, of 'true anti-Semitism' from the Moslem or nationalistic kind. Such a letter suggests the challenge that will one day face a biographical inquiry, not least because the biographical must shade into the critical, especially with a poet who believed that great writers may convert even their weakness into art. There is an Oxford story, a very Oxford story, of how Maurice Bowra was once playing in conversation the donnish game of awarding final degrees – classes of degree – to the poets (a First for Pope, but not for Donne, that sort of thing). His partner: 'Maurice, we've forgotten Eliot.' And he: 'Aegrotat.' 'In the English Universities, a certificate that a student is too ill to attend at an examination.'

After the persecutions

A second avenue would be historical consideration, which involves discriminating one strain of anti-Semitism from

1 – John Malcolm Brinnin, *Sextet* (1981), pp. 269–71.

another. This can easily become insensitive or even callous, but the refusal to make any discriminations at all, historical or social or spiritual, between strains of anti-Semitism would not only involve injustice but would itself harden hearts.

Eliot in 1941 attempted to discriminate between anti-Semitisms in the persecutions perpetrated by Vichy France:

Anti-semitism there has always been, among the parties of the extreme Right: but it was a very different thing, as a symptom of the disorder of French society and politics for the last hundred and fifty years, from what it is when it takes its place as a principle of reconstruction. If this is what is happening, we can only hope that there has been, or that there will be, some organised protest against such injustice, by the French ecclesiastical hierarchy.[1]

This was before the revelation of the full extremity of Nazi anti-Semitic vileness. Even after the revelation, George Orwell in 1948 was strong-minded, though far too burly, about the need to distinguish:

It is nonsense what Fyvel said about Eliot being antisemitic. Of course you can find what would now be called antisemitic remarks in his early work, but who didn't say such things at that time? One has to draw a distinction between what was said before and what after 1934. Of course all these nationalistic prejudices are ridiculous, but disliking Jews isn't intrinsically worse than disliking Negroes or Americans or any other block of people. In the early twenties, Eliot's antisemitic remarks were about on a par with the automatic sneer one casts at Anglo-Indian colonels in boarding houses. On the other hand if they had been written after the persecutions began they would have meant something quite different ... Some people go round smelling after antisemitism all the time. I have no doubt Fyvel thinks I am antisemitic. More rubbish is written about this subject than any other I can think of.[2]

But it won't really do to make 1934 so crucial a date, and not just because of the teetering fact, in Eliot's case, that *After Strange Gods* was uttered in 1933 and published in 1934. For not everybody was anti-Semitic in the 1920s, and moreover the phrase 'the persecutions' ('after the persecutions began') is too

1 – *Christian News-Letter*, 3 September 1941.
2 – To Julian Symons, 29 October 1948; *Collected Essays, Journalism and Letters* (1968; 1970 edition), iv, 509.

convenient for Orwell. The persecution of the Jews antedates Hitler's vile extremity of it; in foreign parts, pogroms did their worst, and in the milder malice of English life a great many wrongs, not all of them unobtrusive, had for centuries been perpetrated against the Jews, including Jews who were Christians, Disraeli for one. Which is to say that there cannot be a fairminded historical account which does not go into a great deal more detail than Orwell felt like mustering in a letter to a friend. Clearly there is something in the insistence that the old English anti-Semitisms, though they were hateful, were mostly not heinous or murderous; were even compatible, for instance, with Disraeli's becoming Prime Minister; were not, to return to that sense of the Eliot phrase, 'particularly anti-Semitic'. Someone who is not a Jew is conscious that it may not be for him or her to say where, and how hard, such particularity bites.

But then political necessity makes strange bedfellows. So it is that Gertrude Himmelfarb, needing to reinstate John Buchan as politically exemplary in some ways and certainly as an ally against certain kinds of misguided sensitivity, cannot bring herself to omit all mention of his 'alleged anti-Semitism' and therefore comes up with an amnesty not only for him personally but for a whole world of suavely brutal bigotry. This is achieved by positing something called the 'innocent anti-Semitism of the clubman'. Here too, as with Orwell, the historical argument is rough and all too ready:

This is not to suggest that Buchan's novels can be acquitted of the charge of anti-Semitism. They were anti-Semitic in the same sense that they were anti-Negro. If the Jews, unlike the Negroes, were not in all ways inferior, they were most certainly different, and as one of Buchan's American heroes said of one of his Jewish heroes (vulgar Americans could be relied on to voice what polite Englishmen only thought), he simply 'didn't like his race'. But this kind of anti-Semitism, indulged in at that time and place, was both too common and too passive to be scandalous. Men were normally anti-Semitic, unless by some quirk of temperament or ideology they happened to be philo-Semitic. So long as the world itself was normal, this was of no great consequence. It was only later, when social impediments became fatal disabilities, when anti-Semitism ceased to be the prerogative of English gentlemen and became the business of politicians or demagogues, that sensitive men were shamed into silence. It was Hitler, attaching such abnormal significance to filiation and physiognomy, who put an end to the casual, innocent anti-Semitism of the clubman. When the conspiracies of the English adventure tale became the realities of German politics, Buchan and others had the grace to realize that what was permissible under civilized conditions was not permissible with civilization *in extremis*.[1]

Like all the most adroit special pleading, this practises not rough justice but rough mercy, combining a profound lack of disinterested attention with a full deployment of a half-truth. Again it is a matter of the glissades, historical and political. On the one hand, Buchan cannot be acquitted of the charge of anti-Semitism; on the other hand, he isn't really to be charged exactly, since his anti-Semitism was of the innocent kind. Granted, a great deal of deft irony plays over these ways of putting things, but the point of the irony is to suggest that prior to Hitler the only anti-Semitism that an Englishman ever had to be conscious of was something that can be called 'social impediments' and never the 'fatal disabilities' of Hitlerian history. Well, social impediments is a comforting and comfortable phrase; it might even be judged appropriate, though not I hope by his friend Gertrude Himmelfarb, to what Lionel Trilling had to endure as a Jew at Columbia in the 1930s.[2] It all comes down to the equivocation in 'permissible' — 'what was permissible under civilized conditions was not permissible with civilization *in extremis*'. 'Permissible' covers a lot of accommodating ground there, because of the difference between can and ought; the *Oxford English Dictionary* says simply, 'That can or ought to be permitted.' The scorn, contempt and humiliation bent upon Jews by those innocent anti-Semitic clubmen can be made light of only by those who do not live within a culture ruled by clubs, and even these had better make sure that they have a sufficiently high-minded extraneous political purpose (anti-

1 – *Victorian Minds* (1968), p. 261. On the other matter of whether Gertrude Himmelfarb is unjust to Buchan in attributing to his work even 'this kind of anti-Semitism', see a correspondence in the *Times Literary Supplement*: Himmelfarb, 27 November–3 December 1987; John Sutherland, 8–14 January 1988; David Daniell, 12–18 February 1988; Himmelfarb, 26 February–3 March 1988; Daniell, 11–17 March 1988.
2 – See Diana Trilling, 'Lionel Trilling: a Jew at Columbia', Appendix to Lionel Trilling, *Speaking of Literature and Society* (1982), from *Commentary* (1982).

Communism, say) such as will allow them to be airy about all such prejudice as falls short of Nazi madness.

At about the same time as he was writing 'Burbank with a Baedeker: Bleistein with a Cigar' (written probably 1918, and published summer 1919), Eliot was scrutinizing *The Education of Henry Adams* (the book was published in 1918, and Eliot's review 23 May 1919). At the time he judged this one of his best essays, though he did not subsequently reprint it. The review and the poem breathe the same world, and even at one point share a turn of utterance; F. W. Bateson pointed out this filament:[1]

Henry Adams in 1858, and Henry James in 1870 (both at still receptive ages), land at Liverpool and descend at the same hotel.

> Burbank crossed a little bridge
> Descending at a small hotel;

(This was not, incidentally, in the poem's first draft, which had 'And Triton blew his wrinkled shell.')[2]

The review speaks explicitly of prejudice and judgement:

When Emerson as a young man stood in his pulpit and made clear to his congregation that he could no longer administer the Communion, he impressed upon them that he had no prejudice and passed no judgment upon those who continued in the practice, but that he could take no part himself – because (in his own words) it did not interest him.[3]

What interested Eliot about Henry Adams was inseparable from prejudice and judgement. The passages which Eliot chose to quote from Adams are a compendium of prejudices; for instance, on 'London society of mid-Victoria. This part of the story will provide most entertainment for English readers'. How casually and internationally diffused was the nocent anti-Semitism of the clubman. There is Adams on the Palgrave family:

Old Sir Francis, the father, had been much the greatest of all the historians of England, the only one who was un-English; and the reason of his

1 – *Eliot in Perspective*, ed. Martin, pp. 39–42; for Bateson, the poem is 'the last and perhaps the best of Eliot's exercises in semi-comic satire'.
2 – *The Waste Land: A Facsimile and Transcript*, p. 131.
3 – *The Athenaeum*, 23 May 1919.

superiority lay in his name, which was Cohen, and his mind, which was Cohen also, or at least not English. He had changed his name to Palgrave in order to please his wife.[1]

In its odious way, this is a masterpiece of *svelte* distaste, exquisitely equivocal. For, after all, Old Sir Francis is being praised, and this partly so that English intellectual life may be disparaged for being snug, and partly so that Adams's anti-Semitic smugness may be veiled in velleities. Then there is the confidence not only that a man's mind may be Cohen (there is some pathos in Henry Adams's perpetual craving that his mind should be Adams – Eliot began his review with a dozen lines pitying Adams for his oppressive forebears), but that to be Cohen is to not be English. And then, since prejudice is always more a matter of sequence, of a fuse, than of an isolated detonation, and since the sequence in such cases is always animated by some sense of a pecking-order, there is the perfectly timed move from expansive anti-Semitism to curt misogyny: 'He changed his name to Palgrave in order to please his wife.' How unmanly of Cohen, or at least not English; and at the same time how all too womanly of his wife. Adams's distaste for Cohen/Palgrave's having been a Jew is matched by his distaste for Palgrave/Cohen's having become a Christian, which he did in the year in which he married a woman whose mother's maiden name, which he then adopted, had been Palgrave. Palgrave *né* Cohen, thanks to his mother-in-law Elizabeth Turner *née* Palgrave: Adams's dark remarking is not likely altogether to have gratified a reviewer who had so many severe things to say about Adams's failings, even though this same reviewer was the poet who had published the previous year a line which has its filaments to Palgrave *né* Cohen: 'Rachel *née* Rabinovitch'.

Adams's equivocations and ironies bring home that it will not do simply to go along with Himmelfarb's equivocal parenthetical irony, '(vulgar Americans could be relied on to voice what polite Englishmen only thought)'. But then Adams does have his own form of vulgarity.

Eliot takes pleasure in Adams's multiplicity of prejudice while

1 – So the quotation in the review; Adams has 'of early England' and 'He changed'.

mildly distancing himself from it by intimating, in a passing allusion, how far Adams is from the truths of Wordsworthian dignity:

The comments of a young man, recollected in septuagenarian tranquillity, are honest, and, though not subtle, are pleasing:

> Barring the atrocious insolence and brutality which Englishmen and especially Englishwomen showed to each other – very rarely, indeed, to foreigners – English society was much more easy and tolerant than American.
>
> Balmoral was a startling revelation of royal taste. Nothing could be worse than the toilettes at Court unless it was the way they were worn . . . Fashion was not fashionable in London until the Americans and the Jews were let loose . . . There was not then – outside of a few bankers or foreigners – a good cook or a good table in London . . . If there was a well-dressed woman at table, she was either an American or 'Fast'. . . . The result was mediaeval, and amusing; sometimes coarse to a degree that might have startled a roustabout [*i.e.* navvy *Eliot's note*] and sometimes courteous and considerate to a degree that suggested King Arthur's Round Table . . .

These are revelations which are now household words, but it is pleasant to find that they were discovered, in 1862, by a serious young American of the best social position and an earnest desire to study the world and improve his mind and manners.[1]

The previous young American in England has met his match.

Adams's vulgarity is bare. 'Fashion was not fashionable in London until the Americans and the Jews were let loose . . .' There is less ambivalence here (though still some, since the English are being snibbed), and there is a less complicated complicity with ugliness of mind; a great deal is let loose when an American speaks of 'the Americans' so, and when he sets up his prejudicial sequence so that to be a Jew is to not be an American: 'the Americans and the Jews'. All the energies of the passages quoted are charged with prejudice: those of sex or gender, of nationality, of royalty, of bankers, of foreigners, and

---

1 – Eliot's ellipses in the review.

of class; and brooding over the whole thing is the highly (*de haut en bas*) equivocal role of tolerance: 'English society was much more easy and tolerant than American.'

Some of these queasy resentful feelings which seethed in Adams, and which were given salience by Eliot in his review, were let loose in Eliot's poem ('The Jew is underneath the lot', or rather 'The jew', in all the poem's printings until 1963). But what made it more than a pathological document – a poem, albeit a riven wrenched one – was Eliot's ear. And his eye. 'A lustreless protrusive eye' is a line which does not lack lustre, and it was the poet in Eliot which caught the glint of the word *protrusive* within a passage from Henry James which figures in the Adams review. 'Every protrusive item' became, with prompt amputation, the 'protrusive eye'; and this becomingly, with fidelity to the original prose and with entire respect for it. So that what is glimpsed, so tactful as not to be protrusive, is a model of literary continuity such as itself constitutes the severest indictment of the muddy roiling of feelings at large in the poem. For Eliot here was not imposing his own pressure upon 'protrusive item' so that he might brutally lop it down to 'protrusive eye'; he was responding to the pressure which James himself had created, the pressure of all the words in the immediate vicinity of 'protrusive item' which made the sub-word 'eye' yearn to protrude:

This doom of inordinate exposure to appearances, aspects, images, every protrusive item almost, in the great beheld sum of things, I regard in other words as having settled upon me once for all while I observed for instance that in England the plate of buttered muffin and its cover were sacredly set upon the slop-bowl after hot water had been ingenuously poured into the same, and had seen that circumstance in a perfect cloud of accompaniments.[1]

James's amazing sentence, the first half of which was prominent in Eliot's review of Adams, teems with things germane to the troubled turbid poem which Eliot was travailing with; for 'Burbank with a Baedeker: Bleistein with a Cigar' is itself a

1 – *The Middle Years* (1917), p. 5. In his review of Adams, Eliot – by substituting an ellipsis for James's phrase 'in the great beheld sum of things' – robs James's perceptive sequence of one of its items, but thereby Eliot brought 'item' within a word of 'I'. Eliot curtailed the quotation at 'cover'.

'doom of inordinate exposure to appearances, aspects, images', rolling in from Henry James himself, from more than one work of Shakespeare, from Marston, Byron, Tennyson, Browning, Gautier and more, all of them offering their protrusive items; and the poem itself finally relinquishes its seeing of circumstances and settles instead for a cloud of accompaniments. 'So the countess passed on . . .': Eliot's frenetic epigraph, itself a cloud of accompaniments, proffers this stage-direction from a masque by John Marston, and so Eliot's later comments on a work by Marston cast a smoky candlelight back upon 'Burbank with a Baedeker: Bleistein with a Cigar'. Sensing 'a peculiar jerkiness and irritability, as of a writer who is, for some obscure reason, wrought to the pitch of exasperation',[1] Eliot was as grudgingly impressed and oppressed by Marston as we may be by Eliot's Marston-minded poem.

But to attend to such things is to decline the third avenue of approach to the matter of anti-Semitism, which is to deal with it by maintaining that it need not be dealt with at all. The dissociative claim is that Eliot's relation to anti-Semitism is one thing, his poems are another. Edmund Wilson is the strongest advocate here; as he made clear in a letter to Van Wyck Brooks in 1957, Wilson was sure that such illiberalisms in Eliot are unimportant and are moreover importantly absent from the poems.

When he is writing for clerical papers or addressing a Conservative dinner, he allows himself reactionary audacities which he rarely hazards with his larger audience. (He did let some of these loose in the lectures collected in *After Strange Gods* – delivered at the University of Virginia, where I suppose he thought it was safe to let his snobberies and antiquated loyalties rip – but when hostile repercussions reached his sensitive ear, he did his best to suppress the volume.) But these dramatically slanted opinions are so dim and make so little sense that I don't see how they can do much damage. I was talking about this just now with Arthur Schlesinger, usually an up-in-arms liberal, and – rather to my surprise – he anticipated my opinion by saying that all this side of Eliot didn't matter. In his poetry and in his personal relations, he is sensitive, gentle, and rather touching. In spite of his assertion to the contrary when I talked to him years ago, he is ready to

1 – 'John Marston', *Selected Essays*, p. 224.

converse with unbelievers, and he is not disagreeable to Jews; and he makes fun of all the old gentilities that he otherwise pretends to represent.[1]

'Gentilities' there has its unperturbed comedy.

There is a great deal in Eliot's poetry that is indeed sensitive, gentle and rather touching; but there is also much that is sensitive, fierce and altogether gripping. Moreover, the lapses from sensitivity do not give warrant for the dissociation of Eliot's anti-liberal convictions from the poetry within which they are one impulsion for their readers as well as for their writer. It is better, not only as ultimately more complimentary to the best in Eliot but also as more illuminating of the poems and the depth of their life, to acknowledge that in so far as Eliot's poems are tinged with anti-Semitism, this – though lamentable – is not easily or neatly to be severed from things for which the poetry is not be deplored or forgiven but actively praised.[2]

There was a weakness, a sliding from something disagreeably true (about the need to classify) into something disagreeably and destructively false (a punitive animus); yet Eliot spoke a truth about what can be done with weakness:

My own view is that Dostoevsky had the gift, a sign of genius in itself, for utilizing his weaknesses; so that epilepsy and hysteria cease to be the defects of an individual and become – as a fundamental weakness can, given the ability to face it and study it – the entrance to a genuine and personal universe.[3]

There was, too, a struggle, in which Eliot more often succeeded than failed.

Shakespeare, too, was occupied with the struggle – which alone constitutes life for a poet – to transmute his personal and private agonies into something rich and strange, something universal and impersonal.[4]

The struggle was lost in the lines which Eliot never published:

1 – 6 October 1957 (*Letters on Literature and Politics*, edited by Elena Wilson, 1977, pp. 548–9).
2 – A. D. Moody writes scrupulously on Eliot and anti-Semitism in Appendix C to his *Thomas Stearns Eliot: Poet*, 'The Christian philosopher and politics between the wars'.
3 – *The Dial*, lxxiii (1922), 331.
4 – 'Shakespeare and the Stoicism of Seneca', *Selected Essays*, p. 137.

> Full fathom five your Bleistein lies
> Under the flatfish and the squids.
> Graves' Disease in a dead jew's eyes!
> When the crabs have eat the lids.
> Lower than the wharf rats dive
> Though he suffer a sea-change
> Still expensive rich and strange

But it is the same struggle which was won in the paired passages which he did publish, passages which are redemptive of the allusion to that song in *The Tempest*, unsentimentally redemptive as *The Tempest* itself is:

> Here, said she,
> Is your card, the drowned Phoenician Sailor,
> (Those are pearls that were his eyes. Look!)

*

> Gentile or Jew
> O you who turn the wheel and look to windward,
> Consider Phlebas, who was once handsome and tall as you.

One can sympathize with those who think that any discriminations within anti-Semitism, even those which ask that it be acknowledged that Hitler changed the world, are gratuitous and indulgent. On the other hand, among the duties of this explosive delicate matter is the one of holding to some sense of the difference between such lines as those which Eliot gave to Gerontion in 1919:—

> My house is a decayed house,
> And the Jew squats on the window sill, the owner,
> Spawned in some estaminet of Antwerp,
> Blistered in Brussels, patched and peeled in London.

— and those which Pound allowed himself in 1948:

> the tip from the augean stables in Paris
> with Sieff in attendance, or not
> as the case may have been,
> thus conditioning.

Meyer Anselm, a rrromance, yes, yes certainly
but more fool you if you fall for it two centuries later
. . .

    from their seats the blond bastards, and cast 'em.
       the yidd is a stimulant, and the goyim are cattle
in gt/ proportion and go to saleable slaughter
with the maximum of docility.

                        (Canto LXXIV)

A part for the victim

One of the many hideous legacies of this century's anti-Semitism
is the pressure to shrink from discussing anti-Semitism and
prejudice for fear of the accusation of 'a retreat to rationality'.
For to distinguish, to discriminate, may so easily become, and
may even more easily be accused of becoming, connivance or
collusion or condoning. So the extremism of prejudice at its
most insane finds itself matched by an extremism of repudiation, and what is repudiated includes all hope of rationally
understanding not only anti-Semitism but any form of prejudice. In the *New Republic*, Leon Wieseltier accused Hannah
Arendt of a deep complicity; insisted that she 'misunderstood
the nature of prejudice, which is precisely a feeling that is not
based upon, and so cannot be revised by, evidence'; and rose to
this conclusive anger at her because 'Arendt blames the victim':

An analysis of prejudice that finds a part for the victim only lessens the
scandal. It is a retreat to rationality, which may be noble. But against such
an analysis the innocence of the victim must be upheld, hard as it is for the
mind to bear. The political wisdom of the Jews was not very great, but they
did not desire to be set upon. Anti-Semitism was an intervention in Jewish
life; it came unbidden from outside. It discriminated against Jews and
tortured them and killed them, all without their consent. When the victim
is innocent, evil is radical. When the victim is an accomplice, evil is —
banal.[1]

This has its dignity. But it is not a sufficient understanding of
prejudice which calls it 'precisely a feeling that is not based

1 – *New Republic*, 7 October 1981.

upon, and so cannot be revised by, evidence'. If prejudice were never able to point to anything which could plausibly be called evidence, had simply and indubitably nothing out there which it could muster, then prejudice would not be so powerful, ubiquitous, and disconcertingly obdurate as it is.

It must indeed be granted that the monstrosity of Hitler's anti-Semitism dwarfs explanation, as the extremity of madness always does; and it must be granted that any discussion of Hitler's anti-Semitism which puts its emphasis upon causes or provocations is in the greatest danger of callousness. But all this is compatible with Wieseltier's being deeply wrong in making the murderous extremity of anti-Semitism synonymous with or conterminous with prejudice; in despairing of the idea that a person could ever be moved from prejudice by evidence; and in insisting that the victim never has a part in prejudice. The same issue of the *New Republic* praised the black sociologist Anne Wortham for 'battling against the combined forces of social-science determinism and welfare-state liberalism, which assign blacks to victim status, she argues, "without any reference to Negroes as the causal agents of their existence"'. The reviewer, Peter Skerry, remarked: 'Of course, this revisionist perspective carries with it a burden that its advocates have not always been willing to bear. For if blacks were active participants in that [American historical] drama, black Americans must also assume some responsibility for its outcome.' The point is not whether Wortham and Skerry are right as historians, or even whether the *New Republic* is as sympathetically vigilant in defence of blacks' rights as of Jews' rights, but simply whether the principle enunciated in Wieseltier's own journal has substance. Would Wieseltier have to argue that in that case blacks were not then victims of prejudice?

'An analysis of prejudice', he insisted, 'that finds a part for the victim only lessens the scandal.' But an analysis of prejudice that – under pressure from the hideousness of Nazi anti-Semitism – finds no part for the victim of very different prejudices: this does not lessen but abolish the chances of the rational reduction of prejudice, a task which cannot afford to say that there is no such thing as any kind of evidence in any of these cases. In the world posited by Wieseltier, there could never be any responsible disagreement as to whether a particular act was or was not an act of prejudice. The fact that there could, appallingly, be no doubt in the case of Hitler and the Jews should not be allowed to petrify or putrefy our entire world into one in which all prejudice is indubitable in being entirely dissociated from any antecedent causes, provocation or evidence. Clearly there are vulture complacencies hovering around my hope, but no more than hover around Wieseltier's despair.

What has to be faced, though, is that no one can write seriously and at length about anti-Semitism without giving offence, and even Nicholas Mosley's scrupulous deliberated biography of his father Oswald Mosley was held by some to have palliated or extenuated his father's evil. One might go further: it must needs be that offences come, but woe to that man by whom the offence cometh. It is unimaginable that anyone could ever judge these matters exactly right, or speak of them without a single failure of tone, or be alive fully to justice and to mercy. The minefield stretches on all sides, and being innocent – or not particularly guilty – will not save any commentator (and certainly not any commentator on T. S. Eliot) from being blown up. Even the demolition squad sows its own bombs; it was thought reasonable for a philosopher in *Scrutiny* in the very month of September 1939 to say as mere say-so that 'the German people are *as a people* politically young; their political philosophy is philosophically immature', and then to proceed: 'Those of us who have not the misfortune to be Germans . . .'[1]

'Kipling made several opportunities for expressing his dislike of Germans; I am not aware that he cherished any particularly anti-Semitic feelings.'

1 – L. Susan Stebbing, *Scrutiny*, viii (1939), 160.

III

PREJUDICE

The nature of prejudice

After Strange Gods was 'A Primer of Modern Heresy'. To its author, who very soon chose not to keep it in print, it came itself to smack of heresy, the driving of a truth to the point at which it becomes a falsehood. The book is desperately controversial, and one of the things of which it despairs is the possibility of worthwhile controversy.

In our time, controversy seems to me, on really fundamental matters, to be futile. It can only usefully be practised where there is common understanding. It requires common assumptions; and perhaps the assumptions that are only felt are more important than those that can be formulated. The acrimony which accompanies much debate is a symptom of differences so large that there is nothing to argue about. We experience such profound differences with some of our contemporaries, that the nearest parallel is the difference between the mentality of one epoch and another. In a society like ours, worm-eaten with Liberalism, the only thing possible for a person with strong convictions is to state a point of view and leave it at that.[1]

Eliot often, and persuasively, offered 'convictions' as the counterpart to 'prejudices', and when his embittered and unbalanced book speaks of the plight of a person of strong convictions in a society 'worm-eaten with Liberalism', we may recall that it is the embittered and unbalanced Hunsden, in Charlotte

---

1 – *After Strange Gods*, p. 13. Eliot's capital L for Liberalism makes a difference, since it points to an institutionalized ideology or political party. 'In the sense in which Liberalism is contrasted with Conservatism, both can be equally repellent: if the former can mean chaos, the latter can mean petrifaction' (*The Idea of a Christian Society*, p. 17).

Brontë's novel *The Professor*, who speaks of the society that is England as 'rotten with abuses, worm-eaten with prejudices'.[1] The triangle of liberalism, prejudice and the worm-eaten defines much of Eliot's diagnosis; dissenting from both the old propensity to indict merely individual weakness and the new propensity to indict merely social injustice, and arguing that the two came to the same thing, Eliot wrote doctrinally in 1937 of Djuna Barnes's *Nightwood*: 'It seems to me that all of us, so far as we attach ourselves to created objects and surrender our wills to temporal ends, are eaten by the same worm.'

Once you think about prejudice you are taken into a great deal of and about Eliot – into the nature and boundaries of his imagination. Reciprocally, once you think about Eliot, you are taken into a great deal of and about prejudice, including how inadequately so momentous a matter has been thought about and argued about. Eliot's work, like much that he admired (*Measure for Measure*, *Coriolanus* and the plays of Jonson), is designed to incite its audience at once to strict judgements upon the world which it presents and to strict thought about the exact grounds on which anyone may validly pass such judgements. For Eliot writes always with a founded sense that the very conditions of modern life which make it more and more urgently essential to be able to pass strong judgements are themselves the conditions which make it less and less possible confidently or unmisgivingly to do so. 'Remorse?' asked a member of Charles Manson's murderous sect: 'What I did was right for me.' She was not being deft, she was divining something about the difficulty which she extraordinarily posed for the age's thinking.

The effects of prejudice are often unquestionable, and yet its nature is highly questionable – not only as morally dubious but as conceptually elusive. One reason why prejudice, though earning its bad name, so often fails even to be arrested is its genuinely being so evasive of definition. Sometimes the public conscience hastens to catch prejudice not in a definition or in an argument but in a metaphor; yet the metaphor then has a way of

1 – Chapter 24.

so fumbling as to let the suspect escape. The Anti-Defamation League, postering the subways with good intentions, tries to capture prejudice within a picture and a slogan: the picture is of athletic hurdlers, one black, one pink, one brown, and one yellow, each clearing a hurdle; and the slogan is:

PREJUDICE An obstacle we must ALL overcome.

One trouble with this is that all the hurdlers look male. Another trouble is that an athletic hurdle really is not an obstacle; on the contrary, an athletic hurdle is the desirable agreed condition for feats of energy and beauty. No hurdle, no loveliness of the hurdlers. Anyway, you don't 'overcome' a hurdle, you clear it, and are properly grateful for it. The competitive *élan* of the hurdlers is rather well limned in the picture, and is at odds with the admonition. Presumably the starting point of the poster was a pun, whether conscious or not, on *race*. Of course you know perfectly well what the poster *means* and wishes and urges; but it is a good thing that you do know in advance, because you couldn't responsibly know it from the muddled poster. The less you ponder the poster, the better. You are to think well of it, not think well about it. Which is one of the things meant by prejudice, that you are to know in advance just what is expected, and that you will not devote any scrutiny to whether the judgement offered has truly been made good.

But what makes good the accusation of prejudice, what makes it stick? Whenever we are accused of prejudice, we realize with dismay how hard an accusation it is to rebut, and yet this is consequentially what makes it a very hard accusation cogently to enforce. To decline to employ an ex-convict, preferring someone with no criminal record: whether this is prejudice or not must bear *some* relation to probabilities and likelihoods, to generalizations which converge upon an individual decision. Yet we acknowledge that we cannot simply appeal later to what indeed happened next (he robbed the mug who did give him a job), since we know that there are such things as self-fulfilling prophecies, and that these are prejudicial. Maybe your spurning him was the last straw; he really would have brought himself to go straight if you could have brought yourself to believe so.

79

True, it is itself a prejudice which assumes that a self-fulfilling prophecy must be a destructive and not a creative act, for trust is just as much a self-fulfilling prophecy as is distrust; yet we have to admit that not even the roundest recidivism on his part will in itself clear us of having been prejudiced, even while those who accuse us will have to admit that his subsequent recidivism is at least relevant to our innocence or guilt. The word prejudice often accuses someone of an error in decision, not solely of an impure state of mind, and it will then partake of the difficulties attendant on even the simplest questions of error in decision since we know that there is no replicable experiment and no 'control'.

One slipperiness of prejudice derives from our being unsure of what bad thing is the opposite of the bad thing prejudice. So here we lack one form of those antithetical terms with which we usually get bearings or get purchase. We are hard put to name this oppositely mistaken relation to true judgement, though we know that there is such a thing as being not too prompt or too selective in judging but too tardy.

Some of the further elusiveness of prejudice is a consequence of its relatedly not being clear or agreed what its good brother or sister is. That is, we mostly get our bearings by conceiving of something undesirable as a damaging extension or travesty of something desirable. We want our children to be happy but not complacent; sensitive but not morbid; brave but not foolhardy; trusting but not credulous. We may figure this distinction as the good side of a coin which has another side, or as the drawing of a line such as asks not only principle but tact. 'Every vice you destroy has a corresponding virtue, which perishes along with it': Anatole France risked complacency but enunciated a risk. Or there was Samuel Butler's thought two centuries earlier: 'Virtues and vices are very near of kin and like the Austrian family beget one another.'

> Unnatural vices
> Are fathered by our heroism. Virtues
> Are forced upon us by our impudent crimes.
>
>   ('Gerontion')

Such apophthegms as France's or Butler's do not propose that we neglect or sophisticate the difference between a vice and a virtue, they simply recall us to how we usually proceed; this, not only because all definition is necessarily contrastive but because of the urgency of these moral and social distinctions.

We may not be entirely at a loss to nominate the good thing which corresponds to the bad thing prejudice; we may even accept Eliot's judgement that the best word for this good thing is *convictions*. Eliot said of Hilaire Belloc: 'His peculiar function is to attack, not arguments, but *prejudices*; and prejudices are attacked, not with arguments, but with *convictions*.'[1] But even 'convictions', which is the strongest candidate, is less than ideal. For one thing, it does not – either by etymology or by usage – stand in any substantial or interesting relation to the components of 'prejudice': the premature prefix and the ill-judged judging. 'Convictions' comes from an entirely different congeries, linguistically and socially. Then for another thing, though 'convictions' is not a weakling of a word, it has at its disposal nothing like the animus possessed by 'prejudice'. The word 'prejudice' or 'prejudiced' itself has a way of being prejudicial, of demanding in advance a bullying superiority over any counter-term which might be mustered; and this prejudicing of the issue is compounded by the increasing propensity of the word to suggest prejudice *against* much more than prejudice *for*. 'A feeling, favourable or unfavourable . . .': but the word has come to have its own prejudice or bias.

Needing to set the vice against this one of its antitheses, G. C. Field settled for 'Prejudice, and its opposite, Impartiality'.[2] But again the terms do not come together with any precision, moving as they do through such different planes, and Field all but admitted as much: 'I have chosen Prejudice and Impartiality as the best terms we have for the two opposites. The opposite of "prejudiced" is, strictly, "unprejudiced". But that has no substantive.' The case of 'unprejudiced' would have been even worse, though, than Field grants, for not only is there no substantive to realize the quality of mind which is the opposite

1 – *English Review*, liii (1931), 245.
2 – *Prejudice and Impartiality* (1932), pp. 2–3.

of prejudice, there is no verb to realize the activity of mind which is the opposite of prejudicing. As a result, 'unprejudiced' summons the absence of a vice and not the presence of a virtue. There is a similar snag with Impartiality, which supplies 'impartial' but does not supply a verb and therefore has the same effect of making the counterpart to prejudice dispiritingly inactive, a weakening which is again audible in the negative form 'impartiality', as if the Devil were acknowledged to have not only the best tunes but the move-making words.

Field calls up the history of the word 'prejudice', but only to dismiss it:

The derivation of the word, to which appeal is sometimes made, helps us little. The Latin *praejudicium*, in the sense from which our word is derived, had a legal meaning, and indicated a previous judgement or precedent which governed the decision in any particular case. As used in this connexion the word conveys no suggestion at all that there is anything wrong about the decision being so governed. In fact, the suggestion is rather the other way. But our word Prejudice unmistakably indicates a bad and undesirable characteristic.

Yet the difficulty is that although prejudice now 'unmistakably indicates a bad and undesirable characteristic', what is unmistakable is a badness and not a characteristic. What exactly characterizes prejudice must be mistakable or the philosopher Field would not have been writing a book about it. So that, when Field concludes 'It is therefore best to leave the history of the word out of account', he is making things harder for himself by taking the easy way out. The history of the word, which includes its originally meaning a useful precedent, is a pointer to the crucial difficulty that everybody has in understanding, controlling, or extirpating prejudice, since the line between an honourable appeal to precedent and a dishonourable appeal to prejudice is a nub.

'The formal word precise but not pedantic' ('Little Gidding'):[1] we are all aware of the further move of distinguishing a virtue from a vice by the expedient of locating the former

[1] – On this and other such discriminations in Eliot, see A. V. C. Schmidt, 'T. S. Eliot and the English Language', *English Studies in Africa*, xxv (1982), 117–43.

within us and the latter within others. I am precise, you are pedantic. Yet this propensity, since it is prejudicial, compounds its force when it is bent upon prejudice itself. I have convictions, you have prejudices. Wisdom then becomes a central term, not only in the large sense but in the daily prudential one of whether it be altogether wise to appeal to, say, precedent. Eliot wrote in 1943:

Already we need another science, the science of the Behaviour of Sociologists. I mean that the moment the sociologist ceases to confine himself to description within his own terms, and to offering dispassionate predictions of the results of two or more alternative procedures, the moment he betrays any emotional interest in what has happened or in what will happen, elements too personal to be part of the 'science' come into play: they appear to us, when we disagree, as *prejudice*, and when we agree, as *wisdom*. I think that Dr Mannheim has a generous share of wisdom, and he would be a singular human being if he had no prejudices.[1]

William Hazlitt took many views of prejudice, among them the conservative one that prejudices themselves may have a generous share of wisdom. 'No wise man can have a contempt for the prejudices of others; and he should even stand in a certain awe of his own, as if they were aged parents and monitors. They may in the end prove wiser than he.'[2] Whether this is a wise way of putting the matter will turn upon how alert the aphorism is judged to be to the dangers it courts. Is Hazlitt's 'may in the end prove wiser' (as against 'are wiser') a rhetorical reservation only, or is it a well-judged prophylaxis against prejudicial complacency? And how much awe is 'a certain awe'? It does sound a very uncertain quantity. Hazlitt is putting his finger on the point while also putting his thumb in the scale.

Hazlitt's admonition acutely aligns a respect for prejudice with a respect for monitors and aged parents. We hear, to right and left, the monitors of conservatism and of liberalism, and have heard them for at least two centuries. The accents of conservatism are most assured in Edmund Burke, confident that we have little or nothing to fear from prejudice.

1 – *Theology*, xlvi (1943), 103.
2 – *Characteristics*, CXXXII.

You see, Sir, that in this enlightened age I am bold enough to confess, that we are generally men of untaught feelings; that instead of casting away all our old prejudices, we cherish them to a very considerable degree, and, to take more shame to ourselves, we cherish them because they are prejudices; and the longer they have lasted, and the more generally they have prevailed, the more we cherish them. We are afraid to put men to live and trade each on his own private stock of reason; because we suspect that the stock in each man is small, and that the individuals would do better to avail themselves of the general bank and capital of nations and of ages. Many of our men of speculation, instead of exploding general prejudices, employ their sagacity to discover the latent wisdom which prevails in them. If they find what they seek, and they seldom fail, they think it more wise to continue the prejudice, with the reason involved, than to cast away the coat of prejudice, and to leave nothing but the naked reason; because prejudice, with its reason, has a motive to give action to that reason, and an affection which will give it permanence. Prejudice is of ready application in the emergency; it previously engages the mind in a steady course of wisdom and virtue, and does not leave the man hesitating in the moment of decision, sceptical, puzzled, and unresolved. Prejudice renders a man's virtue his habit: and not a series of unconnected acts. Through just prejudice, his duty becomes a part of his nature.[1]

Burke trusts his convictions but does not entirely trust himself to make them convincing; hence his resort to the collusive coercions of 'I am bold enough to confess' when he is manifestly issuing a British boast, as again in 'to take more shame to ourselves'. Yet these and other subtractions from Burke's dignity of argument should not blind us to there being some truth in this conservative estimation of prejudice, especially in its appeal to the emergency. The *Oxford English Dictionary* has within its account of prejudice, 'a feeling, favourable or unfavourable, towards any person or thing, prior to or not based on actual experience'. But one difficulty is whether the actual experience has to be one's own, and another is a consequence of there being some actual experiences after which one would be in no position to issue a judgement whether unprejudiced or not. These are emergencies. If I were naively strolling in Central Park

---

1 – *Reflections on the Revolution in France, and on the Proceedings of Certain Societies in London Relative to That Event: in a Letter Intended to Have Been Sent to a Gentleman in Paris* (1790).

at midnight, and there came towards me some tattooed and leathered people swinging baseball bats, to take to my heels would admittedly be an act of prejudice; it would be prior to and not based on actual experience, since I have never seen any such people harm a fly. And of course there are plenty of benign interpretative possibilities; it could be a charity rag on behalf of New York University, or the filming of the sequel to *The Warriors*. But to await the actual experience might not then allow much of a thereafter within which to savour my magnanimity. It would not be much comfort to look up through my one dying eye and to murmur, 'Well at least I wasn't prejudiced.' This may sound a farcical fabrication, but a great deal of urban prejudice defends itself as an instinct of self-defence in an emergency. Sudden fear, alone in a hallway with someone who looks like *that*, would rather be prejudiced than done for. Being unprejudiced may on occasion be something of a luxury. 'Prejudice is of ready application in the emergency.'

Eliot, however, distrusted appeals to an emergency:

That word of prudence, 'emergency', occurs again and again [in Oswald Mosley's programme]; the reader feels coaxed and reassured that there is nothing really revolutionary about all this. (1931)

It [Regionalism] is something of which politicians ought to take thought, if they are capable of thinking in any terms except 'emergencies'. (1931)

It might seem at first that an ally of any sort is welcome in an emergency – and we are always in an emergency. (1933)

But I do not think that practical emergencies are all that matters. (1935)[1]

Such a scepticism about the convenient invoking of emergencies (emergency, another of the tyrant's pleas) is at one with Eliot's being considerably more sceptical about prejudice than was his great predecessor Burke. Eliot, aware of how mammonism had accelerated since Burke's day, would have been more sensitive to the limits of Burke's central analogy. For the limit of the truth of what Burke says is the limit of his analogy. Wisdom is indeed like money, but it is not only *like* money and it is not like *money*

---

1 – *The Criterion*, x (1931), 483, 485; xii (1933), 643; *Time and Tide*, 19 January 1935.

only. Living is more and other than trading upon stock; wisdom is more and other than a bank and capital; 'men of speculation' would do well to think how easily speculation becomes dishonest and bankrupt. The limit of Burke's disinterestedness comes when he refrains from asking whether, if 'prejudice renders a man's virtue his habit', it also renders his vice his habit; when he fails to hear the likelihood of *parti pris* and its gratification in his laudatory sequence 'If they find what they seek, and they seldom fail . . .'; and when he leaves culpably underdescribed that 'just prejudice' to which he has rhetorically conclusive recourse.

It was in 1790 that Burke incorporated this defence of prejudice in his *Reflections on the Revolution in France*. It was in 1793, in his *Enquiry Concerning Political Justice*, that William Godwin gave no less classic expression to the opposite case, liberalism's disavowal of prejudice. To Burke's confidence that we have nothing to fear from prejudice (or at any rate from 'just prejudice' . . .) is opposed Godwin's confidence that for prejudice we need have nothing but disdain.

He soon comes to perceive a considerable similarity between situation and situation. In consequence he feels inclined to abridge the process of deliberation, and to act today conformably to the determination of yesterday. Thus the understanding fixes for itself resting places, is no longer a novice, and is not at the trouble continually to go back and revise the original reasons which determined it to a course of action. Thus the man acquires habits, from which it is very difficult to wean him, and which he obeys without being able to assign either to himself or others, any explicit reason for his proceeding. This is the history of prepossession and prejudice . . . In the mean time it is obvious to remark, that the perfection of the human character consists in approaching as nearly as possible to the perfectly voluntary state. We ought to be upon all occasions prepared to render a reason of our actions.[1]

Here, as in Burke, are the genial coercions of rhetoric ('In the mean time it is obvious to remark . . .'); and there are the limits of a chosen metaphor: the innocent young word 'wean' is asked to take responsibility on its own for a great deal of unspecified argument. That the mere saving of 'trouble' is often at work in

1 – *Enquiry Concerning Political Justice, and Its Influence on Morals and Happiness*, Book I, Chapter V.

prejudice should be granted to Godwin; but no more than Burke does he listen to the tremors that one can hear half-admitted in his account of the matter: 'and is not at the trouble continually to go back and revise the original reasons . . .' Conservatives are always rebuking liberals for being unrealistic, but there truly is something unrealistic about Godwin's programme here. Had we but world enough, and time. But. More than simply *trouble* is involved in *continually* going back and revising the original reasons. Life is finite, and when this goes unacknowledged, lives are lost.

> There will be time to murder and create,
> And time for all the works and days of hands
> That lift and drop a question on your plate;
> Time for you and time for me,
> And time yet for a hundred indecisions,
> And for a hundred visions and revisions,
> Before the taking of a toast and tea.
>
> *
>
> In a minute there is time
> For decisions and revisions which a minute will reverse.
>   ('The Love Song of J. Alfred Prufrock')

Godwin would disturb the universe, personal and social, if he were to insist, as he purports to do, on the mind's never abridging the process of deliberation and on the understanding's never fixing for itself resting-places. Where Burke proposes the salvation of prejudice, Godwin proposes the damnation of habit. But there are such things as good habits. Are there no abridgements of the process of deliberation which are valuable and benign?

In the street a woman is being clubbed to the ground. A full process of deliberation in the matter, though it might save my soul, would not save her life. Does Godwin really want me fully to deliberate, to reconstitute from scratch my entire social and moral commitments? Would it in such a case be a perfection of the human character to approach as nearly as possible to the perfectly voluntary state? I hope that I should not cogitate to myself along such lines as, 'Is it not true that, as the great Greek said, it is better to be dead than alive, best of all never to have been born?' Or, 'Maybe they're filming for Fellini some characteristically subversive moment.' Or, 'Perhaps she has terminal cancer and is being put out of her and our misery.' No, the Englishman likes to think that at such a moment he would be a creature of habit, and would step forward, if only with a deprecating cough and a courteous insistence that though he does not want to interfere in what may be a family quarrel, things do seem to be getting a bit out of hand.

As in the disagreement between I. A. Richards and C. S. Lewis about 'stock responses' (Lewis thought that Richards had a stock response of the wrong kind to stock responses), what happens is that it then becomes not deliberation but *amour propre* which settles the distinction. You are a prey to stock responses, I possess trained instincts.

Burke's conservatism impels him to a defence of prejudice which invites us to see life as little but a succession of emergencies; Godwin's liberalism to a repelling of prejudice which invites us to avert our eyes from all that is emergency. But there are sure to be matters of life and death, as well as matters of daily life, such that it will be an excellent idea 'to act today conformably to the determination of yesterday'.

Yet we live in an age when this siege of contraries is unprecedentedly fierce: never has the accusation of prejudice been more inflamedly important, and yet never has there been so wide an agreement – through the whole range of thought – that no understanding of anything is possible without predicates, preconceptions, and categorial frameworks. You are a prejudiced clique, we are an interpretative community.

In 1944, the year when some of the necessary exacerbations of the matter were being engaged by Eliot and Trilling, Hortense Powdermaker could issue to children this bland soliciting of a liberal unimagination: 'Judgment implies coming to a conclusion after a consideration of all the factors. Prejudice means jumping to a conclusion before considering the facts.' *Probing Our Prejudices*,[1] the book called itself. There was no probing, only a placebo. For there will never be a time when all the factors

1 – (1944), p. 1.

can be considered, since the factors are infinite. In this our life and death, the choice is not between leaving a wholly rational will and leaving an imperfectly rational one, but between leaving an imperfectly rational will and dying intestate. To preach such a blank antithesis of judgement and prejudice as Powdermaker did throughout her book is to sentimentalize judgement and its inevitable painful adjudications. Such illusory encouragement duly issues in disillusionment. A vacancy of open-mindedness helps to precipitate forty years later a book like Allan Bloom's *The Closing of the American Mind*, with its confidence, serenely indiscriminate, that the great vehicle of intellectual advance is the pendulum:

When I was a young teacher at Cornell, I once had a debate about education with a professor of psychology. He said that it was his function to get rid of prejudices in his students . . . I found myself responding to the professor of psychology that I personally tried to teach my students prejudices, since nowadays – with the general success of his method – they had learned to doubt beliefs even before they believed in anything. Without people like me, he would be out of business.[1]

Something a great deal less disarmingly burly is needed if the obligations of principle and of tact are to be met; something much more like Eliot's combination of the tentative and the firm in exactly valuing scepticism, 'the habit of examining evidence and the capacity for delayed decision':

Scepticism is a highly civilised trait, though, when it declines into pyrrhonism, it is one of which civilisation can die. Where scepticism is strength, pyrrhonism is weakness: for we need not only the strength to defer a decision, but the strength to make one.[2]

1 – (1987), p. 42.
2 – *Notes towards the Definition of Culture*, p. 29. Eliot wrote of Valéry: 'The constructive philosopher must have a religious faith, or some substitute for a religious faith; and generally he is only able to construct, because of his ability to blind himself to other points of view, or to remain unconscious of the emotive causes which attach him to his particular system. Valéry was much too conscious to be able to philosophise in this way; and so his "philosophy" lays itself open to the accusation of being only an elaborate game. Precisely, but to be able to play this game, to be able to take aesthetic delight in it, is one of the manifestations of civilised man. There is only one higher stage possible for civilised man: and that is to unite the profoundest scepticism with the deepest faith. But Valéry was not Pascal, and we have no right to ask that of him' ('Leçon de Valéry', *Paul Valéry Vivant*, 1946, p. 76).

The precision of this is bracing, for what validates Eliot's distinction between the good thing which is scepticism and the bad thing which is pyrrhonism, a parody or paroxysm of scepticism, is that civilization can die of it because pyrrhonism is a kamikaze of the intellect. Pyrrhonism is suicidally aggressive, in that if its claims are true its claims must be false: we can know nothing with certainty – except this knowledge itself. Eliot in 1917 visited the same justified scepticism upon the extremities of pragmatism: 'And of course we can always accuse the pragmatist of believing his own doctrine in a sense which is not pragmatic but absolute – in other words, of eating his cake and having it too.'[1]

William Empson observed that life involves maintaining oneself between contradictions that can't be solved by analysis,[2] and in practical terms there would be much to be said for quitting prejudice's conceptual tussle and concentrating on navigating between Scylla and Charybdis; when Eliot published his late lecture 'Scylla and Charybdis',[3] his thinking was fostered by his having long valued such navigation. He had praised John Bramhall: 'His thinking is a perfect example of the pursuit of the *via media*, and the *via media* is of all ways the most difficult to follow.'[4] Eliot often felt obliged to be hard on liberalism's softness, but he did not have a soft spot for conservatism's hardness: 'In the sense in which Liberalism is contrasted with Conservatism, both can be equally repellent: if the former can mean chaos, the latter can mean petrifaction.'[5]

Yet even if one were finally to acquiesce in the principle of a happy mean and in a trust in tact, it is salutary to see how very difficult the question of prejudice is, conceptually, even for

1 – *New Statesman*, 29 December 1917. This review speaks of prejudice and its filaments: 'Those who have read philosophy with complete detachment from any schools have trained themselves to look for just those aspects of any author which are most personal; have followed with keenest interest his doubts, his prejudices, his hesitations, his confessions, here and there, of failure; have sought always for the peculiar flavour of the man's thought in the man's own words.'
2 – Note to his poem 'Bacchus'.
3 – (1952); *Agenda*, xxiii (1985).
4 – 'John Bramhall', *For Lancelot Andrewes*, p. 42.
5 – *The Idea of a Christian Society*, p. 17.

dedicated and resourceful thinkers. In 1954 Gordon W. Allport published what is still the standard work on the subject, *The Nature of Prejudice*. (It is the book to which Ingeborg Day turned when she was dismayed by a startling rush within her of anti-Semitic feeling.)[1] Allport is aware of the difficulties and of the problems; he is alive to the challenge, not only within life but to his arguments, of his having to grant that 'rubrics are essential to mental life, and that their operation results inevitably in prejudgments which in turn may shade into prejudice'.[2] But such shadings would supply so little momentum for his book, or indeed for any strong general argument about prejudice (as against delicate elicitings in particular cases), that Allport is obliged to mount a bolder distinction between prejudgements and prejudices. He plumps for this one, complete with italics to outfrown any hecklers:

Here we have the test to help us distinguish between ordinary errors of prejudgment and prejudice. If a person is capable of rectifying his erroneous judgments in the light of new evidence he is not prejudiced. *Prejudgments become prejudices only if they are not reversible when exposed to new knowledge.*[3]

But no amount of italicizing can save this definitional assurance from ringing hollow. It is the shift in the tenses which constitutes its sleight of mind, for the proposition that 'if a person is capable of rectifying his erroneous judgements in the light of new evidence he is not prejudiced' offers no way of dealing with the question of whether he *was* prejudiced; and to say that 'Prejudgments become prejudices only if they are not reversible when exposed to new knowledge' is to maintain, for instance, that nobody could ever utter a death-bed prejudice (since this would evacuate the matter of reversibility when exposed to new knowledge). All a dying man could utter would be a prejudgement. Which is absurd. Rectification in the light of new evidence (*pace* Leon Wieseltier)[4] is very germane to prejudice, but it

1 – *Ghost Waltz* (1980).
2 – *The Nature of Prejudice* (1954; 1958 edition), p. 24.
3 – p. 9.
4 – See p. 74 above.

cannot in itself constitute 'the test to help us distinguish between ordinary errors of prejudgement and prejudice', since what it will mostly distinguish is people who continue to be prejudiced from people who don't.

It is not that I can create or cite a more adequate account of the theory and principles of prejudice than Allport's. But his account remains crucially unsatisfactory; it is weak exactly where it cannot afford to be. The strength, paradoxically, of the best post-Allport book known to me is its honest elaboration of the perplexities of the whole question, not its then itself being able to untie the perplexities. Barry Glassner's *Essential Inter-actionism: On the Intelligibility of Prejudice* (1980) engages in much genuine probing, not only of prejudice but of prejudice-studies. It concedes, for instance, that 'Prejudicing persons do base their prejudices on empirical data, on observations'; and though it goes on at once to say, 'at least in terms of which techniques they choose to accomplish their prejudicing' (which might seem a substantial retraction), the words 'at least' – in Glassner's context – are not just an evasive way of saying 'though only in terms of . . .'. 'At least' grants that it probably isn't only this, and that a difficulty or problem about prejudice's relation to data still exists, for Glassner continues:

Hence, some liberal proposals to diminish prejudice by exposing preju-diced persons to their targets tend not to work, partly owing to the ability for prejudicing persons to incorporate new information into their simplifi-cation.[1]

'*Partly owing*' puts up its small stubborn resistance to one's natural wish that the failure of such exposure be entirely a matter of the cunning immovable flexibility of the prejudiced mind.

Glassner's book is to be honoured for saying that 'We will see throughout our inquiry that indeed the line between prejudicing and "normal" social-mental phenomena is either very thin or non-existent'[2] – but those last words do rather give the game away. 'Or non-existent'? It is strange that the appropriate praise

1 – *Essential Interactionism* (1980), p. 102.
2 – p. 85.

for his scrupulous and pertinacious inquiry into the intelligibility of prejudice should be that so many of its findings could have been published in the *Journal of Negative Results*.

Glassner is aware of how tempting it is for the opponent of prejudice to deploy the same hyperactive generalization which is being deplored: 'By lumping a group of people together and calling them "prejudiced" or "abnormal" or "subjects", social scientists have been able to do comparisons of "them" and "us"'; but this is 'a prejudicing strategy itself.'[1] Glassner's words are all the better as a warning because they are felt as a warning to himself as well as to others. Their point is the one which moved Eliot in 1935 to exclaim, 'How easy it is to see the servitude of others, their obedience to prejudice, to the group among which they live, to the collective will of their progenitors – and how difficult to recognize and face our own!'[2]

In 1984 *Tribune* disowned a stupid 'Vote Labour' poster which mindlessly flourished gender-roles, but *Tribune* then perpetuated quite the wrong flourish of its own. 'It is the sort of unthinking sexism which could only have been produced by a committee of middle-aged men.' *The Times*, gleeful that the poster was in fact the unaided work of 'a young female cartoonist', duly bit the biter: 'I say, *Tribune*, if thinking in stereotypes is prejudiced, aren't your comments on "middle-aged men" both sexist and agist?'[3]

Or there was the review-article by Michael Dummett, 'Power and Prejudice', in the *London Review of Books*.[4] Dummett cogently rejected palliations:

Senior police officers in Britain frequently condone the existence of racially prejudiced policemen by remarking that the Police are only a cross-section of society. They fail to recognise that such prejudice, exhibited by a policeman, has far more malign effects than similar prejudice manifested by a private citizen, and that it ought to be grounds for instant dismissal.

At which point, Dummett was excited to a 'prejudicing strategy' of his own:

1 – p. 120.
2 – *Time and Tide*, 19 January 1935.
3 – *The Times*, 17 November 1984.
4 – 7–20 October 1982.

In fact, however, racial prejudice is far *more* prevalent among policemen than amongst the public at large, for an obvious reason: the kind of personality that is attracted to the police force as a profession is more liable to be infected by racism than are most other types of personality.

The appeal here is to a fully authoritative and emptily unspecified body of findings about those prejudicial conveniences, personality-types, which is why Dummett falls back upon the obvious coercion: 'for an obvious reason'. 'The kind of personality that is attracted to the police force . . .': this is itself infected by just such exacerbated breeziness as seethes in racial prejudice. The matter would be put like this, here of all places, only by someone who has never had any intention of asking himself whether, for instance, *he* has been infected by possessing the kind of personality that is attracted to philosophical professorship as a profession. 'How easy it is to see the servitude of others, their obedience to prejudice, to the group among which they live, to the collective will of their progenitors – and how difficult to recognize and face our own!'

Perception and preception

How deep does prejudice reach? Does there come to our rescue a firm difference in kind between, on the one hand, social stereotyping and, on the other, the operations of perception itself, or is there a quagmire of gradation? For philosopher-psychologists of perception, perception is the crucial mutation of preception, 'a previous conception or notion; a preconception, presumption'. There is no innocent eye, no possibility of perceiving other than by courtesy of prepossession and therefore of what will inevitably on occasion be prejudice. 'To perceive', says Richard Gregory, 'is to read the present in terms of the past to predict and control the future.'[1] So much, under one aspect, for Godwin's hope that we might defy the impulse to act today conformably to the determination of yesterday.

A characteristic title for a Gregory essay is 'On how so little

1 – *Concepts and Mechanisms of Perception* (1974), p. xix.

information controls so much behaviour'. Gregory is blithe about this disparity whereas Eliot wasn't, but the finding is one that Eliot would have acknowledged, just as Eliot would have appreciated both Jerome S. Bruner's insistence that 'perception involves an act of categorisation' and Bruner's title, *Beyond the Information Given* (1974). For the alternative to going beyond the information given may be going nowhere, just as the alternative to our behaviour's being controlled by so little information may be the even more tyrannical control exerted by the proliferation of possibilities. Paralysis has its fascinations, for fascination is paralysis. One of Gregory's instances is the sight of a spoon in a cup of coffee; you take out the spoon, and it proves to be a fork. But what you saw was a spoon; you didn't interrogate your preception-perception by wondering whether it was something other than what you had every reason to expect, despite the possibility that the whole thing was an optical illusion or an experiment in perception set up by your friendly neighbourhood psychologists. You saw a spoon, and quite right too even if you were wrong this once.

For D. H. Lawrence, 'Thought is a man in his wholeness wholly attending.' True. (Or a woman.) But thought is no less a matter of a trained responsible *dis*attending, as when we recognize that the art of reading prose requires something which becomes second nature (meaning that it is never nature at first): a creative disattending to the line-endings, which are effected by the compositor not the composer and which therefore are to carry no information. Poetry creates and transmits information through line-endings; prose does not. In poetry a line-ending is a word-processor's 'hard return'; in prose, it is a 'soft return'. We have to be educated into principled ignoring, which is sometimes an ignoring of what might look like information but isn't, and is sometimes a harder thing, an ignoring of genuine information which we are obliged to discount lest we be shattered by an information-explosion or a possibility-paralysis.

Psychologists of perception are usually conservative, and think well of habit and prejudice, as Gregory does:

Prejudices we may represent as systematic refusal to consider data which are relevant to certain kinds of decision. Now this refusal might well be useful (since the decision device is limited in its capacity) because if all relevant data were used for each important decision, too much time would be required for each decision. Prejudices might well be important for the business of 'getting on with it' . . . Human prejudice is useful in saving thinking time: clearly it would be intolerable to have to consider all relevant possibilities.[1]

One snag there is the relation of 'it would be intolerable' to being intolerant. Yet conservatives are not alone in believing in the need to get on with it; Mark Rutherford from his very different political perspective observed that 'There is always a multitude of reasons in favour of doing a thing and against doing it. The art of debate lies in presenting them; the art of life lies in neglecting ninety-nine hundredths of them'.[2] This antithesis – the art of debate and the art of life – is reasonable, and yet there is a third term, something which is neither debate nor life though partaking of both: art. The art of art might then be thought to consist in doing justice to the obligations both of the art of debate, which presents the multitude of contrary reasons, and of the art of life, which neglects for honourable reasons ninety-nine hundredths of them.

Art would therefore have its own obligation, a balance or reconciliation such as is characteristic of art; and part of this obligation would then consist in being sensitive to the dangers of complacency which lurk within even so humane a conservative confidence as Gregory's:

The past is usually a reliable guide, and our memory contains vastly more information than can be transmitted in reasonable time by the sensory channels even when the relevant information is available – which is rarely the case.[3]

To perceive is to ignore. Up to a point. In the words of Mary Douglas:

In the normal process of interpretation, the existing scheme of assumptions tends to be protected from challenge, for the learner recognizes and absorbs cues which harmonize with past experience and usually ignores

1 – *Concepts and Mechanisms of Perception*, pp. 533, 639.
2 – *More Pages from a Journal* (1910), p. 247.
3 – *Concepts and Mechanisms of Perception*, p. 598.

cues which are discordant. Thus, those assumptions which have worked well before are reinforced. Because the selection and treatment of new experiences validates the principles which have been learned, the structure of established assumptions can be applied quickly and automatically to current problems of interpretation. In animals this stabilizing, selective tendency serves the biological function of survival. In men the same tendency appears to govern learning. If every new experience laid all past interpretations open to doubt, no scheme of established assumptions could be developed and no learning could take place.[1]

Yet there is always a question to be pressed, in one of two forms. Can a distinction be made, in the generalized terms of philosophy, between a proper prejudging and an improper prejudicing? Or can such a distinction be made in the more local terms of principle and tact? Drawing up a theory, or drawing the line. A poet such as Eliot might draw the line, simply though not easily, by tact's incarnation, not by theory at all. He might incorporate and enact within his poetry a double vigilance: a distrust of prejudice, and a distrust of the distrust of prejudice. But the philosopher will have different responsibilities. Mary Douglas, thinking anthropologically, has retorted to the Paris graffito of 1968, 'Ears have walls' (itself a retort to the wartime warning about spies: 'Walls have ears'), that 'Ears must have walls'.

Legitimacy must be clothed in magic, words must be made into things, blocks, hedges, compartments are the conditions of knowledge. Thinkers must recognize the destructive lure of the natural system of symbols, equally when it devastates category boundaries as when it wrongfully closes them.[2]

We are enabled to listen to something only by not hearing everything. But the theoretical problems (of 'wrongfully' and rightfully) do not dissolve, as may be glimpsed in a crucial variant in the wording of the prefatory note to Mary Douglas's anthology *Rules and Meanings* (1973):

Each person confronted with a system of ends and means (not necessarily a tidy and coherent system) seems to face the order of nature, objective and

1 – *Implicit Meanings* (1975), pp. 51–2.
2 – *Natural Symbols* (1970), p. 200.

independent of human wishes. But the moral order and the knowledge which sustains it are created by social conventions. If their man-made origins were not hidden, they would be stripped of some of their authority.

The last two sentences found themselves quoted on the book's jacket – with one small alteration for drama and sales: 'If their man-made origins were not hidden, they would be stripped of much of their authority.' But if 'some' can be silently upped to 'much', why cannot 'much' be upped to 'all'? What is at stake is both the judgement of authority and the authority of judgement, and to say – *tout court* – that knowledge is created by social conventions is to leave no safeguard against the further escalation, after 'some' becomes 'much', into this: If their man-made origins were not hidden, they would be stripped of all of their authority.

Two men of genius attended to this matter last century. They came at it from different angles, and they wrangled – not always genially – about their differences of temperament and of aegis. They were brothers. Both William James and Henry James were profoundly inaugurative, and it is therefore the more weighty that they give such eloquent testimony to the knottiness of prejudice, its being so entwined with human necessities. William James believed that 'The great thing, then, in all education, is to *make our nervous system our ally instead of our enemy*. It is to fund and capitalize our acquisitions, and live at ease upon the interest of the fund'.[1] James's metaphor shows his continuity with Burke ('the general bank and capital of nations and of ages'); Eliot was more critical of capitalism than this,[2] but the preceding sentence of James anticipates an insistence of Eliot's: 'Our problem being to form the future, we can only form it on the materials of the past; we must *use* our heredity, instead of denying it.' For William James, writing here more as the founder of modern psychology than as a follower of ancient philosophy,

1 – *The Principles of Psychology* (1890), i, 121–2.
2 – 'I still believe that such words as *work* and *thrift* have potent moral significance, though their real moral value has been distorted by the capitalist system, a distortion which seems unlikely to be straightened out in any merely socialist system. *Property* is another such word' (*The Criterion*, xi, 1932, 274).

the crucial term was habit; against Godwin's contempt for habit must be set James's estimation of it, an estimation which includes though it is not limited to an esteem for it:

Habit is thus the enormous fly-wheel of society, its most precious conservative agent. It alone is what keeps us all within the bounds of ordinance, and saves the children of fortune from the envious uprisings of the poor. It alone prevents the hardest and most repulsive walks of life from being deserted by those brought up to tread therein. It keeps the fisherman and the deck-hand at sea through the winter; it holds the miner in his darkness, and nails the countryman to his log-cabin and his lonely farm through all the months of snow; it protects us from invasion by the natives of the desert and the frozen zone. It dooms us all to fight out the battle of life upon the lines of our nurture or our early choice, and to make the best of a pursuit that disagrees, because there is no other for which we are fitted, and it is too late to begin again. It keeps different social strata from mixing. Already at the age of twenty-five you see the professional mannerism settling down on the young commercial traveller, on the young doctor, and the young minister, on the young counsellor-at-law. You see the little lines of cleavage running through the character, the tricks of thought, the prejudices, the ways of the 'shop', in a word, from which the man can by-and-by no more escape than his coat-sleeve can suddenly fall into a new set of folds. On the whole, it is best he should not escape. It is well for the world that in most of us, by the age of thirty, the character has set like plaster, and will never soften again.

This is itself too armed in habit, grindingly supporting the class-system and the economic system in its harshest form: we fund and capitalize our acquisitions, and live at ease upon the interest not only of the mind, and thus it is that we are protected from the envious uprisings of the poor. Though James has the decency to take no pleasure in what he sees as the case, he is here oppressively grim. Against a liberal hopefulness about the infinite plasticity of man, he pits a conservative hopelessness, one for which too high a price is exacted. Social arrangements are encouraged to insist that they are the human condition and the will of God. In his obduracy James does not here invite such generosity as Gray's 'Elegy Written in a Country Churchyard' was accorded by Empson, Empson being able at once to criticize the political coercion and to concede the irreducible truth within such induration of social inequity into tragic necessity:

Full many a gem of purest ray serene,
The dark unfathomed caves of ocean bear:
Full many a flower is born to blush unseen,
And waste its sweetness on the desert air.

What this means, as the context makes clear, is that eighteenth-century England had no scholarship system or *carrière ouverte aux talents*. This is stated as pathetic, but the reader is put into a mood in which one would not try to alter it . . . By comparing the social arrangement to Nature he makes it seem inevitable, which it was not, and gives it a dignity which was undeserved . . . And yet what is said is one of the permanent truths; it is only in degree that any improvement of society could prevent wastage of human powers; the waste even in a fortunate life, the isolation even of a life rich in intimacy, cannot but be felt deeply, and is the central feeling of tragedy. And anything of value must accept this because it must not prostitute itself; its strength is to be prepared to waste itself, if it does not get its opportunity. A statement of this is certainly non-political because it is true in any society, and yet nearly all the great poetic statements of it are in a way 'bourgeois', like this one; they suggest to many readers, though they do not say, that for the poor man things cannot be improved even in degree.[1]

Yet William James does write with poignancy about these tragic submissions; his imagination is chastened as well as impassioned, and he makes no exception for himself. Life on these terms may be – or may often be – hell, but at least it is not 'a Hell for the *other people*'. 'The hell to be endured hereafter, of which theology tells, is no worse than the hell we make for ourselves in this world by habitually fashioning our characters in the wrong way.'[2] We are not then created to be other than creatures of habit, and the only question is whether we shall be the creatures of good or of bad habit.

We only live, only suspire
Consumed by either fire or fire.
('Little Gidding')

To dissent from James's vision of life here is not simply to disown it; and the vision is the more unignorable because it

1 – *Some Versions of Pastoral* (1935), p. 4–5.
2 – *The Principles of Psychology*, i, 127.

emanates from someone whose lifelong courage defied habit (habits of innumerable kinds) to the point of risking and enduring madness.

Thirty years earlier, William James's younger brother had sketched, at twenty, his own more youthful and less tragic sense of these things. In a letter of 1 November 1863 to Thomas Sergeant Perry, Henry James rotated exquisitely and exactly the innumerable facets of prejudice, facets many of which Eliot was to crystallize in poetry. There is a taunting contrariety between, on the one hand, the Jamesian ambition to be one of those on whom nothing is lost (incarnate in the multifariousness of his findings, the urgings, velleities, and concessions with which in the lovely long letter his thinking makes its supple way) and, on the other hand, his acknowledgement that prejudice itself has to be valued for its making possible the desirable and even indispensable losing of at least some of the countless considerations which would otherwise overwhelm all thinking and feeling. In replying to Perry's 'little dissertation on prejudice', Henry James creates something more than a dissertation, something more undulating and diverse.

Your letter contains a little dissertation on prejudice, suggested by a book you had been reading (Locke on the Human Understanding), in which you do me the honour to ask me my opinion two or three times. It is a subject I have thought on not at all (like every other subject), and upon which I shrink from giving a judgement to you who have been reading Locke, even as a little child paddling among the chance waves that roll up about his feet on Newport beach, shrinks from following the strong man who ventures forth into the great ocean. – I agree with you perfectly that "prejudice is one of the worst evils which afflict humanity"; but I hardly think that it is one which each man can take in hand for himself and drive away. Every one knows the injustice of it, but few people are conscious that they possess it. Wilfully, intentionally prejudiced persons are very rare. Every one certainly is more or less prejudiced, but "unbeknown" to themselves. Is not a prejudice a judgement formed on a subject upon *data* furnished, not by the subject itself, but by the mind which regards it? (This is a very crude definition, but it will show you what I mean). These *data* are the fruits of the subtlest influences, – birth, education, association. Unless carefully watched they insinuate themselves into every opinion we form. They grow to be the substance of our very being. So far are they from being subjects of consciousness that they almost become vehicles thereof. They exercise, then, a great weight in our judgements. They are so intimately connected with every mental process, that they insidiously pervert our opinions, discolour and distort the objects of our vision. The opinion is consciously formed, perhaps; but not appreciatively, critically. That is we are conscious of it when formed, but not during formation. Now, all opinions which we consciously hold for any time, receive in a measure the sanction of conscience. And then – who shall gainsay them? They have been stamped at the royal mint: let them pass current. However false they may be, however base the metal of which they are composed, they have undergone an ordeal which renders them supremely valid in our eyes. You will say we cannot impose them on others. Certainly not. But when others reject them they become doubly dear to ourselves. We treasure them up. We gloat over them in private. We become millionaires of self-complacency. – This of course is the very height of prejudice. – But there is no-one whose judgements are *all* preconceived. And even the most prejudiced people when convinced that they *are* so are willing to correct themselves. But the question is to find out where the prejudice lies, to distinguish the true from the false. This is immensely difficult – so much so, that I should fear a man setting to work on his own hook would find it impossible. We know when we lie, when we kill, when we steal; when we deceive or violate others, but it is hard to know when we deceive or violate ourselves. You will say that a prejudice violates others – their rights, their claims, etc. Certainly it does when it is practically carried out; and *then* we can straightway take cognizance of it, measure it, reform it or cast it off. But as long as it is held as a mere opinion, I suppose it only violates some abstract standard of truth and justice. It cannot be denied, however, that we have mighty few opinions that we are not desirous to act upon. – Cannot you imagine the state of irresolution and scepticism and utter nothingness a man would be reduced to, who set to work to re-cast his old opinions, pick them clean of prejudice and build them up into a fairer structure? I'm afraid that he would find he had pulled out the chief corner stones, and that the edifice was prostrate, and he almost crushed in its ruins. In his desire to believe nothing but what his reason showed him to be true, I think he would end by believing nothing at all. It is a question whether he would not have attained the chief felicity of man; whether it is *not* better to believe nothing than to believe falsely; whether scepticism is not preferable to superstition. But it is a question which I can't answer. It seems to me like a choice between lunacy and idiocy, – death by fire – or by water. We were certainly born to believe. The truth was certainly made to be believed. Life is a prolonged reconciliation of these two facts. As long as we squint at the truth instead of looking straight at it – *i.e.* as long as we are prejudiced instead of fair, so long we are miserable sinners. But it seems to me that this fatal obliquity of vision inheres not wholly in any individual but is some indefinable property in the social atmosphere. – When by some concerted effort of humanity the air is purified then the film will fall from our eyes and (to conclude gracefully) we shall gaze undazzled at the sun!!!! How I do run on! You will certainly fear to broach any further question of morals THIS being the penalty. In reading the above over I am struck with its great dogmatism and crudity. It is probably all wrong or even all nothing. At all events, supply a query after every assertion and enclose the whole in a great parenthesis and interrogation point, or even scratch it all out.[1]

James has the right ending there, up first to a comically religious revelation, and then down to querying any judgement he has given upon prejudice, to the point of inviting the cancellation of it all – even while not himself scratching it all out. The final three sentences of postscript are pure *postjudice*.

The movement of the thought throughout, as of waves and tides, which is adumbrated in James's evocation of Newport beach, is true to the necessary undulation, ebb and flow: but . . . but . . . but . . . but . . . but [these five within nine lines] . . . but . . . but . . . But . . . But . . . But . . . but . . . but . . . But . . . however . . . But . . . But . . . Given this sequence of roundings upon himself as well as upon the matter, it is astonishing that James does not emerge as a dervish. 'But me no buts' – unless your subject is the complexities and perplexities of prejudice. James eludes all the various complacencies which lurk, and, where his brother was unmisgivingly to urge us 'to fund and capitalize our acquisitions, and live at ease upon the interest of the fund', Henry James warns against the propensity to 'become millionaires of self-complacency. – This of course is the very height of prejudice'.

Prejudication

Ten years after Eliot's death, William Empson wrote in the *T. S. Eliot Review*:

I was asked to reflect about the politics of Eliot, and after making the attempt felt rather surprised to conclude that he hadn't got any. He was not

1 – *Letters*, edited by Leon Edel, i (1974), 45–7.

(so to speak) brought up to have any, because an aesthete rather boasted of having none; he inherited a healthy crop of family prejudices, but did not feel committed to them.[1]

There is a quizzical tension to this, since aesthetes in Eliot's young days were drawn towards socialism, whereas those who believe themselves to be without politics are usually only taking it for granted that conservatism is not *politics* but simply the way life is. Several of the healthy crop of Eliot family prejudices proved unhealthy, but fortunately Eliot found it both his duty and his instinct for survival to resist in some degree his family. His greatest personal decisions all necessitated such resistance, though none of them made the mistake of then being dictated by some determination not to be dictated to by his powerful family: his change of profession, his leaving his country, and his marrying so against his family's wishes. These went with his decision to be an artist, which prompted him to the traditional blasphemy that had been voiced by Pope: 'To follow Poetry as one ought, one must forget father and mother, and cleave to it alone.'[2] Or, in Eliot's words, compounding the grave blasphemy:

The Arts insist that a man shall dispose of all that he has, even of his family tree, and follow art alone. For they require that a man be not a member of a family or of a caste or of a party or of a coterie, but simply and solely himself.[3]

Eliot's relations with his notable family were not really such as to make it likely, then, that he would be uninquiringly committed to those family prejudices; his art is often engaged rather with probing not only those prejudices but prejudice itself.

It is not clearly true (Empson was mischievous) that Eliot had

1 – *T. S. Eliot Review*, ii (1975); *Argufying* (1987), p. 364. Empson has a slightly, but crucially, different sense of this from that of William M. Chace in his discriminating study of *The Political Identities of Ezra Pound and T. S. Eliot:* 'For although one may assume that Eliot absorbed roughly the same basic predilections and prejudices from his genteelly declining, New England-connected family as Pound did from his, Eliot rejected his American origins so thoroughly in later life that it seems presumptuous to try to make much of them' (p. 109).
2 – To Jervas, 16 August 1714.
3 – 'A Romantic Aristocrat', *The Sacred Wood*, p. 32.

no politics; it is clearly true that he was aware that others did have politics. But his political vigilance, his distrust of political manipulation, was by no means limited to watching the Left. Substantiating his claim that 'I am as scary of Order as of Disorder',[1] he wrote to his good friend Bonamy Dobrée in 1930:

I think we are in agreement that 'Order' and 'Authority' are more dangerous catchwords now, than 'Liberty' and 'Reform' were fifty or seventy-five years ago. Order and Authority may point more directly to the yellow press and the crook capitalists than Liberty and Reform pointed to Socialism. I am terrified of the modern contempt of 'democracy'.

Prejudice is a matter of politics and of philosophy. Of all American and English poets, Eliot was the most professionally trained and talented as a philosopher. It is because of this, and not despite it, that he offered not a philosophical encompassing of prejudice's issues but a poetic incarnation and enactment of them. He will have been struck by the propensity of his philosophical mentor F. H. Bradley simultaneously to depress and to elevate the word 'prejudice' by so often prefacing it with a pejorative or prejudicial epithet: 'blind prejudice'; 'thoughtless prejudice'; 'groundless prejudice'; 'crassest prejudice'; 'irrational prejudice'; 'a mere prejudice'; 'the merest prejudice'. Without this inculpation, 'prejudice' might be countenanced, and yet one effect of the opprobrious adjectives is to exculpate any *un*-epitheted prejudice.

Eliot's apprehension of scepticism was affected by Bradley's crucial distinction between two forms of it. It took Bradley more than four hundred pages of *Appearance and Reality* to move from a direct asseveration to a rounded or circular one. From this, on p. xii (the roman numerals of a preface):

By scepticism is not meant doubt about or disbelief in some tenet or tenets. I understand by it an attempt to become aware of and to doubt all preconceptions. Such scepticism is the result only of labour and education, but it is a training which cannot with impunity be neglected.

To this, on pp. 428–9:

1 – *T. S. Eliot: The Man and His Work*, ed. Tate, pp. 84–5.

An honest and truth-seeking scepticism pushes questions to the end, and knows that the end lies hid in that which is assumed at the beginning. But the scepticism (so-called) of Common Sense from first to last is dogmatic.[1]

What in Bradley is a philosophical relation of an end to a beginning, a relation contained within the conscious acquiescence in an assumption, was in the end to become for Eliot a circling back which was simultaneously poetic, literary, personally ancestral, and doctrinal:

> We shall not cease from exploration
> And the end of all our exploring
> Will be to arrive where we started
> And know the place for the first time.
> Through the unknown, remembered gate
> When the last of earth left to discover
> Is that which was the beginning;
>
> ('Little Gidding')

'We have to return to where we started from, but the journey has altered the starting place: so that the place we left and the place we return to are the same and also different'.[2] It is in thinking of Valéry that Eliot is moved to say this, Valéry being uncoincidentally one whose scepticism rivalled even Bradley's own.[3]

Eliot as an artist came to rest in religious comprehensions of philosophical unresolvabilities.[4] He chose the more-than-profession of artist instead of the profession of philosopher, and the art itself he often made out of scepticism about philosophy. 'The root cause of the vagaries of modern philosophy – and perhaps, though I was unconscious of it, the reason for my dissatisfaction with philosophy as a *profession* – I now [1952] believe to lie in the divorce of philosophy from theology.'[5]

1 – *Appearance and Reality* (1893; second edition 1897).
2 – 'Leçon de Valéry' (1946).
3 – See p. 89.
4 – Piers Gray addresses this question: 'But is Eliot implying that an act of faith is necessary because, intellectually, we can never construct a coherent world?' (*T. S. Eliot's Intellectual and Poetic Development 1909–1922*, p. 164).
5 – Introduction to Josef Pieper, *Leisure the Basis of Culture* (1952), pp. 14–15.

It was Bradley who had done most to lay bare the unresolv-abilities and to find the foundation of all thinking in an act of faith, in assumptions (which proved to be for Eliot 'assumptions up to heaven', in Tennyson's words), and in a confidence that, though prejudice was often dishonourable, prejudication was always the condition even of our being able to conceive of honour or dishonour.

Bradley's first book was entirely devoted to *The Presuppositions of Critical History* (1874).[1]

History must ever be founded on a presupposition; and the scepticism which saw in the succession of historical writings a series of fictions, where the present was transported into the bygone age, was thus and so far justified: but the insight into the ground of the partial justification will exhibit, I hope, the source of the general mistake.

Paley protested against that which he called a 'prejudication'. We have seen the reason why every history is necessarily based upon prejudication; and experience testifies that, as a matter of fact, there is no single history which is not so based, which does not derive its individual character from the particular character of the author. There is no such thing as a history without a prejudication; the real distinction is between the writer who has his prejudications without knowing what they are, and whose prejudica-tions, it may be, are false, and the writer who consciously orders and creates from the known foundation of that which for him is the truth.

It is when history becomes aware of its presupposition that it first becomes truly critical, and protects itself (so far as is possible) from the caprices of fiction.[2]

'(So far as is possible)': the brackets do not succeed in protecting Bradley's thought against the infection of a more virulent scepticism, pyrrhonism. (So far as is possible): (and how far is that, exactly?)

Bradley's demonstrations of insubstantiality were largely believed by Eliot, who (in 1923, seven years after completing his dissertation) contemplated Bradley with a hushed awe laced with solemn banter:

1 – Piers Gray illuminates this work of Bradley's (*T. S. Eliot's Intellectual and Poetic Development*, pp. 103–6); he drily makes good his observation that 'We are left with the following conclusions from "The Presuppositions of Critical History", conclusions which, in fact, are problems.'
2 – Bradley, *Collected Essays* (1935), i, 20–1.

All we can do is to accept these data and follow our argument to the end. If it ends, as it may well end, in zero, well, we have at least the satisfaction of having pursued something to the end, and of having ascertained that certain questions which occur to men to ask, are unanswerable or are meaningless. Once you accept his theory of the nature of the judgment, and it is as plausible a theory as any, you are led by his arid and highly sensitive eloquence (no English philosopher has ever written finer English) to something which, according to your temperament, will be resignation or despair – the bewildered despair of wondering why you ever wanted anything, and what it was that you wanted, since this philosophy seems to give you everything that you ask and yet to render it not worth wanting.[1]

Bradley is to philosophy what Henry Adams was to culture, though with this crucial proviso, that Bradley understood the process: Adams was for Eliot 'A Sceptical Patrician',

aware, as most Bostonians are, of the narrowness of the Boston horizon. But working with and against conscience was the Boston doubt: a scepticism which is difficult to explain to those who are not born to it. This scepticism is a product, or a cause, or a concomitant, of Unitarianism; it is not destructive but it is dissolvent . . . Wherever this man stepped, the ground did not simply give way, it flew into particles.[2]

The forked root of the matter for Bradley, as for many others, is the inseparability (not the indistinguishability) of perception from preception. Eliot had a sudden lapse of critical vigilance when, writing of allegory and the visual imagination in his book on Dante, and asking the reader 'to clear his mind, if he can, of every prejudice against allegory', he averred: 'it is the allegory which makes it possible for the reader who is not even a good Italian scholar to enjoy Dante. Speech varies, but our eyes are all the same.'[3] One knows what Eliot means, and there is something in it, but to put it like that is to make it sound (prejudicially, by being uncharacteristically imperceptive about perception) as if eyes, unlike tongues, did not have to be educated. Our eyes are not all the same when it comes to seeing imaginatively; we have to be trained to see, and the training of a twentieth-century American or Englishman is very different from that of a

1 – *Vanity Fair*, February 1924.
2 – *The Athenaeum*, 23 May 1919.
3 – 'Dante', *Selected Essays*, p. 243.

fourteenth-century Italian, as Eliot's own vivid argument acknowledged in his previous paragraph:

Dante's is a *visual* imagination. It is a visual imagination in a different sense from that of a modern painter of still life: it is visual in the sense that he lived in an age in which men still saw visions. It was a psychological habit, the trick of which we have forgotten, but as good as any of our own.

Bradley was more clear-sighted than to say that speech varies but our eyes are all the same. 'We see what we perceive; and the object of our perceptions is qualified by the premises of our knowledge, by our previous experiences.'[1] Knowledge and experience come together there, and Eliot, the author of a dissertation which became *Knowledge and Experience in the Philosophy of F. H. Bradley,* knew that among his most import-ant experiences was his experience of Bradley's thought. Eliot found the Marxist materialistic interpretation of history insuffi-ciently critical, and his insistence on this (in 1929) brought together his Bradleyan conviction about history, his political allegiance, and his religious faith (trusting to revelation since rationality is not rational at its foundations), all of these finding their focus in a double use of the word 'prejudice'. First,

I must hasten to declare that I have cleared my mind of any prejudice against what communists or Marxians calls the 'materialist theory of history'.

Second,

Like every other interpretation of history, it asserts itself to be the 'fundamental' interpretation: and if one went into the matter thoroughly, one would question it, not from the point of view of any other interpre-tation, but from the point of view of an observer who believes that any interpretation of history is merely a selection of a particular abstracted series of causes and effects, and is valid only from a particular point of view. I suspect that the materialistic interpretation derives much of its cogency (like any other) from a sentimental prejudice: namely, for this interpretation, that the most important thing is that human beings should be fed and clothed and sheltered (which is not self-evident). I believe, that

1 – *Collected Essays,* i, 15.

is, that any interpretation of history being a selection, is preceded by a valuation, which is a postulate and cannot be justified rationally.[1]

For just as perception entails preception, so to construe is to construct. As Eliot said in his dissertation on Bradley: 'Knowledge is invariably a matter of degree: you cannot put your finger upon even the simplest datum and say "this we know". In the growth and construction of the world we live in, there is no one stage, and no one aspect, which you can take as the foundation.'[2]

Eliot on prejudice

The relations of prejudice to prejudication are clearly of the greatest philosophical complexity, and it would be vain for someone who is not a philosopher to hope to clarify them. All that is intended here is to suggest the persistence and variety of Eliot's engagement. Eliot is from the beginning preoccupied with prejudice because it constitutes an intersection of philosophy, psychology, politics, and art. In the words that summarize a paper by Eliot at Josiah Royce's seminar on 24 February 1914:

To sum up, explanation is an act which tries with indifferent success to bring the particular under the universal; description tries to stay in the particular as given, but in spite of itself transforms the given by the interpretation it gives to it.[3]

Or there are the terms of Eliot's introduction to his mother's verse-play *Savonarola*:

The role played by interpretation has often been neglected in the theory of knowledge. Even Kant, devoting a lifetime to the pursuit of categories, fixed only those which he believed, rightly or wrongly, to be permanent, and overlooked or neglected the fact that these are only the more stable of a vast system of categories in perpetual change.[4]

1 – *The Criterion*, viii (1929), 684–6.
2 – *Knowledge and Experience in the Philosophy of F. H. Bradley*, p. 151.
3 – *Josiah Royce's Seminar, 1913–1914: as recorded in the notebooks of Harry T. Costello*, edited by Grover Smith (1963), p. 121.
4 – Introduction to Charlotte Eliot, *Savonarola* (1926), p. viii.

Psychology is no less enmeshed with prejudice, because of classification. Eliot wrote in a review of Sri Ananda Acharya in 1918:

There is, moreover, extremely subtle and patient psychology in the later [Indian] writers; and it should be the task of the interpreter to make this psychology plausible, to exhibit it as something more than an arbitrary and fatiguing system of classifications.[1]

Politics engages prejudice because of stereotypes. And art, because of convention, 'a preparedness, a habit, on the part of the public, to respond in a predictable way, however crudely, to certain stimuli'.[2]

That Eliot, with a good deal of knowledge and self-know-ledge, was wary of prejudice, of its dangers and those of supposing that it simply should or could be eradicated, may be shown by an abbreviated anthology from his prose writings (abbreviated, in that one could supply an annals-anthology throughout Eliot's writing life, explicitly on the matter of prejudice):

1916
Now it follows almost inevitably, if one holds a theory of conscience similar to Dr. Rashdall's, that conscience will consist in the usual structure of prejudices of the enlightened middle classes.[3]

1919
Mr. Lynd ought to turn loose his passions, his curiosities, even his prejudices – if he will make them distinct and evident.[4]

1923
The critic, one would suppose, if he is to justify his existence, should endeavour to discipline his personal prejudices and cranks – tares to which

1 – *International Journal of Ethics*, April 1918. Also *After Strange Gods*, p. 40: 'A good half of the effort of understanding what the Indian philosophers were after – and their subtleties make most of the great European philosophers look like schoolboys – lay in trying to erase from my mind all the categories and kinds of distinction common to European philosophy from the time of the Greeks.'
2 – *The Athenaeum*, 14 May 1920.
3 – *International Journal of Ethics*, October 1916.
4 – *The Athenaeum*, 13 June 1919.

we are all subject – and compose his differences with as many of his fellows as possible, in the common pursuit of true judgment.[1]

1924

If it be objected that this is a prejudice of the case, I can only reply that one must criticize from some point of view and that it is better to know what one's point of view is.[2]

1927

Mr. Russell's words will stir the hearts of those who employ the same catchwords as himself. He has a wholly unreasoning prejudice in favour of freedom, kindliness and such things, and the same unreasoning prejudice against tyranny and cruelty.[3]

Middleton was a great observer of human nature, without fear, without sentiment, without prejudice.[4]

1928

A new Remy de Gourmont could 'dissociate' these ideas of Nationalism, of Class, of Race into their local components; and there is also the Religious Idea (not discussed by M. Benda) to be dissociated (with special reference to an actual controversy in England) into components such as conviction, piety, prejudice and politics. Each of these subjects would take a chapter by itself.

Sometimes, when an historian has exactly the same bias as ourselves, we have the optical illusion of no bias at all; to many people Gibbon or Mr Lytton Strachey seem to possess the virtue of detachment, instead of the virtue of a pleasant bias. The judgment of any historian must depend both on the degree of his prejudice and (I am afraid) upon our moral judgment of the prejudice itself.[5]

1931

The elders have had the satisfaction of throwing off prejudices; that is, of persuading themselves that the way they want to behave is the only moral way to behave; but there is not much in it for those who have no prejudices to reject.[6]

1 – 'The Function of Criticism', *Selected Essays*, p. 25.
2 – 'Four Elizabethan Dramatists', *Selected Essays*, p. 114.
3 – *The Criterion*, vi (1927), 178–9.
4 – 'Thomas Middleton9, *Selected Essays*, p. 169.
5 – *Cambridge Review*, 6 June 1928.
6 – 'Thoughts after Lambeth', *Selected Essays*, p. 367.

One must, in considering a writer like Lawrence, confess what will be called one's prejudices, and leave the rest to the reader.[1]

1933

Instead of the sophistication of the man [Anatole France] who knows all about the past, who has understood all philosophies and faiths and seen through them, infinitely learned, infinitely 'intelligent' (magic word), and infinitely weary, weary; instead of that kind of humbug he [André Gide] offered us the sophistication of the daring mind, freed from all prejudices and inhibitions (how that word fatigues one!), exploring all possibilities, willing to try anything – the slave, not of the past, but of the future.[2]

1934

Nor can we safely, without very critical examination, dig ourselves in stubbornly to a few dogmatic notions, for what is a healthy belief at one time may, unless it is one of the few fundamental things, be a pernicious prejudice at another.

The personality thus expressed, the personality which fascinates us in the work of philosophy or art, tends naturally to be the *unregenerate* personality, partly self-deceived and partly irresponsible, and because of its freedom, terribly *limited* by prejudice and self-conceit, capable of much good or great mischief according to the natural goodness or impurity of the man: and we are all, naturally, impure.[3]

1935

I suggest that he [C. H. Norman] is making a mistake, and that he is weakening the expression of a conviction, by reinforcing it with a prejudice.[4]

1937

More [Paul Elmer More], like Babbitt, seems almost to have been born in a state of emancipation from the prejudices of his time and place. Many people give the appearance of progress by shedding the prejudices and irrational postulates of one generation only to acquire those of the next: by 'keeping up to date'.[5]

1940

It is through the science of theology only that we can hope to bring to our

1 – *The Criterion*, x (1931), 774.
2 – *The Criterion*, xii (1933), 470.
3 – *After Strange Gods*, pp. 19, 63.
4 – *New English Weekly*, 31 October 1935.
5 – *Princeton Alumni Weekly*, 5 February 1937.

own consciousness, and so dispose of, the unconscious assumptions, bias and prejudice which impair social thinking.[1]

1944

If we censure an eighteenth-century critic for not having a modern, historical and comprehensive appreciation, we must ourselves adopt towards him, the attitude the lack of which we reprehend; we must not be narrow in accusing him of narrowness, or prejudiced in accusing him of prejudice.[2]

1947

But when Johnson held an opinion which seems to us wrong, we are never safe in dismissing it without inquiring why he was wrong; he had his own 'errors and prejudices', certainly, but for lack of examining them sympathetically we are always in danger of merely countering error with error and prejudice with prejudice.[3]

1948

I dare say that some readers will draw political inferences from this discussion: what is more likely is that particular minds will read into my text a confirmation or repudiation of their own political convictions or prejudices. The writer himself is not without political convictions and prejudices; but the imposition of them is no part of his present intention.[4]

1950

We are all, in fact, trying to persuade other people: that is, we appeal to their emotions, and often indeed to their prejudices, as well as to their reason; and the best we can do is to see *as well as* (to our reason) does not become *instead of* (to our reason). We can at least *try* to understand our own motives, passions, and prejudices, so as to be conscious of what we are doing when we appeal to those of others. This is very difficult, because our own prejudice and emotional bias always seem to us so rational.[5]

1952

My aims in writing this preface are, first, to affirm my belief in the importance of the author and of this particular book; second, to warn the reader against premature judgment and summary classification – to persuade him to hold in check his own prejudices and at the same time to be patient with those of Simone Weil.[6]

1 – *Christendom*, x (1940), 103.
2 – 'Johnson as Critic and Poet', *On Poetry and Poets*, p. 164.
3 – 'Milton II', *On Poetry and Poets*, p. 147.
4 – *Notes towards the Definition of Culture*, p. 16.
5 – 'The Aims of Education', *To Criticize the Critic*, p. 123.
6 – Preface to Simone Weil, *The Need for Roots* (1952), p. v.

1956

So the critic to whom I am most grateful is the one who can make me look at something I have never looked at before, or looked at only with eyes clouded by prejudice, set me face to face with it and then leave me alone with it.[1]

Eeldrop and Appleplex

In May 1917, the month when *Prufrock and Other Observations* was advertised, Eliot published in the *Little Review* a prose dialogue the preoccupation of which was prejudice. He never reprinted it. 'Eeldrop and Appleplex' has been read as a conversation between Eliot and Pound; it should be read as itself in dialogue with that dialogue of Fontenelle on prejudice which Pound translated and published in the same month in *The Egoist*.

'Eeldrop and Appleplex' is a deep, witty, and honourably uneasy exploration of prejudice, of stereotyping and of the classifying of people. At its heart are these exchanges, which need to be fully quoted if they are to be fairly judged:

Both were endeavoring to escape not the commonplace, respectable or even the domestic, but the too well pigeon-holed, too taken-for-granted, too highly systematized areas, and, – in the language of those whom they sought to avoid – they wished 'to apprehend the human soul in its concrete individuality'.

'Why', said Eeldrop, 'was that fat Spaniard, who sat at the table with us this evening, and listened to our conversation with occasional curiosity, why was he himself for a moment an object of interest to us? He wore his napkin tucked into his chin, he made unpleasant noises while eating, and while not eating, his way of crumbling bread between fat fingers made me extremely nervous: he wore a waistcoat café au lait, and black boots with brown tops. He was oppressively gross and vulgar; he belonged to a type, he could easily be classified in any town of provincial Spain. Yet under the circumstances – when we had been discussing marriage, and he suddenly leaned forward and exclaimed: "I was married once myself" – we were able to detach him from his classification and regard him for a moment as an unique being, a soul, however insignificant, with a history of its own,

1 – 'The Frontiers of Criticism', *On Poetry and Poets*, p. 117.

once for all. It is these moments which we prize, and which alone are revealing. For any vital truth is incapable of being applied to another case: the essential is unique. Perhaps that is why it is so neglected: because it is useless. What we learned about that Spaniard is incapable of being applied to any other Spaniard, or even recalled in words. With the decline of orthodox theology and its admirable theory of the soul, the unique importance of events has vanished. A man is only important as he is classed'.[1]

*

'What you say', replied Appleplex, 'commands my measured adherence. I should think, in the case of the Spaniard, and in the many other interesting cases which have come under our attention at the door of the police station, what we grasp in that moment of pure observation on which we pride ourselves, is not alien to the principle of classification, but deeper. We could if we liked, make excellent comment upon the nature of provincial Spaniards, or of destitution (as misery is called by the philanthropists), or on homes for working girls. But such is not our intention. We aim at experience in the particular centres in which alone it is evil. We avoid classification. We do not deny it. But when a man is classified something is lost. The majority of mankind live on paper currency: they use terms which are merely good for so much reality, they never see actual coinage'.

'I should go even further than that', said Eeldrop. 'The majority not only have no language to express anything save generalized man; they are for the most part unaware of themselves as anything but generalized men. They are first of all government officials, or pillars of the church, or trade unionists, or poets, or unemployed; this cataloguing is not only satisfactory to other people for practical purposes, it is sufficient to themselves for their "life of the spirit". Many are not quite real at any moment. When Wolstrip married, I am sure he said to himself: "Now I am consummating the union of two of the best families in Philadelphia" '.

Eliot was to encompass the range of his contrarious thoughts on dramatic poetry by casting them – true to drama – entirely in dialogue, as 'A Dialogue on Dramatic Poetry' (1928). In 'Eeldrop and Appleplex', the range of his thoughts on prejudicial classification asked a substantial allotment of dialogue, because

---

1 – 'This Spaniard was in fact José Maria de Elizondo, a priest Pound had met in Madrid in 1906 and again with Eliot in 1917'; 'looking at Elizondo (referred to only as the "fat Spaniard"), Eeldrop and Appleplex . . .' (James Longenbach, *Modernist Poetics of History*, 1987, pp. 154–5). But what matters to 'Eeldrop and Appleplex' is the opposite, that the Spaniard be a complete stranger.

of the acknowledged partiality endemic to the understanding of prejudice, but it would have sentimentalized the problems of prejudice to have furnished no narrative viewpoint external to Eeldrop's and Appleplex's – as if points of view could be contemplated except from what has to be itself a point of view. 'To realize that a point of view is a point of view is already to have transcended it.'[1] In 'Eeldrop and Appleplex' the nub is the puzzled yearning for a 'pure observation' such as is 'not alien to the principle of classification, but deeper'.

The continuity of such a prose-fable with the poems is evident, and what saves the prose from complacency is the admission that you should not think that just because you are a poet the case is altered: 'or trade unionists, or poets, or unemployed'. Unemployed is what anxious parents think a young poet is.[2] The sudden impinging of the remark of a total stranger – 'I was married once myself' – impels us into the world of Eliot's poems, where, as in life, we are always hearing that which we have not chosen to listen to, and where we usually have the unlovely choice either of having to judge on insufficient evidence, by prejudicially assimilating to a trusted classification, or of having to abdicate judgement altogether. I was at dinner at a restaurant in London and heard – hearing this only – a man at the next table say to the woman he was with: 'And in the three years we've been married, she hasn't once been down to the squash courts to see me play.' Was it wrong of me to feel a rush of rich suspicion, to be virtually and virtuously sure that this was a bad man and probably even a jerk? ('I was married once myself.') Yet would it be humanly possible, or right, to hear the tremulous indignation of 'And in the three years we've been married . . .' and *not* judge it in some way? Judgement is not

1 – *Knowledge and Experience in the Philosophy of F. H. Bradley*, p. 148. The thought of 'points of view' remained of the greatest importance to Eliot; he approved the selection of his prose made by John Hayward under the title *Points of View* (1941).

2 – 'I don't think that any parents have ever brought a child up with a view to his becoming a poet; some parents have brought up their children to be criminals; but for good and loving parents a poet is almost the last thing they could want their child to be, unless they thought it was the only way of saving him from becoming a criminal' (*To Criticize the Critic*, p. 82).

intervention; in any case, it would have been too late to persuade the woman that I was a better person than the person she was with, since her eyes were already molten with sympathy and more.

'Eeldrop and Appleplex' is about being able to be neither comfortable nor altogether uncomfortable with stereotypes. These days we are supposed to be nothing but uncomfortable with them, though many of the people who are loudest in denunciation of stereotypes are also loudest in demanding 'role-models'; this, although a role-model is nothing but a stereotype of which you approve. The crux is this: is a stereotype inherently an abuse, or is a stereotype something which can all too easily be abused?

'The moral will is deplorably given to stereotypes': this asseveration of Helen Vendler deplores not the wrong uses to which stereotypes are put but any use of them. She regrets Adrienne Rich's stereotyping in itself ('It is for the sake of Rich's own good intentions . . . that I wish she would consider more closely her aesthetic means'):

Stereotypes (the uncomprehending mother-in-law, the vicious cop) not only exist, but exist in sufficient numbers to have given rise to the stereotype; but they have no more place in art in their crude state than the grasping Jew or the drunken Irishman. Shylock, in Shakespeare's imagination, grows in interest and stature so greatly that he incriminates the anti-Semitism of Belmont.[1]

This braves the sentimentalists in acknowledging that social realities do to some degree give rise to social stereotypes, and it even risks conceding this not just of the vicious cop (fair game for readers of the *New York Review of Books*) but of the grasping Jew and the drunken Irishman. But the insistence that such stereotypes have no place in art in their crude state is not persuasive as it stands. Shakespeare's superb way of avoiding such crudity, by having Shylock grow in interest and stature, does not have to be the only responsible way of escaping or offsetting crudity. It is true by definition that art, being fine, cannot be simply crude, but it would not follow from this that

1 – *New York Review of Books*, 17 December 1981.

stereotypes should not have a place in art in their crude state, since there is no reason why the stereotyping should not itself then be 'placed' by the work of art, contemplated with 'a suspicious and interrogating eye' and understood. This would not be the same as making the state of the stereotype itself uncrude, but would be the provision of an uncrude setting, context, or ethos. This would be to engage something intrinsic not only to the stereotyped character but also to our own ways with stereotypes.

Sander L. Gilman has assembled a great deal of very interesting and shocking material in his *Difference and Pathology: Stereotypes of Sexuality, Race, and Madness*; but he havers about stereotyping, being at most willing to forgive it because otherwise we are going to be more anxious than we can bear: 'I believe that stereotyping is a universal means of coping with anxieties engendered by our inability to control the world.' He therefore deplores the 'Manichean perception of the world' and 'the pathological personality' while himself offering the most clear-cut Manichean them-and-us 'division of the world', enforcing it with a 'rigid line of difference' of exactly the kind he affects to deplore:

Stereotypes arise when self-integration is threatened. They are therefore part of our way of dealing with the instabilities of our perception of the world. This is not to say that they are good, only that they are necessary. We can and must make the distinction between pathological stereotyping and the stereotyping all of us need to do to preserve our illusion of control over the self and the world. Our Manichean perception of the world as 'good' and 'bad' is triggered by a recurrence of the type of insecurity that induced our initial division of the world into 'good' and 'bad'. For the pathological personality every confrontation sets up this echo. Stereotypes can and often do exist parallel to the ability to create sophisticated rational categories that transcend the crude line of difference present in the stereotype. We retain our ability to distinguish the 'individual' from the stereotyped class into which the object might automatically be placed. The pathological personality does not develop this ability and sees the entire world in terms of the rigid line of difference. The pathological personality's mental representation of the world supports the need for the line of difference, whereas for the non-pathological individual the stereotype is a momentary coping mechanism, one that can be used and then discarded once anxiety is overcome. The former is consistently aggressive toward the

real people and objects to which the stereotypical representations corres-
pond; the latter is able to repress the aggression and deal with people as
individuals.[1]

It is shocking though not surprising to find a book which so
stigmatizes stereotypes seeking its own salvation in such a Sheep
and Goats division – vacantly circular in its professionalized
self-righteousness – as that between the pathological personality and the non-pathological one. '*We* retain *our* ability to
distinguish the "individual" from the stereotyped class.' The
Pharisee stood and prayed thus with himself, God, I thank thee,
that I am not as other men are, extortioners, unjust, adulterers,
or even as this pathological personality.

The inadequacy of Gilman's argument is clear here: 'This is
not to say that they are good, only that they are necessary.' First,
Gilman does not realize a moral and spiritual world within
which such a distinction would make sense, such a world as that
of the Christian paradox, 'For it must needs be that offences
come, but woe to that man by whom the offence cometh', or of
Eliot's related conviction about the difficult concept of 'just
wars': 'It is almost impossible to say anything about the subject
without being misunderstood by one or both parties of *simpli-
fiers*. (Yet Æschylus, at least, understood that it may be a man's
duty to commit a crime, and to accomplish his expiation for
it.)'[2] Second, Gilman reserves the right to use the word *good*
for his own ends without quotation marks, only to put it within
the quotation marks of enlightened evacuation when it comes to
the next stage of his argument: 'into "good" and "bad"'. 'We
can and must make the distinction between pathological stereotyping and the stereotyping all of us need to do to preserve our
illusion of control over the self and the world': but you will not
learn from Gilman's book what the distinction is exactly, except
that the bad form of stereotyping is the one done by sick people.
As for 'our illusion of control over the self and the world':
control over the self and the world is not an illusion, and it is

1 – *Difference and Pathology* (1985), pp. 12, 18.
2 – Another of Eliot's penetrating bracketings, a central aside (*The Criterion*, xv,
1936, 664).

merely a professional sentimentality to say so, as we know every time we bite back a rude remark or are the beneficiaries of a safe landing in a 'plane. Such control is less than fully adequate, but it hardly seems so in comparison with Gilman's argument.

Thought about 'the crude line of difference' needs to be more refined than Gilman's, not least if it is to attend to art. If art too purposefully shuns what Vendler calls the 'crude state' of things, it does not so much refine itself as attenuate itself. Eliot accepted the need for 'a preparedness, a habit, on the part of the public, to respond in a predictable way, however crudely, to certain stimuli'. Eliot said that 'the Elizabethan drama was aimed at a public which wanted *entertainment* of a crude sort, but would *stand* a good deal of poetry'.[1] He acknowledged that the vigorous crudity of popular art (itself so animated by stereotypes) needs to be sufficiently present for the act of creative refinement to be substantial. Granted, the refinement might very valuably take the form of a character's transcending the stereotype, as Shylock does, but it could also take the form of the art's transcending the stereotype. It is such contextualizing which Eliot chooses, a network which – because it does not offer indubitabilities of judgement – has the effect of implicating the reader in just such 'prejudicing strategies' as are at work within the world of the poem and may (of course) be at work within 'the man who suffers and the mind which creates'.[2] It is this which makes Eliot's poems grow in interest and stature so that they incriminate both such prejudice as does not acknowledge that it would be justified only in an emergency *and* such credulity about prejudice (as to its easy distinguishability from indispensable prejudgement, for instance) as constitutes a prejudice about prejudice.

It will sometimes seem that Eeldrop's high thought is true: 'For any vital truth is incapable of being applied to another case: the essential is unique. Perhaps that is why it is so neglected.' But could anybody possibly live by or with such a truth? We live by neglecting as well as by applying, and must not neglect the principled case to be made for some forms of neglect.

1 – 'The Possibility of a Poetic Drama', *The Sacred Wood*, p. 70.
2 – 'Tradition and the Individual Talent', *Selected Essays*, p. 18.

Suspending judgement may be comfortable, but only if it is unaware that there is a sword of Damocles. Suspicion is uncomfortable, itchy, always craving assurance. 'The Love Song of J. Alfred Prufrock' incites its readers to the shrewd suspicion which is prejudice but the poem should also make them suspect their own wish – all too human and far too dangerous – to harden suspicion into certainty. In 'Gerontion' the process is pushed to another extremity. The induration of a suspicion into a fervent indubitability can be heard in Stephen Spender's account of 'Gerontion'.

> In the juvescence of the year
> Came Christ the tiger
>
> In depraved May, dogwood and chestnut, flowering judas,
> To be eaten, to be divided, to be drunk
> Among whispers; by Mr. Silvero
> With caressing hands, at Limoges
> Who walked all night in the next room;
> By Hakagawa, bowing among the Titians;
> By Madame de Tornquist, in the dark room
> Shifting the candles; Fräulein von Kulp
> Who turned in the hall, one hand on the door.

Spender is moved to a precipitate collusion with an animus within the lines:

Eliot excels in this poem in an effect at which he always shows great brilliance: condemning attitudes by attaching to them names and gestures which are in themselves prejudicial. By merely inventing a name like 'Fräulein von Kulp' he can evoke in us the punishing hatred we have felt in a lodging house, say in Vienna, for some unknown person in the next room who keeps us awake all night by expectorating in a peculiarly disgusting manner which we involuntarily seize on as being the expression of her central European personality. Eliot invents names for such targets of what seems an atavistic righteous indignation.[1]

It is true to Eliot's power that his poetry can trigger in otherwise sane men such paroxysms, that from the pad of the poem such rocketing feelings can be launched. Spender re-lives,

1 – *Eliot* (1975), p. 65.

and therefore in some way relieves, one of the worst nights of his life, and is eager to betray himself to us. But does Eliot have no intention deeper, more humane, and more self-interrogating, than such caricature? Spender, like Hugh Kenner on 'The Love Song of J. Alfred Prufrock', makes it all sound monstrously easy for a rhetorician of brilliance: 'By merely inventing a name like "Fräulein von Kulp" ', Eliot can incite all that, and we should feel nothing but an admiring equanimity at this. But Eliot does not choose to give only 'when our attention is distracted'. He is more attentive to 'atavistic righteous indignation' than those three words suggest; he is more attentive, likewise, not only to such an effect but to how it is effected. Which is why it is *not* self-evident that these people are being condemned or are targets exactly. We may suspect them of the sinister or the warped, but no more than we should suspect the poem's thinker of being sinister or warped. 'With caressing hands': you will find this menacing only if you do not want to be caressed by Mr Silvero, and you mistake the poem if you read it as if he were simply a stranger to you (with no right even to seem to have caressing hands) when Eliot has so created the poem as to ensure that Mr Silvero, like the rest of them, exists in a world so wholly strange to you as to make the distinction between strangers and others meaningless to you.

Or there is the line: 'By Hakagawa, bowing among the Titians'. It is a quintessential Eliot line, fostered alike by beauty and by fear, and not all of its fear is a fear of how unknown, how mysterious, the figure of Hakagawa is there; some of the fear is of how unknown, how mysterious, are our own responses to the thought of him. If we are moved to ask, with some hostility, how accessible the art of Titian truly is to someone by the name of Hakagawa, then we should presumably be moved by the same token to ask how accessible to someone by the name of Ruskin is the art of Hokusai. If Hakagawa is not an English name, nor is Titian, anglicized though it be. Eliot believed that there was such a thing as 'the mind of Europe', but he also believed that it was a long time since there had been many minds able to apprehend the mind of Europe. And is Hakagawa bowing in oriental homage or is he bowing like perfectly occidental gallery-goers, the better to see a detail of the paintings? John Crowe Ransom's evocation of the scene is subtly and distinctly different, twice over, from Eliot's line when Ransom writes of 'Hakagawa bowing before his Titians'.[1]

One touch of genius in the line is 'among the Titians', with its disconcerting reminder that paintings may be physical objects available for unique ownership in a way which is much less true of books (despite the investment cult of manuscripts, limited editions or association copies); this is why you can speak in this sense of Titians though you cannot speak of Shakespeares or Eliots. Owning a Henry James is much less valuable than owning your gratitude to him. Say, for his touch of genius in originating the phrase 'among the Titians':

In spite of those few dips and dashes into the many-coloured stream of history for which of late Kate Croy had helped her [Milly Theale] to find time, there were possible great chances she had neglected, possible great moments she should, save for to-day, have all but missed. She might still, she had felt, overtake one or two of them among the Titians and the Turners; she had been honestly nursing the hours, and, once she was in the benignant halls, her faith knew itself justified.

(*The Wings of the Dove*, Book Fifth, Chapter VII)

Milly Theale at the National Gallery is alien to Hakagawa at whatever gallery, national or private, he may occupy. James's evocation is international comedy dipped and dashed with pastoral; it takes place among the Turners as well as among the Titians; it is 'benignant'; and the question of Milly's 'faith' is secular, a cultural confidence. Eliot pounced upon 'among the Titians'; placed 'faith' within the largest vistas; and relocated his unreal citizens so that they were no longer within 'the benignant halls' of the National Gallery but within the malignant halls of the international gallery of Gerontion's dry brain. Milly's social decency – 'she had been honestly nursing the hour' – becomes Gerontion's grim threat: 'I would meet you upon this honestly.' And 'the many-coloured stream of history', which is James's courteous nod in the direction of the poetic National Gallery of Shelley and Keats, becomes darkened to the maze of modern history or rather of history modernly seen:

1 – *T. S. Eliot: The Man and His Work*, ed. Tate, p. 155.

> Think now
> History has many cunning passages, contrived corridors
> And issues, deceives with whispering ambitions,
> Guides us by vanities.

Such are some of the energies which seethe within the line

> By Hakagawa, bowing among the Titians;

and the one thing we must not do with the line is prejudicially cramp it to being in essence a scoffing at Orientals who suppose that they can appreciate the attractions of Europe.

The idea of the National Gallery had been with her from the moment of her hearing from Sir Luke Strett about his hour of coming. It had been in her mind as a place so meagerly visited, as one of the places that had seemed at home one of the attractions of Europe and one of its highest aids to culture, but that – the old story – the typical frivolous always ended by sacrificing to vulgar pleasures.

'Gerontion' is a poem about sacrifices, pre-eminently the sacrifice made by Christ and the ones offered to him; it is not a poem which solicits 'the typical frivolous'. The poem must not be sacrificed to the vulgar pleasures either of a prejudicial devouring of Hakagawa or of a prejudicial devouring of Eliot.

> The tiger springs in the new year. Us he devours. Think
>   at last
> We have not reached conclusion, when I
> Stiffen in a rented house. Think at last
> I have not made this show purposelessly
> And it is not by any concitation
> Of the backward devils.
> I would meet you upon this honestly.

IV

TONE

Matters of life and death

Matters of prejudice, preconception and perception are intimate
with questions of tone. A child is beguiled with the question,
innocent on the page: 'Would you rather a gorilla attacked you
or a tiger?' Furrowing of the brow, and then, tentatively, 'The
gorilla, maybe? as kind of more human?' Whereupon: 'Oh, I'd
rather the gorilla attacked the tiger.'

For, as the parent may have to spell out to the child, the
question had not been 'Would you rather a *gorilla* attacked you
or a *tiger*?', but 'Would you rather a gorilla attacked *you* or a
tiger?'[1] The child is tricked by its intelligible preconception;
the presumption was that you had to choose between grim
alternatives, not that you were being asked whether you would
choose to be attacked or not. Yet the warrant is that the
question's weirder slant is improbable only, not impossible.
Imagine a modern saint, Malcolm Muggeridge say, on television
as usual, reading out this question sent up by the audience, and
at once grasping the opportunity for proud humility: 'Oh, I'd
much rather a gorilla attacked *me* than a *tiger*; "Tiger, tiger,
burning bright/In the forests of the night"; "Everything that
lives is holy" – everything except, of course, "man, proud man,
Dressed in a little brief authority"; "Only man is vile" ' – and so
on. One can fairly imagine it; so the question's unexpected
twist, the antithesis not of *gorilla* and *tiger*, but of *you* and *tiger*,
is fair enough. The twist, plainly, depends upon the straight face

1 – A good old joke; Hugh Rowley, *Puniana* (1867), p. 55: 'Which would you
rather, that a lion ate you or a tiger? Why, you would rather that the lion ate the
tiger, of course!'

of the printed page, the studied neutrality with which print can, when it chooses, mislead you as to the choices.

Again within such a world of fictitious violence, a fiercer twist is given to the same kind of misconstruing, or misconstruction, in the film *The Conversation*. Gene Hackman plays a private investigator. At the start of the film, he is bugging the conversation of two young lovers. He hears one of them say 'He'd kill us if he got the chance'; that is, 'He'd *kill* us if he got the chance.' Our sympathies (like the investigator's own, which are hard-bitten but soft-centred) are with the poor imperilled lovers, certainly not with the man spying on them or with the man (the husband) who has hired such a spy. For the lovers are young, and are nice to look at, and are walking in the open air, in a happy public square, while the investigator, the better to violate their privacy, lurks within a van. But as the events fall, the investigator comes to realize that what he heard was not 'He'd *kill* us if he got the chance' (the pitiful words of people in danger of being murdered), but 'He'd kill *us* if he got the chance' – the pitiless words of people in danger of being murderers. The realization comes too late to save the husband's life.

The film plays less fair than does the children's joke. For the presumption – as to where to direct our pity and fear – with which the film legitimately works upon us (a presumption which amounts to prejudice, well-intentioned and then having hellish consequences) is much less legitimate in its working upon the investigator. Professionally it is inconceivable that he would have so misheard the fatal words, however strong the pressure upon him of dismay at the squalor of his work. For the fatal words were altogether audible, not resting with artful blankness on a page. Could a private eye afford to have such a tin ear? If, in the interests of truth and criticism, you re-visit the film, you hear the discrepancy between the tape as it was first enunciated: 'He'd KILL us if he got the chance'; and the tape as it is finally recognized: 'HE'D kill US if he got the chance.' Not even the Hackman-man, guilt-ridden and out of sorts on a bad day, would have misconstrued *that*. The film came out of the Watergate time, and itself partakes of the current sleaziness, so that not even Hackman's remarkable performance as a Jacobean malcontent can altogether authenticate it. Yet the *donnée* of the film is well worth receiving: incarnating that how we hear even the simplest words is instinct with our preconceptions and prejudices. For *The Conversation* has some of the strengths of Jacobean tragedy, of such art – in Eliot's terms – as understands the necessity for 'a preparedness, a habit, on the part of the public, to respond in a predictable way, however crudely, to certain stimuli'.[1] And the central imaginative stroke in the film is its relating this sense of such a preparedness on the part of its public (the audience) to just such an unexpected preparedness on the part of a crucial agent within the film itself, the investigator who is the cunning yet unwitting audience for the words, 'He'd kill us if he got the chance.'

These are matters of life and death, in the film and even in the joke, but only of imaginary lives and deaths. So carry further the relation of preconception or prejudice to tone and intonation, through more sombrely to the real-life murder, and the subsequent execution, which were to do much to abolish capital punishment in Britain. In 1952 Christopher Craig and Derek Bentley broke into a warehouse. Bentley was apprehended by the police. Craig shot and killed a policeman. Bentley was said to have uttered the words, 'Let him have it, Chris.'

It was denied by Bentley, and by Craig, that Bentley said those words. It is not to be denied that he was executed because of them. Bentley, who did not have the gun (or indeed a gun), and who did not shoot anyone, and who had been for fifteen minutes in the hands of the police when the murder was committed, and for whom the jury had recommended mercy, was executed. Craig was not executed, for at sixteen he was under age. Bentley was nineteen. At which point even fiercely retributive citizens felt some unease.

Lord Goodman, deploring the fiercely retributive Lord Goddard, put the issues very clearly, though one might wish to add a rider:

Fifteen minutes after the arrest of Bentley, when he had not stirred or made any effort to escape, he is alleged to have shouted at his companion – who

1 – *The Athenaeum*, 14 May 1920.

was putting up a determined defence – words which have now become historic in our forensic annals: 'Let him have it, Chris.'

The words, if spoken, were represented and rightly so as a direction and encouragement to Craig to shoot the officer. But a crucial question was whether they were uttered. The probabilities seem very strongly against it and were never put to the jury by Lord Goddard. The probability that a boy so timid, of such poor mental quality that he lacked the resolution to run away when left by himself or to make any attempt to escape, should suddenly fifteen minutes later have burst into this Hollywood idiom seems remote in the extreme but, in any event, there was no reason to believe that the words had the slightest effect on Craig. He was busily shooting away regardless of anything that might have been said to him, and needed no encouragement.[1]

Lord Goodman's last point attends essentially not to Bentley's being guilty but to exactly what Bentley would have been guilty *of* in uttering such a provocation. Lord Goodman's previous point, about the likelihood of Bentley's having said it at all ('The probabilities seem very strongly against it', and in the next sentence 'The probability . . . seems remote in the extreme'), is seriously underdescribed; it is not clear upon what this psychologicalizing confidence rests, as to a man's (or a boy's, for either word takes a side as to whether he should have been executed) not being at all likely to utter such a cry if he had made no effort to escape. And 'Let him have it' was not *only* a Hollywood idiom, not least because the influence of Hollywood was worldwide. On the other hand, Lord Goodman neglects one reasonable plea for Bentley when he, Goodman, insists that 'The words, if spoken, were represented and rightly so as a direction and encouragement to Craig to shoot the officer'. For though the words must have been an incitement if they were indeed uttered as the 'Hollywood idiom' – 'Let him have it', they wouldn't have to be uttered so; they *could*, after all, have been said as simple English, meaning no more than 'Let him have it', or 'Let the policeman have the gun.' True, it may be thought improbable that Bentley would have used a phrase which is slightly formal (as against, say, 'Give him the gun, Chris'); but then some improbability, as Lord Goodman says, attaches to

1 – *Times Literary Supplement*, 8 April 1977.

the Hollywood idiom too. We all, necessarily, resolve such improbabilities or likelihoods by reference to preconceptions which can become prejudices, and Bentley's words (if he uttered them) have to be interpreted one way or other, though his denial of having said them entailed that he could not also claim to have said them unaggressively; it might nevertheless be urged that, in the absence of any tape-recording which would have settled the question of the exact tone in which someone uttered words as momentous as this particular 'Let him have it, Chris', it would be better not to hang a boy. Or a man.

Last of these instances which constitute a hinge between prejudice and tone is a key testimony in the case of Mrs Harris. Jean Harris was found guilty in 1981 of murdering her lover Dr Tarnower. Her plea was that she had gone to him to be put out of her love-misery, and that the gun – which she had intended would be turned upon her – had gone off accidentally and had (she thought at first) inflicted no more than a flesh wound upon him. Diana Trilling, in her book *Mrs. Harris*, is as sceptical of this as the jury had proved to be:

How could Mrs. Harris maintain that when she'd left the bedroom she'd thought that the doctor had suffered nothing worse than a hand injury, when both she and Aurnou [her defence lawyer] had conceded that immediately on her return to the bedroom she'd said, 'Oh, Hi, why didn't you kill *me*?' meaning that she knew she had killed *him*?

But of this good question a question can itself then be asked: How could Mrs Trilling maintain that the crucial testimony here was 'Oh, Hi, why didn't you kill *me*?' ('meaning that she knew she had killed *him*') when 250 pages earlier in her book the testimony had been recorded as this: 'Oh Hi, why didn't you kill me?'?

Mrs. Harris sat on the doctor's bed and at one moment 'bended down and she touch the tip of her hand to his face and she said, "Oh Hi, why didn't you kill me?"' [1]

The emphasized (italicized) *me* has indeed to mean that she knew she had killed *him*; but the unemphasized unitalicized one

1 – *Mrs. Harris* (1981), pp. 328, 86.

which was originally recorded is in fact compatible with Mrs Harris's own story, one possible intonation then being 'Oh, Hi, *why* didn't you *kill* me?', meaning that he should have done as she had wished, and should have inflicted her suicide upon her. The point is that on p. 86, when Mrs Trilling first records the policeman's testimony, she has in a sense not yet reached her verdict, but by p. 328 she has, and 'me' is now to be heard as something far more damaging: '*me*'. Mrs Trilling concurs with the jury's verdict, Guilty; so do I, but the incrimination of Mrs Harris should not turn upon even the most minute change in the testimony, a change for which no warrant is produced.

The world of Mrs Harris may seem remote from that of T. S. Eliot and his poetry. Yet Eliot, as *Sweeney Agonistes* and *The Family Reunion* attest, was aware of such murderous amatory hatreds. *The Waste Land* is among other things a despatch from the front-line of a Great War, the one between the sexes. What swung the case against Mrs Harris, and indeed did for her, was the letter of hers which was produced as evidence that her feelings were not suicidal towards herself but murderous towards Tarnower. She writhes in remonstration at Tarnower's latest usurping mistress:

Give her all the money she wants, Hi – but give me time with you and the privilege of sharing with you April 19. There were a lot of ways to have money – I very consciously picked working hard, supporting myself, and being with you. Please, darling, don't tell me now it was all for nothing. She has you every single moment in March. For Christ sake give me April. T. S. Eliot said it's the cruelest month – don't let it be, Hi.[1]

This is appalling, but because it is vulgar, not because of any other impercipience. There is something very true to Eliot's poem in this intimacy of resentment, and there is something very Eliot-like in the alluding itself, wrested and bitterly alive. For Mrs Harris's writhing is a memory of the participial writhing and rounding in Eliot's turn of his lines; her twisting sequence – *sharing, working, supporting, being* (compounded then by the pressure from *darling* and *nothing*) – is itself mixing memory and desire, breeding resentment out of the dead love.

1 – *Mrs. Harris*, p. 261.

April is the cruellest month, breeding
Lilacs out of the dead land, mixing
Memory and desire, stirring
Dull roots with spring rain.
Winter kept us warm, covering
Earth in forgetful snow, feeding
A little life with dried tubers.

But then the tawdry tragedy of Mrs Harris and Dr Tarnower is of the sort foresuffered in 'Eeldrop and Appleplex'.[1] Eeldrop laments the fact that 'A man is only important as he is classed. Hence there is no tragedy, or no appreciation of tragedy, which is the same thing.' Appleplex is to muster a 'measured adherence' to this. The transition from the one speaker to the other is created by murder:

In Gopsum Street a man murders his mistress. The important fact is that for the man the act is eternal, and that for the brief space he has to live, he is already dead. He is already in a different world from ours. He has crossed the frontier. The important fact that something is done which can not be undone – a possibility which none of us realize until we face it ourselves. For the man's neighbors the important fact is what the man killed her with? And at precisely what time? And who found the body? For the 'enlightened public' the case is merely evidence for the Drink question, or Unemployment, or some other category of things to be reformed. But the mediaeval world, insisting on the eternity of punishment, expressed something nearer the truth.

Eeldrop's final gravity there is a gravitation in Eliot, though it was to be ten years before he joined the Church.

Frustration at a recalcitrant world

There is a good definition of tone in the *Oxford English Dictionary*, good not because it catches the word once and for all but because unusually for a dictionary it welcomes 'negative capability' and allows the word responsibly to elude it in the end.

1 – *Little Review*, May 1917.

A particular quality, pitch, modulation, or inflexion of the voice expressing or indicating affirmation, interrogation, hesitation, decision, or some feeling or emotion; vocal expression.

This leaves happily unresolved, unresolvable even, the question – 'expressing or indicating' – of how an inflexion of the voice could express something without indicating it or indicate it without expressing it. For there is, after all, something respectably elusive about the very relation of tone to expressing and to indicating. As for the final shot at definition, 'vocal expression', this is attractive in the modesty with which it reconciles itself to never getting the matter exactly right, for clearly 'vocal expression' can be held to define *tone* only if one already knows just what expression is here on the face of that difficult and various word 'expression'.

Perhaps then a figure of speech may better catch what is needed than a definition. Tone has been called the expression on the face of the words; you may know exactly whose face your eyes are meeting but may still need reassurance as to just what expression is on that face. Or there might be a larger figure of speech, invoking not only face-language but body-language, and then tone becomes not only the expression on the face of the words but the posture intimated by the body of the words. Tone, more abstractly though not more thinly, may likewise be understood as how something is being offered and so how it is to be taken. A true and persuasive writer, like any other true and persuasive user of the language, will know how to control the transmission and reception of tone. He or she will also know how and when (and why) not exactly to control tone, or rather exactly not to, but this – though a wonderful achievement – matters because it is a negative capability that is related first of all to an assured positive capability. First, then, some indication of one way in which a writer may positively control tone.

In his novel *The Tragic Muse*, Henry James is to make manifest that Miriam Rooth has now started to bring to realization her remarkable powers as an actress: Peter Sherringham, after an absence from her, is more than surprised when he hears her. James's famous cry to the novelist, 'Dramatise, dramatise', is here to be brought to bear upon rendering a character who is herself in the most literal sense dramatizing, being confidently an actress; the challenge to the novelist is therefore in a way a double one. James rises to it, assisted by a pun, at once direct and discreet, on the word 'act'.

Miriam was in the act of rolling out some speech from the English poetic drama –
   'For I am sick and capable of fears,
    Oppressed with wrongs and therefore full of fears'.
He recognised one of the great tirades of Shakespeare's Constance and saw she had just begun the magnificent scene at the beginning of the third act of "King John", in which the passionate injured mother and widow sweeps in wild organ-tones the entire scale of her irony and wrath . . . Peter listened intently, arrested by the spirit with which she attacked her formidable verses. He had needed to hear her set afloat but a dozen of them to measure the long stride she had taken in his absence; they assured him she had leaped into possession of her means.

(Book First, Chapter XIX)

It is a magnificent evocation of wonder at someone's powers, and one question that it happily raises is that of James's own leaping into possession of *his* means. At the heart of James's art here is his inerrancy in choosing that particular couplet of Shakespeare's art. *King John* is not the play that would first come to mind if one were seeking the especial opportunity for an actress to show that she had leapt into possession of her means. What moved James then to swoop upon this very couplet?

> For I am sicke, and capeable of feares,
> Opprest with wrongs, and therefore full of feares.

(III, i)[1]

Dramatize, dramatize: James felt the inherently dramatic force of these two lines, felt them as supremely right for and ripe for an answering force in an actress. And the inherently dramatic is here a matter of the way in which the lines have their vocal stage directions so unmistakably built in, have their tone so

---

1 – Quotations from Shakespeare are from the first Folio.

indubitably awaiting vocal realization. For Shakespeare had seen, and James now felt, the endemic effect within English verse of ending two successive lines with the same word; more, pair of words, not just *fears* echoed as *fears*, but *of fears* echoed.

> For I am sicke, and capeable of feares,
> Opprest with wrongs, and therefore full of feares.

What this terrible turn intimates is the meeting of an irresistible force and an immovable object: Constance's cry for justice meeting a power obdurate in its corruption. Nothing will bring back her loved dead; nothing will bring vengeance upon the wrongdoers; nothing will stop her continuing to cry against this recalcitrance in the nature of things. The effect – an effect where the tonal strength is indistinguishable from an excruciating human apprehension – is at once simple and double. Constance cannot and should not swallow her plight, and so she cannot digest it; but nor can she spit it out. The words stick in the throat of her lines.

> For I am sicke, and capeable of feares,
> Opprest with wrongs, and therefore full of feares.

One has only to transpose the monosyllabic plural nouns (which would scarcely affect the rhythm even) to see how the clenched bite of the lines is incorporate within the grim rhyming turn. Listen instead to this:

> For I am sicke, and capeable of feares,
> Opprest with feares, and therefore full of wrongs.

And at once the hideous log-jam of feeling has been eased, for Constance has been able to move on, to put the fears to some small degree behind her. Whereas as Shakespeare wrote it, and as James and his heroine realized it, there is no moving on, no remission from something which is at once a lock-jaw and the wild organ-tones of her irony and wrath; Constance fled and pursued transverse a resonant fugue. Indeed, as Shakespeare rendered it (James pared it for his effect), Constance's lines are more continuingly paralysed and mobile, beating for ever upon the same doors in vain:

> Thou shalt be punish'd for thus frighting me,
> For I am sicke, and capeable of feares,
> Opprest with wrongs, and therefore full of feares,
> A widdow, husbandles, subject to feares,
> A woman naturally borne to feares.
>
> (*King John*, III, i)

James had no need to give salience to all these undevouring gnawings, though Miriam Rooth gave voice to them all in the voice of Shakespeare's Constance; James plucked out the root of the matter, the contrariety made real in the tone of an anguished voice, the contrariety between the undying will to move the heavens and the stony-hearted stubbornness of things. The effect, essentially dramatic in making so unblinkingly clear how the lines simply have to be heard, is certainly more than verbal but it is nothing unless it is first of all verbal, and it speaks as if it is unanswerably in the grain of the language.

> For I am sicke, and capeable of feares,
> Opprest with wrongs, and therefore full of feares.

The voice has to be at once gingerly and brave, picking its way across the red-hot stones.

We may call this a matter of technique, but only if we go on to concur with Eliot, that we cannot say at what point 'technique' begins or where it ends.[1] This particular turn, which we slight if we think of it as a 'device', is alive in some of Eliot's greatest lines, alive as they are to the grain of the language.

> Unreal City,
> Under the brown fog of a winter dawn,
> A crowd flowed over London Bridge, so many,

1 – 'Preface to the 1928 edition', *The Sacred Wood*, p. ix.

136

> I had not thought death had undone so many.
> > (*The Waste Land*)

The life of these lines is active in the turn of the grim rhyme, at once more richly a rhyme than any other could be, since it is the repetition of the very word itself, and yet more poverty-stricken than a rhyme could be, since it is not truly a *rhyme* at all, is not a creative cooperation of two things but instead has what is here the singleness of a consternation without parallel.

This penetrating singularity is, though, compounded; it is an obdurate paralysis, for as with the turn within *King John* the repetition is so stationed at the ends of the successive lines ('so many', 'so many') as to convey both the utmost will to know, judge or understand (an imagination at full stretch, seeking fully to comprehend), and at the same time an immovable admission that the scale of all this is beyond comprehension. *So many. So many.* The lines do more than merely convey, they create this siege of contraries. I had not, Heaven knows, been naive or unimaginative about how many are dead, whether literally or in the death that is modern industrial civilization, but *so many* . . . The thought staggers belief, while embodying too a stubborn insistence that belief is only staggered, not felled.

Again, as with 'of fears', there is the double repetition, not only of *many* but of *so many*. The tension, incarnate in the unmistakable tone (tone itself etymologically deriving from the Greek for tension and stretching), is felt in this inability either to incorporate or to disown the vistas of 'so many'. We have only to replace the infinite compounded suggestiveness of 'so many', urged twice in awe, with our large number –

> A crowd flowed over London Bridge, so many,
> I had not thought death had undone such millions –

to feel the tension dissolve into complaisance. The voice would be hard put to act out 'such millions', would have to melo-dramatize it, in order to carry any rhetorical conviction, whereas 'so many' has the quiet unanswerability of true drama, and the voice does not have to reach for any acting out, it has only to react.

What is always said is that these two lines are from Dante. This is true, and Eliot's note both speaks his and bespeaks our consciousness of this:

63. Cf. Inferno III, 55–57:

> si lunga tratta
> di gente, ch'io non averei creduto
> che morte tanta n'avesse disfatta.

But a great allusion is a metaphor, created not only out of pertinent likeness but out of pertinent unlikeness, and there are two igniting unlikenesses in the way in which the poet of London Bridge uses the poet of Florence. First, Eliot drops the epithet which Dante had attached to his crowd, his '*lunga* tratta' (an epithet variously translated as 'long', 'vast', 'endless'), and instead Eliot reconstitutes the epithet as the phrase 'so many' – a phrase for which there is warrant in Dante (though not till two lines later) but not an exact precedent. The effect of the first line of Eliot's couplet, then, is radically different from Dante; in Dante, the lines flow syntactically forward (flow over the line-ending too): 'si lunga tratta / di gente' (such a long stream of people), whereas in Eliot the line circles back upon itself, anticipating the way in which the second line of the couplet will circle back too. 'A crowd flowed over London Bridge, so many': the mind turns back, turns round, as with the might of waters. Moreover 'so many' operates very differently from what would have been not the reconstitution of 'si lunga tratta' but only the new placing of its epithet. 'A crowd flowed over London Bridge, so endless': that would have circled, but differently, less weightily and less amazedly, for it would simply have supplied a delayed adjective for 'crowd'. But 'so many' is no such thing. For 'so many' asks us to imagine a plural to which 'many' can attach itself, and there has been no plural, only the word which is massively singular and yet which is itself a plurality: 'A crowd'. We have to supply a spectral plural for 'many' to depend from or upon: people, shades, souls. From without, a crowd is single, but from within, plural; wait one more moment and we shall be so within it as to hear the very sighs. Dante has no counterpart to what Eliot is effecting here.

But then nor does Dante have any counterpart to the effect of *so many . . . so many* at the ends of the successive lines. For such an effect is not possible within terza rima, within a rhyming sequence that rolls and flows *aba bcb cdc*. More exactly, it is only in the utmost extremity that *terza rima* is ever so moved to deny its essential being; an extremity of wonder, a divine stasis. There is no such moment here in Dante's lines, enlisted as they are in an army of all-but-unalterable law. So that when Eliot creates his lines:

> A crowd flowed over London bridge, so many,
> I had not thought death had undone so many.

– he does so by courtesy of Dante, yes, but with a manifest distance between his own creation and Dante's, a distance which must qualify any simple identification of Eliot's dead with Dante's dead, a distance embodied in a turn of the phrasing which is unthinkable in Dante's staple verse-form. But then the genius of the uninflected language in relation to rhyming is too different from that of Italian for *terza rima* ever to have been able to thrive in the vicinity of London Bridge. It was to be Eliot's simplicity of genius in 'Little Gidding' to fashion some counterpart to *terza rima*, yet crucially different in its pacing, out of the pure alternation of lines with feminine and lines with masculine endings.

Eliot's initial imaginative stroke was to displace 'lunga' and then to refashion it as something which anticipated the 'tanta' of Dante ten words later. There is no equivalent to this first 'so many' in Dante. Dante does indeed give us a *later* 'many' which Eliot's succeeding line so faithfully follows: 'I had not thought death had undone so many' ('ch'io non averei creduto / che morte tanta n'avesse disfatta'), but there is all the difference in the world (and in the next world) between having *so many* turn twice and having it, or rather 'tanta', turn once only. And no less a difference in having 'tanta' come once within the line as against having 'so many' enforce its tonal destiny, there in the grain of the language, at the end of two successive lines.

There is of course a grain to the particular lines too, and 'so many', 'so many', has to be heard within the tissue of all that

Eliot creates here.[1] There is, for instance, the fearful negativity given to the simple word *Under*, at the beginning of its line, by the pressure of the negative prefix Un- at the beginning of the previous line, 'Unreal City', as well as of the negative prefix un- in the ensuing 'undone'; it is as if *Under* were at last perceived, with fixated clarity, to be a word of deep negation:

> Unreal City,
> Under the brown fog of a winter dawn,
> A crowd flowed over London Bridge, so many,
> I had not thought death had undone so many.

And there, transversely threading the lines, is the sequence *Under . . . London . . . undone*. What makes 'undone' so perfect is not only its simple fidelity to Dante's simplicity ('disfatta'), or its congruence of steely directness and understated dignity: 'I had not thought death had undone so many', but its inescapable precipitation: *Under . . . London . . . undone*. If Under and London were to have a child, its name would be Undone.

It is a rhyme which Byron had used with weighty levity: disaster in the shipwreck would have been speedy

> But for the pumps. I'm glad to make them known
> To all the brother tars who may have need hence,
> For fifty tons of water were upthrown
> By them per hour, and they had all been undone
> But for the maker, Mr Mann, of London.
> (*Don Juan*, Canto II, xxix)

It is, too, a rhyme which Eliot was to use with hollow gravity in *The Rock* (1934):

---

1 – Such as Calvin Bedient remarks: 'The figure "A crowd flowed over London Bridge" mimics the significantly unrecognized natural flow of the river below – as if taking the side of bridges, of human society and furthering artifice, in the ancient enmity between bridges and rivers. But this flow, in actuality a death-flow, the spineless flow of the undone, lacks all joy of freeing motion, as signalled by the stiff sound of "A crowd flowed", a stiffness only lightly relieved by the flowing over of long *o* in "flowed over"' (*He Do the Police in Different Voices*, 1986, p. 65).

Ill done and undone,
London so fair
We will build London
Bright in dark air,
With new bricks and mortar
Beside the Thames bord
Queen of Island and Water,
A House of Our Lord.

This is feeble stuff, with 'Thames bord' sounding not like medieval loveliness but like the Thames Water Board, and with the twice-tolled rhyme of *London* with *undone* halving the efficacy. Eliot, resilient in his redemptive genius, would later do much better by thi‹ Ill done and undone', when he re-created it in 'Little Gidding' as 'things ill done and done to others' harm'. But Eliot never made more of the rhyme of *London* and *undone* than when in *The Waste Land* he apparently made very little of it, ensconcing it unobtrusively within lines which are pinioned by the tonal half-Nelson of 'so many', 'so many'.

A poet may be great in his triumphs over the grain of the language, but the condition of such triumphs is his acknowledging such a grain, and so there is need here for a small anthology such as will give body to the claim that this particular turn is not only in *King John* and in *The Waste Land* but is in the grain of the language, a turn offered as an instance of what it is for tone to be unmistakably enforced, to have its stage directions built in.

Shakespeare's art both constitutes and is constituted of such a grain. There is in *Henry VI Part III* a great speech with which most of us are familiar from the film of *Richard III*, Laurence Olivier having felt free to liberate it. Richard's irresistible force fears that it may be up against an immovable object. The speech revolves the crown; the word itself figures at the end of the line, which is where it is happy to be: the word 'crown' should always be either at the beginning or the end of its line, since only there can it enact itself; unlike, say, the word 'cummerbund', which is well advised to seek the middle of any line of verse in which it finds itself. Shakespeare releases the word 'crown', then, at the end of a line; having tipped off our attentive ears, he goes away from the word for two lines and then returns to it as the end of two successive lines. For here is Richard's overpowering will to command, to check and to o'erbear, confronting something which may overpower even such will.

> Then since this Earth affoords no Joy to me,
> But to command, to check, to o're-beare such,
> As are of better Person than my selfe:
> Ile make my Heaven, to dreame upon the Crowne,
> And whiles I live, t' account this World but Hell,
> Untill my mis-shape'd Trunke, that beares this Head,
> Be round impaled with a glorious Crowne.
> And yet I know not how to get the Crowne,
>
> (*Henry VI Part III*, iii, ii)

The speech soars to its over-reaching climax: 'Be round impaled with a glorious Crowne'. *Crowne* crowns the line, the sentence, the verse paragraph even. And yet it has to be succeeded by the grimly concessive 'And yet': 'And yet I know not how to get the Crowne'. The direct rapacity of 'get', stooping like a bird of prey from the height of the 'glorious' way of speaking, is violently piercing. Yet the effect of the line is not only of this fierce change of plane but of being still imprisoned within the same plane. For it is the level repetition of the word 'Crowne', out at the end of the promontory of the line, which so enforces this trammelled troubled tone, compounded of undying ambition and unyielding resistance. It is a real question in the play whether Richard does ever get the crown in the true sense of what it is to wear the crown; or to put the point differently, it is a real question whether a crown is something that one *can* 'get'.

The tone, the tension again, is realized in the obduracy of the terminal repetition:

> Be round impaled with a glorious Crowne.
> And yet I know not how to get the Crowne,

Richard, who finds his only joy in commanding, checking and o'erbearing others, is here compelled to command, check and o'erbear himself, or at least the part of him that runs before himself to market.

Again we can see the hiding-places of the lines' power if we respectfully tamper with their very words. This time, though, we need not fashion our own smaller phrasing ('I had not thought death had undone such millions'), since a poet of real gifts refashioned the lines in 1700. Colley Cibber, after all, is responsible for some of the best lines that Shakespeare never wrote in *Richard III*. 'Off with his head. So much for Buckingham.' Or there is the piercing moment after Richard's nightmare-night before the last battle: 'Richard's himself again.' Olivier's Richard said this into the ear of his beautiful white horse, Richard not being a man to make such an admission – of having *not* been himself – to another man; it was a touch of the truest highest camp, Olivier giving the words all of his tongued cluck. In Cibber's adaptation of *Richard III*, then, we meet the imaginative depredations of a real writer. What Cibber makes of the speech from *Henry VI Part III* is lesser art but is art:

> Then since this Earth affords no joy to me,
> But to Command, to Check, and to Orebear such,
> As are of Happier Person than my self,
> Why then to me this restless World's but Hell,
> Till this mishapen trunk's aspiring head
> Be circled in a glorious Diadem.
> But then 'tis fixt on such a heighth, O! I
> Must stretch the utmost reaching of my Soul.[1]

Cibber is quite wrong to think that a diadem is more glorious than a crown; he is gulled into thinking that a diadem is the higher because it sounds higher of diction, Cibber having set himself to maintain 'a heighth' of diction as Shakespeare so acutely did not ('And yet I know not how to get the Crowne'). But Cibber misjudges more than the diction; in speaking not once of the crown, where Shakespeare had spoken thrice, he slackens the very stretching, the tension and the tone, which the lines must embody. Cibber does effect something real, there in

1 – Cibber's *Richard III* is conveniently excerpted in *Shakespeare: The Critical Heritage*, volume 2, 1693–1733, edited by Brian Vickers (1974), pp. 101–28.

the stretched-out sequence of monosyllables which arrives so aptly at the dissyllables of 'utmost reaching':

> But then 'tis fixt on such a heighth, O! I
> Must stretch the utmost reaching of my Soul.

But how much less strong this is than the pincer-jaws which Shakespeare fashions, or rather sees Richard fashioning for himself:

> Be round impaled with a glorious Crowne.
> And yet I know not how to get the Crowne,

Shakespeare knows how to get such a crowning triumph of his art.

There is, as one might have hoped, a moment in *Macbeth* which outdoes this one in *Henry VI*, outdoes it not in completeness of achievement but in being a greater kind of achievement, even as *Macbeth* itself is of a greater kind than the superb *Richard III*. The exchange between Macbeth and Lady Macbeth after the murder of Duncan shudders at the thought of the murder and of the grooms, monstrously framed. The heart of the lines is the word *Amen*. It moves from within the line to the end of a line; Amen is a word which asks to be at the end of wherever it finds itself; and then, having again alerted our attentive ears, Shakespeare goes away from it for one line, only to return to it with redoubled force at the end of two successive lines.

MACBETH: One cry'd God blesse us, and Amen the other,
                  As they had seene me with these Hangmans hands:
                  Listning their feare, I could not say Amen,
                  When they did say God blesse us.
LADY MACBETH: Consider it not so deeply.
MACBETH: But wherefore could not I pronounce Amen?
                  I had most need of Blessing, and Amen
                  Stuck in my throat.

                                            (II, ii)

It is one of the greatest moments in Shakespeare, an incomparable feat of that dramatic art which at once takes you fully within another's feelings and at the same time keeps you at an extraordinary distance from them; the distinction between sympathy and empathy never more clear, or the uselessness of such an uncritical concept as that of 'identifying with'. And the artistic triumph, the human horror, are there in the spiritual lock-jaw which clamps upon Amen. Macbeth has cut his own vocal cords. 'But wherefore could not I pronounce Amen?': *pronounce* is desperate in its asking so little and therefore being denied so much. Then the move into the immobility of the riven:

> But wherefore could not I pronounce Amen?
> I had most need of Blessing, and Amen
> Stuck in my throat.

The word sticks in the throat of the lines. Macbeth can neither swallow the thought of what it is to say Amen, nor spit it out. This is even more than that fine thing 'language as gesture' (the phrase is R. P. Blackmur's), it is language there within the body, the catch in that throat by which we breathe and eat and speak. To the very end of his story, Macbeth has most need of blessing, and Amen sticks in our throat. It is impossible to read the lines, to hear them in one's inner ear, without the fullest sense – a matter of tone and of more than tone – of how they are inexorably to be pronounced, for they are sentences pronounced both by and upon Macbeth.

> But wherefore could not I pronounce Amen?
> I had most need of Blessing, and Amen
> Stuck in my throat.

When Wordsworth had the courage to tell of how the hiding-places of his power were closing, he thereby opened them. Once more a great force of will finds itself obliged to concede a recalcitrance in the nature of things, and so here too the inevitable turn is the invariable resource:

> the hiding-places of my power
> Seem open; I approach, and then they close;
> I see by glimpses now; when age comes on,
> May scarcely see at all, and I would give,
> While yet we may, as far as words can give,

A substance and a life to what I feel:
I would enshrine the spirit of the past
For future restoration.

> (*The Prelude*, 1805, XI, 335–42)

'I would give', in its unegotistical sublimity, is the counterpart to the Miltonic height:

> That to the highth of this great Argument
> I may assert Eternal Providence,
> And justifie the wayes of God to men.

> (*Paradise Lost*, I, 24–6)

'I would give' has all the very different Wordsworthian strength of purpose, even as it has then to move at once to the profound concession which is made by the rhyming recoil of 'give' upon itself:

> and I would give,
> While yet we may, as far as words can give,
> A substance and a life to what I feel:

It is every poet's aspiration, and it impeccably combines commonalty and individuality in the unique use that it makes of the indispensable turn.

Resistance is likewise commensurate with intensity of will in the quiet accents of a later Wordsworthian poet, Edward Thomas. Memory both is and is not within conscious control; how elusive memory is, as much our master as our servant, and how mysterious is a name. 'Old Man' is a poem not only about the name, or rather the names, of a plant but about the deep plantedness of names; the word 'name' moves from within the line to a commanding position at the end of the line, as 'names'; Thomas then goes away from it for one line, only to return to its double return. Nothing could be less vague than this effort of patient acquiescence, this achieved irresolvability. The poem opens:

> Old Man, or Lad's-love, – in the name there's nothing
> To one that knows not Lad's-love, or Old Man,
> The hoar-green feathery herb, almost a tree,

> Growing with rosemary and lavender.
> Even to one that knows it well, the names
> Half decorate, half perplex, the thing it is:
> At least, what that is clings not to the names
> In spite of time. And yet I like the names.

It is a poem which perfectly judges the accommodation that it reaches with imperfection, the mind fully bent upon that which must remain half perplexed. 'And yet': it has a very different energy from the 'And yet' of Richard ('And yet I know not how to get the Crowne'), and yet the source of the energy is the same: the sense of what exactly we are intimating in English when we end two successive lines with the same word or words ('the names', 'the names'). What is intimated, unmistakably, is a refusal of the will to yield before that which in its otherness will itself never yield to the will. The turn, the recoil, is always waiting to crystallize into *And yet*.

> Even to one that knows it well, the names
> Half decorate, half perplex, the thing it is:
> At least, what that is clings not to the names
> In spite of time. And yet I like the names.

That, there's no getting round.

All of these instances have been in blank verse, mostly because of the Shakespearean mastery from which one should start, and because one particular kind of clarity attaches in blank verse to such salient rhyming or repetition. But clearly blank verse has no monopoly of the effect, the contrariety incarnate in the turn. So, before returning to Eliot, let me give an instance where the effect is alive within another verse-form.

Robert Lowell's poem 'Caligula' begins by seizing the horrid pun in *like*: 'to make me like you'. It ponders the grim affinities which had come over the ages to nickname a twentieth-century American poet 'Cal' (touched with Caliban, yes, but centrally Caligula).

> My namesake, Little Boots, Caligula,
> you disappoint me. Tell me what I saw
> to make me like you when we met at school?

The poem interrogates the conjunction of the body politic and the body personal, incarnating a conviction that the imperial psychopathology is at one with an immitigable revulsion from the emperor's own person. The poem is in heroic couplets, the form which in our Augustan literature worked so strongly both within and against Augustan and Caesarean energies, a form designed to promulgate public values and order, a form rationally instinct with horror at madness. Each couplet is a plank, firmly in position in order to build a platform which is to be at once highly personal and extendedly political. In Lowell's fearful poem, you can hear that Caligula has suddenly gone off his head when without warning the couplet is poleaxed.

The ugliness of Caligula's body is being remorselessly itemized. Behind the sequential hatred is the loving convention which itemized the beauties of the loved one's person, a medieval and renaissance convention which had been scratched though not lacerated by Olivia in *Twelfth Night*.

O sir, I will not be so hard-hearted: I will give out divers scedules of my beautie. It shalbe Inventoried and every particle and utensile labell'd to my will: As, Item two lippes indifferent redde, Item two grey eyes, with lids to them: Item, one necke, one chin, & so forth.

(I, v)

'I will not be so hard-hearted'; but Caligula had been, and Lowell was compelled to be. 'Item, one necke': this lodged with Lowell, and like Caligula but in horror at him Lowell butchered all such loveliness.

> *Item*: your body hairy, badly made,
> head hairless, smoother than your marble head;
> *Item*: eyes hollow, hollow temples, red
> cheeks rough with rouge, legs spindly, hands that leave
> a clammy snail's trail on your soggy sleeve . . .
> a hand no hand will hold . . . nose thin, thin neck –
> you wish the Romans had a single neck![1]

The rhymes inch obdurately on: *head/red; leave/sleeve;* and then the inspired lunacy of *neck/neck.* 'Item, one necke': 'a single neck'. It is the single thing said by Caligula which the

---

[1] – Lowell's ellipses within the poem.

world will never forget, and a supreme instance of sheer power coming up against sheer resistance: 'you wish the Romans had a single neck!' The exclamation-mark wouldn't have to be a shriek-mark; even whispered, the line would have its cutting edge, there in the tonal turning of the rhyme, an expression at once of total will and of total frustration. Instead of the doubleness of the couplet, the singleness of a single neck.

Lowell is not the only twentieth-century poet to apprehend that in the matter of single necks we have changed all that. These days a Caligula, thanks to the technology of mass murder, would not have his work cut out. The Romans do now have a single neck, as do the Italians, the Europeans, and even the human race.

Caligula out-Richards Richard III, and a Hitler can now out-Caligula Caligula. Lowell's horrifying inwardness with such lunacy is there in his simple deep decision to adapt the Shakespearean turn, that doubly unyielding repetition at the end of two successive lines, to the fundamentally non-Shakespearean form of the heroic couplet. The artistic superiority of Lowell over some good contemporary poets who have likewise sought to capture this new vulnerability of the human neck is in a sense a technical triumph, though we cannot say at what point technique begins or where it ends. Howard Nemerov issues his words 'To the Rulers': I hear you praying

> Your prayer, that used to be Caligula's too,
> *If they all only had one neck* . . . It's so
> Unnecessary and out of date. We do.[1]

This won't do, not just because it so announcingly cups its hands, or because it whinges instead of shuddering, but because Nemerov has not hit upon any corporeal embodiment, there in the very tissue of his verse, for the aggression of 'one neck'. His lines remain high-mindedly expository. Tennyson, in the first published version of 'A Dream of Fair Women' (1832), perpetrated this stanza about Iphigeneia:

> 'The tall masts quivered as they lay afloat,
>   The temples and the people and the shore.

1 – Nemerov's ellipsis.

> One drew a sharp knife through my tender throat
> Slowly, – and nothing more.'

This was very vulnerable, and someone duly vulned it. For Tennyson had handed a knife to the reviewer Croker, and Croker cuttingly affected to misunderstand: 'what touching simplicity – what pathetic resignation – he cut my throat – "*nothing more!*" One might indeed ask, "*What more*" she would have?'[1]

Saul Steinberg has reported:

I made another drawing of a hero fighting a giant baby. A giant baby can be very dangerous. You cannot reason with him: he cannot be controlled. If we were subjected to 6-month-old babies with iron muscles, we would all be murdered.[2]

Along Steinberg's lines, Roy Fuller has made a better shot than Nemerov's at updating and outdating Caligula, though a less appalling one than Lowell's. Fuller starts from the monstrous infantilism of sheer will-power finding itself sheerly frustrated.

Outside the Supermarket

> Grasping with opposite hand the side of his pram
> As though an idle sceptre or marshal's baton,
> A look of serious surveillance on his face,
> This infant for an instant restores to me
>   The sense of mankind's worth.
>
> No matter that soon he'll be in floods of tears;
> Who can blame his frustration at a recalcitrant world?
> Thus wept Isaiah over Jerusalem.
> Long years must pass before like Caligula
>   He weeps for a single neck.

This wrings the neck of Wordsworth's eloquence, of 'The Child is father of the Man', and compared with Nemerov the poem tries with a keener eye the axe's edge of Caligula. But it does not strike a monstrously right form for its horror. 'Who can blame

1 – *Quarterly Review*, April 1833.
2 – Harold Rosenberg, *Saul Steinberg* (1978), p. 29.

his frustration at a recalcitrant world?': this is very well said, but it is something less than the quintessential embodiment of such frustration and recalcitrance in the unyielding turn:

> For I am sicke, and capable of feares,
> Opprest with wrongs, and therefore full of feares.

> A crowd flowed over London Bridge, so many,
> I had not thought death had undone so many.

> Be round impaled with a glorious Crowne.
> And yet I know not how to get the Crowne,

> But wherefore could not I pronounce Amen?
> I had most need of Blessing, and Amen
> Stuck in my throat.

>   when age comes on,
> May scarcely see at all, and I would give,
> While yet we may, as far as words can give,
> A substance and a life to what I feel:

> At least, what that is clings not to the names
> In spite of time. And yet I like the names.

> a hand no hand will hold . . . nose thin, thin neck –
> you wish the Romans had a single neck!

Very different though these all are, they yet have in common that their tone is definitely and unmistakably indicated, and that the heart of their tone is a deep will deeply frustrated, an animated paralysis caught in the turn of the lines' repeated ending.

Eliot is intrepid as a poet, and nowhere more so than when he acknowledges trepidation. This is not only perturbation or involuntary trembling, it is a 'vibratory or reciprocating movement'. The reciprocating movement may then issue in a locked immobility. Then the key to this sense of imprisonment may take this turn.

> I have heard the key
> Turn in the door once and turn once only

> We think of the key, each in his prison
> Thinking of the key, each confirms a prison
> (*The Waste Land*)

Confirmed, indeed. Or there is the tonal power, welcoming and sinister, which is so fearfully inviting early in *The Waste Land*. Eliot may triple the trepidation, by making the repeated line-end have the weight not just of one word (*prison/prison*), or of two words (*so many/so many*) but of three, darkly beckoning from within the shadow of the parenthesis:

> Only
> There is shadow under this red rock,
> (Come in under the shadow of this red rock),
> And I will show you something different from either
> Your shadow at morning striding behind you
> Or your shadow at evening rising to meet you;
> I will show you fear in a handful of dust.
> (*The Waste Land*)

This is the old turn newly armed, for there is something very disconcerting about rhyming, so to speak, the three words 'this red rock' out in the open with the same three words entrenched within their cunning canny brackets. These lines constitute one of Eliot's greatest triumphs, in their astonishing play of the cadences and the sense against the punctuation's demand.[1] The ear registers no disturbance from Eliot's bracketed line, but the eye should be disturbed by its so being 'something different' from the ear. For if there is one thing which would be thought to be stable, it is that if bracketed words are removed, there will be no stumble but an unbroken syntactical 'striding'. Puttenham said of the parenthesis: 'when ye will seeme, for larger information or some other purpose, to peece or graffe in the middest of your tale an unnecessary parcel of speach, which neverthelesse may be thence without any detriment to the rest'.[2] Johnson defined a parenthesis as 'A sentence so included in

1 – Here I draw on a page from my essay on Geoffrey Hill, in *The Force of Poetry* (1984), p. 308.
2 – *The Arte of English Poesie* (1589), III, xiii.

another sentence, as that it may be taken out without injuring the sense of that which encloses it: commonly marked thus ( )'. So that when you exclude such 'intercluding' ('Parenthesis, an intercluding . . .'), your stride can pick up where it left off. Yet what happens if we exclude Eliot's intercluded parenthesis?

> Only
> There is shadow under this red rock,
> And I will show you something different

The sense is so precarious as to sound deranged; a reader is therefore pressed to let the words '(Come in under the shadow of this red rock)' come in, or come out from the shadow of their brackets, in order that there may then be the sane sequence: 'Come in under the shadow . . . And I will show you'. It is a revolutionary moment in English poetry, in the mildness of its violence, the intrepidity with which it realizes trepidation. Such a parenthesis, compounded by the two-handed engine of the turn at the line-end, deepens the meaning of Puttenham's definition of a parenthesis as 'your first figure of tollerable disorder'. Eliot had not arrived at this eerie profundity in his earlier version of these lines, in the poem which was in galley proof for publication in *Poetry*, where in October 1915 Eliot published three poems. 'The Death of Saint Narcissus' did not have the sanity of its opening sequence 'Come . . . And I will show you . . .' endangered by any intervening brackets.

> Come under the shadow of this gray rock –
> Come in under the shadow of this gray rock,
> And I will show you something different from either
> Your shadow sprawling over the sand at daybreak, or
> Your shadow leaping behind the fire against the red rock:
> I will show you his bloody cloth and limbs
> And the gray shadow on his lips.[1]

1 – *Poems Written in Early Youth* (1950).

V

AN ENGLISH ACCENT

The sound of sense

It was Robert Frost who gave wholehearted support to the truth, or rather a half of it, about tone and unmistakability. Being the best of those modern poets who are not modernists (though modernizers have dug up his corpus in order post-humously to baptize it), Frost is Eliot's worthiest antagonist. He is so, not because Eliot would deny Frost's one principle, but because Frost would deny one of Eliot's.

Frost had only one crucial critical idea, which is one more than most of us ever have. He returned to it refreshingly. It is 'the sound of sense'.

I alone of English writers have consciously set myself to make music out of what I may call the sound of sense. Now it is possible to have sense without the sound of sense (as in much prose that is supposed to pass muster but makes very dull reading) and the sound of sense without sense (as in Alice in Wonderland which makes anything but dull reading). The best place to get the abstract sound of sense is from voices behind a door that cuts off the words. Ask yourself how these sentences would sound without the words in which they are embodied:

> You mean to tell me you can't read?
> I said no such thing.
> Well read then.
> You're not my teacher.

*

> One – two – three – go!
> No good! Come back – come back.
> Haslam go down there and make those kids get out of the track.

Those sounds are summoned by the audile imagination and they must be positive, strong, and definitely and unmistakeably indicated by the context. The reader must be at no loss to give his voice the posture proper to the sentence.[1]

This gives classic expression to one half of the truth, and it has the virtues to which it swears loyalty: it is itself positive, strong and definitely and unmistakably indicated. Its loyalty is not misplaced, except only in the insistence that there be loyalty to this one principle only. Though Frost's poems are often less single-minded than this, Frost as a commentator on poetry was entirely clear about not just the supremacy but the totality of the principle. 'The reader must be at no loss to give his voice the posture proper to the sentence.' 'Never if you can help it write down a sentence in which the voice will not know how to posture *specially*.'

There is an anecdote of an actress's encounter with Frost:

As soon as she met Frost, she asked if he really believed there was only one way to read a good poem. Yes he did. Oh no, Mr. Frost, you must know better than that, for if that were true then all actors and actresses reading lines from Shakespeare's best plays would read them in much the same way – or at least in as nearly the same way as possible. But they never do that. Instead, they demonstrate in their performances that there are many different ways to read – and to interpret – one and the same poetic passage. Frost answered pleasantly by saying that if such ambiguities occurred in any of Shakespeare's plays, the fault must lie with Shakespeare as poet. You mean, said Florence Eldridge, that you can do with words what Shakespeare didn't do? Smiling, Frost answered, yes. Not amused, Miss Eldridge abruptly turned her back on the poet, and walked away.[2]

For Frost, if on occasion Shakespeare wrote so that you do not know, definitely and unmistakably, the posture proper to the sentence, then the less Shakespeare he.

The objection to the principle, or rather to its claim to a monopoly, is not that it makes too much of responsibility but that it makes too little. For the mark of greatness is not only

1 – 4 July 1913 (*Selected Letters*, edited by Lawrence Thompson, 1964, pp. 79–81).
2 – Lawrance Thompson, *Robert Frost: The Years of Triumph* (1970), p. 427.

wisely to exercise responsibility but wisely to delegate it. What is at issue is the responsibility for responses. Frost takes the entire responsibility, in a way which is something less than the greatest give and take, less than something given and taken.

Frost is an admirably decisive writer, preferring therefore to steer nearer to the rock of coercion than to the whirlpool of abdication. Abnegation is not his style, either. This confident strength, this being at no loss, creates the electric limits of most of his best poems; the loveliness of 'Never Again Would Birds' Song Be The Same' is a consequence of the unexpected gentleness with which Frost here informs this enduring conviction of his, not only pondered but enacted in the poem, a conviction that is much more than declared:

> He would declare and could himself believe
> That the birds there in all the garden round
> From having heard the daylong voice of Eve
> Had added to their own an oversound,
> Her tone of meaning but without the words.
> Admittedly an eloquence so soft
> Could only have had an influence on birds
> When call or laughter carried it aloft.
> Be that as may be, she was in their song.
> Moreover her voice upon their voices crossed
> Had now persisted in the woods so long
> That probably it never would be lost.
> Never again would birds' song be the same.
> And to do that to birds was why she came.

Eliot did not lack respect for this principle of the 'tone of meaning', the sound of sense, not least because otherwise the counter-principle could never be effectual. But he did not grant Frost's premise, that the essentially dramatic nature of poetry has to be mediated by, and only by, an unmistakable posture in the body of the words, by the building in of indubitable stage directions. Eliot believed that there was an equal and opposite counter-principle, and that it too was a genuinely dramatic principle. Eliot would have considered Frost 'a Heretic: that is, a person who seizes upon a truth and pushes it to the point at which it becomes a falsehood'.[1] 'For heresy, which consists in emphasising one aspect of the mystery to the exclusion of the other, is a natural tendency of the mind.'[2]

Eliot has one of the speakers in 'A Dialogue on Dramatic Poetry' (1928) ask 'what great poetry is not dramatic?'[3] But though this was a rhetorical question in the mouth of mouthpiece B, it was a real one, a lifelong one, for B's creator. Eliot held to the conviction that there was indeed something dramatic in all great poetry, as one might likewise contend that there is something riddling in all great poetry. But there is also such a thing as a riddle, and there is drama. Eliot resisted the English propensity to honour Shakespeare that side idolatry and to make supreme not just Shakespeare's achievement but Shakespeare's chosen kind, as if ('Dramatise, dramatise') all great literature would be drama if only it could. Eliot's recurrent reminder of Dante's achievement is not only a matter of setting an art that embodies a great philosophy or theology against one that does not, but is also an insistence that even the greatest achievements in art are acknowledgements of inescapable sacrifice. Or not *even* such, but especially such, since if art on the scale of Shakespeare or Dante is yet forced to acknowledge sacrifice, how much more must this be true of lesser art. 'Now, to some extent, the sacrifice of some potentialities in order to realize others, is a condition of artistic creation, as it is a condition of life, in general.'[4]

Eliot's reply to Middleton Murry's *Shakespeare* constitutes one of his most unanswerable parentheses:

(I question one assertion of a more general kind: on p. 135 Mr. Murry affirms that 'drama is the highest and fullest form of poetry'. I should say that in the highest and fullest forms of poetry there is a dramatic element; but I doubt whether the highest and fullest poetry has to take the form of drama. For any form of poetry restricts one's liberty; and drama is a very peculiar form: there is a great deal that is high and full poetry that will not go into that form. Drama was, I think, less of a restriction to Shakespeare

1 – 'Second Thoughts about Humanism', *Selected Essays*, p. 488.
2 – *Listener*, 16 March 1932.
3 – 'A Dialogue on Dramatic Poetry', *Selected Essays*, p. 51.
4 – 'What is a Classic?', *On Poetry and Poets*, p. 60.

than it has ever been to any other dramatic poet; but I do not see how we can assert that it is a higher and fuller *form* than that used by Homer or that used by Dante.)[1]

The dramatic element could for Eliot, though not for Frost as commentator, be realized in either of two opposite ways. There is an analogy in Eliot's twofold account of music and the lyric:

Now there are two kinds of 'music' in verse. One is that of the lyrics of Shakespeare or Campion, which *demand* the kindred music of the lute or other instrument . . . And Donne's is the second kind of musical verse: the verse which suggests music, but which, so to speak, contains in itself all its possible music.[2]

Eliot has many other thoughts at this point in his radio talk, including the standing of ideas in poetry, but one might invoke simply the distinction he makes here between two relations which poetry may have to music, a distinction which might seem to leave us with nothing to say of the lyric, but which instead clarifies the intrinsic duality of whatever we may be impelled to say. For lyric poetry either is poetry which builds its music into itself, lyrical in being musical, or it is the opposite: poetry which demands to be accompanied by music and is therefore enabled – though not required – to be not more but less musical in itself. A lyric either exercises or delegates its responsibility to music; this does not mean that we have to despair of saying anything useful about the lyric, it means that we are from the start confronted with two equal antithetical thrusts which together sustain the great arch of lyric art. If we insist on a singleness of critical statement, then the most we will be able to maintain is that a lyric is a poem to which music stands in an especially salient relation. But the double principle will permit an expansion of this, into the understanding that a lyric is a poem which either builds music into itself, or positively builds music out – in the confidence that this obligation responsibly delegated will then be responsibly met. Met by 'the kindred music of the lute or other instrument'.

Brought back then from the lyric to the dramatic, the double

1 – *The Criterion*, xv (1936), 709.
2 – *Listener*, 12 March 1930.

principle offers itself as this: given that the dramatic element is that to which stage directions stand in an especially salient relation, the dramatic is animated either by building stage directions in or by positively building them out. The posture proper to the sentence is one kind, a tonal kind, of stage direction. Whether in stage-drama or not, a dramatic effect will be the precipitation either of delegating or of exercising responsibility for decisions as to tone. What is definitely and unmistakably indicated by the context may be not one decided tone but rather a delegation of the decision.

'We begin, all of us, with every prejudice against Dryden's "heroic drama"': so began, with a reminder of prejudice, the *Listener*'s reprinting of another radio talk, on 'Dryden the Dramatist',[1] in 1931. Here Eliot touched on 'the nature of the *dramatic* in poetic drama, as distinguishable from the *poetic* in poetic drama': 'the problem is much more of a tangle than it looks.' The tangle thickens, and Eliot is like one lost in a thorny wood. Then suddenly he cuts through to a lucid instancing of what is at issue:

But to make my point a little clearer I will take parallel passages from *Antony and Cleopatra* and from *All for Love*. In the former play, when the soldiers burst in after Cleopatra's death [a soldier then crying, 'What worke is heere Charmian? Is this well done?'] Charmian is made to say

> It is well done, and fitting for a princess,
> Descended of so many royal kings.
> Ah, soldier!   (*dies.*)

Dryden's Charmion says

> Yes, 'tis well done, and like a Queen, the last
> Of her great race. I follow her.
>   (*Sinks down and dies.*)

Now, if you take these two passages by themselves, you cannot say that the two lines of Dryden are either less *poetic* than Shakespeare's, or less *dramatic*; a great actress could make just as much, I believe, of those of

1 – 22 April 1931. As collected in *John Dryden: The Poet: The Dramatist: The Critic* (1932), the talk preceded these words with a page on Dryden's body of plays. The 1932 text (pp. 29–31) is quoted here, as more exact (for instance, Eliot rightly has 'Dryden's Charmion', not 'Dryden's Charmian').

Dryden as of those of Shakespeare. But consider Shakespeare's remarkable addition to the original text of North, the two plain words, *ah, soldier*. You cannot say that there is anything peculiarly *poetic* about these two words, and if you isolate the dramatic from the poetic you cannot say that there is anything peculiarly dramatic either, because there is nothing in them for the actress to express in action; she can at best enunciate them clearly. I could not myself put into words the difference I feel between the passage if these two words *ah, soldier* were omitted and with them. But I know there is a difference, and that only Shakespeare could have made it.

If in some game I had to instance one paragraph from Eliot to show that he was a great critic, I should choose this, from a radio talk which he never himself reprinted. For it is an act of genius in the critic to see that the act of genius in the artist was the cry 'Ah Souldier'. After all, you or I would on the face of it be capable of creating the words 'Ah Souldier'. Yet Eliot swoops upon those two plain words, supporting his impulse by remarking that they are an addition to the original text of North's translation from Plutarch. 'I could not myself put into words the difference I feel between the passage if these two words *ah, soldier* were omitted and with them. But I know there is a difference, and that only Shakespeare could have made it.'

Charmian's great moment stirs the life of the play. Eliot would, for instance, have been sensitive to the effect of her dying upon an incompleteness; her cry completed, yes, but not her line or her cadence. Death, after all, is not always so considerate as to allow us perfectly to round off what we were saying, as Charmian has only just discovered in having to complete the last words of the dying Cleopatra. But in Dryden's Charmion the poignancy of this incompleteness of the line is vitiated by the movement into the histrionically egotistical.

> Yes, 'tis well done, and like a Queen, the last
> Of her great race. I follow her.

Eliot, fascinated as he was by the hideous human propensity to self-dramatize, would have been struck by this sad slide. Shakespeare's Charmian, who dies upon the uncomplaisant words 'Ah Souldier', says nothing of herself at all; her great love for Cleopatra is evidenced not in what she says of herself but in what she ringingly affirms of her royal mistress; evidenced, too, not in what she says, but in what she does. 'It is well done.' In the completeness of her love and of her self-abnegation (the scene is Shakespeare's greatest evocation of a true sisterhood), there is no room for the self-assertion of 'I'. But when Dryden eschews the two plain words, it follows that there will be a flash of self-aggrandizement in his Charmion such as makes her more consciously and less truly a heroine in her suicide:

> Yes, 'tis well done, and like a Queen, the last
> Of her great race. I follow her.

There is nothing in Shakespeare's Charmian to match this *superbia*, fortunately. It is for Dryden's Charmion to insinuate, 'And I, though not a Queen, am – as you may notice – behaving no less nobly.'

An adequate account of Eliot's insight and of Shakespeare's art would delight in showing the reciprocity of Charmian's moment with a great deal else in the play. But in terms of tone, and of the sound of sense, the nub is the simple exclamation 'Ah' in 'Ah Souldier'. An exclamation is especially demanding in the matter of tone, since an exclamation has no meaning other than its tone. The meaning of any word or phrase can clearly be altered by its tone, as when – the door having been let swing in your face – your clipped '*Thank* you' means something other than an expression of gratitude. But an exclamation such as Oh or Ah means nothing more (or less) than the tone in which it is uttered; an exclamation is a vacuum waiting to be filled with a tone. Oh and Ah and Eh are pregnant with potentiality. One reason why there are very few great poems in English with the exclamation 'Yuk' in them is that Yuk is lamentably unsatisfactory as an exclamation, having only one possibility as to its tone and therefore annulling the special power of exclamation.

'Ah Souldier' (there is no exclamation mark in the Folio): it is definitely and unmistakably indicated that here Shakespeare is not definitely and unmistakably indicating the posture proper to the cry, the expression on the face of the word. The Ah may be a cry of triumph over the soldier, since the women have outwitted the soldiers and outsoldiered them. Or it may be a cry of pain, since dying is not necessarily painless. Or it may be a cry of resignation. Or some combination of these. Not that the words are a Rorschach blot, designed to reveal no more than our own projections. There is not an infinite number of plausible ways of hearing 'Ah Souldier', but there are several ways. The responsibility for settling upon the best response has been manifestly delegated by the artist, since Shakespeare is perfectly capable of making these things crystal-clear when he chooses to do so; delegated as a practising playwright should often delegate it and as all artists should sometimes delegate it. Within a narrow insistence upon the sound of sense, 'Ah Souldier' would have to be judged a failure; buttressed antithetically, though, it is – in Shakespeare and for Eliot – a triumph.

Yes, we tread a circle in interpreting any such moment. For we choose the best tone for it by bringing to bear upon any particular moment our sense of the play as a whole, and yet we arrive at a sense of the play as a whole only by interpreting such moments. We should acknowledge this without being thrilled to bits by it.

The fact that the tone is *not* definitely indicated, indeed is definitely not, might be something dramatized within the character, or might be something solicited from us, something that asks not the character's decision but ours. A novelist may semi-dramatize this indecision within a character, a novelist being free to report that which a dramatist is obliged to render. George Eliot exercises the novelist's prerogative in *Felix Holt*:

'Dear me, what a splendid little boy, Mrs Transome! why – it cannot be – can it be – that you have the happiness to be a grandmamma?'

'Yes; that is my son's little boy.'

'Indeed!' said Lady Debarry, really amazed. 'I never heard you speak of his marriage. He has brought you home a daughter-in-law, then?'

'No,' said Mrs Transome, coldly; 'she is dead.'

'O – o – oh!' said Lady Debarry, in a tone ludicrously undecided between condolence, satisfaction, and general mistiness.[1]

---

1 – Chapter VII. George Eliot has an ear for these things; there is the conversation about money, between Rosamond Vincy and Lydgate, in *Middlemarch* (Book VI, Chapter LVIII):

'What can *I* do, Tertius?' said Rosamond, turning her eyes on him again. That little speech of four words, like so many others in all languages, is capable by varied vocal inflexions of

The crucial thing is that any mistiness be the character's, not the author's.

Frost too seized upon 'Oh' as crucial to tone. He complained in 1916 that American poetry was then

meaningless twaddle, with a few worn-out tones. You know what I mean by tones? I'll explain . . . Take, for instance, the expression 'oh'. The American poets use it in practically one tone, that of grandeur: 'Oh, Soul!' 'Oh Hills!' – 'Oh Anything!' That's the way that they go. But think of what 'oh' is really capable; the 'oh' of scorn, the 'oh' of amusement, the 'oh' of surprise, the 'oh' of doubt – and there are many more.[1]

'Oh' is understood here not as an object that may be tonally rotated to catch a different light, or even a hole that may be filled, but a vacuum that must be filled. The twaddling habit of using 'Oh' in practically one tone, that of grandeur, had not only impoverished the tones of American poetry but had nullified the particular worth and opportunity of exclamations, their naturally inviting a diversity of tonal embodiments. It is witty of Frost to rise to 'Oh Anything !', since this is at once preposterous and authentic; even the words 'Oh Anything' could conceivably find their way into great poetry. Shakespeare had his momentum of O's:

> Why then, O brawling love, O loving hate,
> O any thing, of nothing first created.
>
> *(Romeo and Juliet, I, i)*

And the Shakespearean genius of Dickens delighted in these potentialities of Oh and Ah. Dickens's son records the voicing of a song about Guy Fawkes:

———

expressing all states of mind from helpless dimness to exhaustive argumentative perception, from the completest self-devoting fellowship to the most neutral aloofness. Rosamond's thin utterance threw into the words 'What can *I* do!' as much neutrality as they could hold.

Yet those who find the novelist prejudiced against Rosamond may remark that George Eliot does not throw much neutrality into the unacknowledged change which she makes from the question mark to the exclamation mark there. Still, one knows what Eliot (T. S.) means when he lets lurk within brackets this thought: '(And I am quite sure that Rosamond Vincy, in *Middlemarch*, frightens me far more than Goneril or Regan.)' ('The Three Voices of Poetry', *On Poetry and Poets*, p. 93.)
1 – Thompson, *Robert Frost: The Years of Triumph*, p. 68. The ellipsis is Frost's (or Thompson's).

To each verse there was a chorus of the good old-fashioned sort, with an 'oh, ah, oh, ri fol de riddy oddy, bow wow wow' refrain, and a great part of the point of the joke lay in the delivery of the introductory monosyllables; the first 'oh' being given, as it were, with incredulity, or a tone of inquiry; the second 'ah' strongly affirmatively, and the last 'oh' with an air of one who has found conviction not without difficulty.[1]

American poets needed Frost's goading then, but it was an American novelist who had brought out just how full, how unvacuous, the little word 'Oh' could be made by a practised European, even while seeming to be almost nothing:

'I don't know whether you know Lord Mark.' And then for the other party: 'Mr. Merton Densher – who has just come back from America.'

'Oh!' said the other party while Densher said nothing – occupied as he mainly was on the spot with weighing the sound in question. He recognised it in a moment as less imponderable than it might have appeared, as having indeed positive claims. It wasn't, that is, he knew the 'Oh!' of the idiot, however great the superficial resemblance: it was that of the clever, the accomplished man; it was the very specialty of the speaker, and a deal of expensive training and experience had gone to producing it.

(*The Wings of the Dove*, Book Sixth, Chapter IV)

A vacuum has its aggressive opportunity, nocently there within an innocent Oh, lurking perhaps in a studied neutrality. James had been a citizen of a country which has a national anthem beginning with O or Oh; this may be asking for trouble, since immediately prior to the anthem there may no longer be an indisputable context of patriotic reverence; perhaps the anthem is awaiting someone like Jimi Hendrix to insist upon a very unexpected tone for that opening Oh, and to make it gutter. A nation may be on firmer ground if it takes as the first word of its anthem *God*. But it was an American soon to become an Englishman who created the inimitable run, itself imitating the jazzy sequence:

> But
>
> O O O O that Shakespeherian Rag–
> It's so elegant
> So intelligent

1 – *Interviews and Recollections*, edited by Philip Collins (1981), i, 132.

Eliot's intelligence, at once critical and creative, valued the principled dubiety which could on occasion unsettle the 'tone of meaning'. The value is akin to that of wit, of which Eliot said, with a profundity both tentative and firm: 'It involves, probably, a recognition, implicit in the expression of every experience, of other kinds of experience which are possible.'[1] It is the mark of drama signally to acknowledge that other kinds of experience are possible, partly because of the many-voiced nature of theatre, and partly because of the delegating that is essential to it: 'You are deliberately writing verse for other voices, not for your own, and you do not know whose voices they will be.'[2] The dramatic element, even off the stage and on the printed page, will always partake of some such recognition of other voices, perhaps voices from a farther room. This has its relation not only to wit but to humour; Eliot said of the dramatic sense as it flourishes in real life off stage: 'It is a sense which is almost a sense of humour (for when anyone is conscious of himself as acting, something like a sense of humour is present).'[3]

Imagination in a reader, as in a writer, practises a width of acknowledgement, while genius as an actor may be able to utter words both so that their posture is unmistakable *and* so that we are simultaneously made aware that the words could, with only the slightest difference of angle, have been heard very differently – and that this possibility is to the point, this 'recognition, implicit in the expression of every experience, of other kinds of experience which are possible'. In a critique of *The Waste Land* unparalleled for prompt acumen, Conrad Aiken in 1923 said of Eliot: 'with this capacity or necessity for being aware in his own way, Mr. Eliot has a haunting, a tyrannous awareness that there have been many other awarenesses before.'[4] But what protects Eliot against being tyrannized over by these previous awarenesses, and protects us against being tyrannized over by his, is his understanding that it is not just a matter of previous

1 – 'Andrew Marvell', *Selected Essays*, p. 303.
2 – 'Poetry and Drama', *On Poetry and Poets*, p. 79.
3 – ' "Rhetoric" and Poetic Drama', *Selected Essays*, p. 41.
4 – *New Republic*, 7 February 1923; reprinted in *T. S. Eliot: The Man and His Work*, ed. Tate, p. 196.

awarenesses. His art is aware of other ways of being aware here and now.

Of '*theatrically* dramatic value in verse' and '*poetic* dramatic value', Eliot said: 'Shakespeare, of course, made the utmost use of each value; and therefore confuses us in our attempt to estimate between the minor Elizabethans and Dryden, for neither they nor Dryden had such vast resources.'[1] This praise of Shakespeare implies the analogous double principle, of the tone of meaning and the vacuum of tone. No one has any difficulty in recognizing (both as seeing and as valuing) Shakespeare's triumphs of the unmistakable sound of sense, whether on the stage or on the page.

REGAN: If you will come to me,
      (For now I spie a danger) I entreate you
      To bring but five and twentie, to no more
      Will I give place or notice.
LEAR: I gave you all.
REGAN: And in good time you gave it.
LEAR: Made you my Guardians, my Depositaries,
      But kept a reservation to be followed
      With such a number.

                                (II, iv)

There is no doubt of the posture proper to these life-and-death sentences, caught in the doubled retorting of 'give': *give/gave/gave*; caught, too, in the touching indeflectibility of Lear, who – cruelly interrupted by the vista of geological resentment, which retorts his word upon him ('And in good time you gave it') – nevertheless finds courage enough, and dignity enough, not to permit his syntax to be interrupted, not to have to begin again. It is essential to the effect (poignant and invigorating) that Lear overrules Regan, duly, with that simple maintenance of his pronouncement implicit in his carrying on with 'Made you . . .', not recommencing with 'I made you' or 'And made you': the steeling of himself is thrilling.

LEAR: I gave you all.
REGAN: And in good time you gave it.

1 – *John Dryden* (1932), pp. 29–30.

LEAR: Made you my Guardians, my Depositaries,
But kept a reservation to be followed
With such a number.

Such poetry is perfectly in accord with Frost's principle; but Shakespeare's greatness is in the reconciliation of these feats with those of the counter-principle. The existence and the worth of such a 'reservation' (as to a decided tone) have been less recognized, partly for the good reason that they are necessarily consequent upon the achievements of the sound of sense.

There are two moments in *Macbeth* of the utmost simplicity, where the meaning of the words is not in question and where if you could speak a foreign language at all, you would be ashamed to be unable to translate. Both moments are disconcerting to anybody who lacks '*Negative Capability*, that is when man is capable of being in uncertainties, Mysteries, doubts, without any irritable reaching after fact & reason'.[1] For the point of the piercing simple moment is that it should be illuminating because of its dubious light.

LADY MACBETH:　　　　　　　I have given Sucke, and know
How tender 'tis to love the Babe that milkes me,
I would, while it was smyling in my Face,
Have pluckt my Nipple from his Bonelesse
　　　Gummes,
And dasht the Braines out, had I so sworne
As you have done to this.

MACBETH:　　　　　　　　If we should faile?

LADY MACBETH: We faile?
But screw your courage to the sticking place,
And wee'le not fayle.

(I, vii)

How does Lady Macbeth say 'We faile?'? Does she say it with incredulous contempt, one of her spurs to prick the sides of his intent? Or does she say it with more solidarity, with an encouragement to stoicism, to a shouldering? (How much weight, and exactly what weight, are we to attach to the Folio's question-mark, 'We faile?'? And how clear can we be about the

1 – Keats, to George and Tom Keats, 21, 27 (?) December 1817; *Letters*, edited by Hyder Edward Rollins (1958), i, 193.

proportions of 'But' as *Only* against 'But' as *Yet*, in 'But screw your courage to the sticking place'?) Or does she say it, 'We faile?', since after all she is both hard as nails and tensely vulnerable, with a sudden appalled gaze into the abysmal possibility, with something of a momentary faltering such as will later issue in her sleep-walking and her suicide?

> They don't understand what it is to be awake,
> To be living on several planes at once
> Though one cannot speak with several voices at once.
> (The Family Reunion, II, i)

Each of these ways in which Lady Macbeth's words may be said has something to be said for it. A great actress might blend something of each, or might strongly, definitely and unmistakably say it in one particular way, or might say it in one way while indicating that there are other kinds of experience which are possible. What is clear is that this is not clear, and that this is unlikely to be incompetence on the part of this particular playwright.

The wish to batten down the sense is not ignoble, though it is here misplaced; the wish leads some people to claim that Lady Macbeth's ensuing admonition, 'But screw your courage to the sticking place, / And wee'le not fayle', surely settles the matter. Yet one thing which is certain is that the ensuing words ensue, and they can never tell us for sure whether in their robust reassurance they are the continuing of an imperturbable impulse within Lady Macbeth, or are, on the contrary, the recovery from a lapse ('We faile?', in momentary dismay) which had threatened her steadiness. Perhaps the current of her words flows straight on in unperturbed confidence; but perhaps the stream had unexpectedly met an obstacle in Macbeth's unexpected interjection ('If we should faile?'), and had briefly been forced to back up or back away ('We faile?'), only to plunge on into what is less self-assurance than self-reassurance. In which case, the courage that is to be screwed to the sticking-place is as much her own as his. And that's true too.

Robust writers are often impatient with such critical cogitations, which seem to them a pseudo-agon. Henry Fielding is very funny on this, and yet if you were to direct *Othello*, or act it, or even hear it within the theatre of your head, could you evade such decisions?

I then observed Shakespeare standing between Betterton and Booth, and deciding a difference between those two great actors concerning the placing an accent in one of his lines: this was disputed on both sides with a warmth which surprized me in Elysium, till I discovered by intuition that every soul retained its principal characteristic, being, indeed, its very essence. The line was that celebrated one in *Othello*:

> *Put out the light, and then put out the light.*

according to Betterton. Mr Booth contended to have it thus:—

> *Put out the light, and then put out* THE *light*

And so the accent is bandied; and then the text, by a natural momentum, emended.

At last it was agreed on all sides to refer the matter to the decision of Shakespeare himself, who delivered his sentiments as follows: 'Faith, gentlemen, it is so long since I wrote the line, I have forgot my meaning. This I know, could I have dreamt so much nonsense would have been talked and writ about it, I would have blotted it out of my works; for I am sure, if any of these be my meaning, it doth me very little honour'.

(*A Journey from This World to the Next*, Book I, Chapter VIII)

Effective, this, but very broad and bluff.

There is in *Macbeth* even more of a black hole than 'We faile?', in the dark scene in which Macduff learns of the murder of his household.

MACDUFF: My Children too?
ROSS: Wife, Children, Servants, all that could be found.
MACDUFF: And I must be from thence? My wife kil'd too?
ROSS: I have said.
MALCOLM: Be comforted.
Let's make us Med'cines of our great Revenge,
To cure this deadly greefe.
MACDUFF: He ha's no Children. All my pretty ones?
Did you say All? Oh Hell-Kite! All?
What, All my pretty Chickens, and their Damme

At one fell swoope?

(IV, iii)

The unspeakable pain of the scene is there at the crux: 'He ha's no Children.' English could not be more basic; if I. A. Richards had pared our tongue to fifty words of Basic English, could he have done without the four words 'He has no children'? And yet the words are notoriously cryptic for all their unmistakable directness and clarity. If 'He' is Macbeth, does Macduff answer Malcolm's incitement to revenge with the flat truth (one that is central to the play) that Macbeth has no children? No hope of a complete revenge there. Or does Macduff not *answer* Malcolm (the scene is built out of massive incomprehensions and incommunicabilities), but rather brood upon how it can be that Macbeth has done such a thing? Then the words comprise no sharp retort upon Malcolm, but instead a smouldering illumination of the Macbeths' darkest despair. 'No Sonne of mine succeeding'. 'I have given Sucke . . .' It may have been idle to speculate, in a sub-Bradleyan way, upon 'How many children had Lady Macbeth?', but it was worse than idle of A. C. Bradley's opponents, it was crassly indifferent to the play's plot and impulse, to deny that childlessness lacerated and goaded Macbeth and Lady Macbeth. Or is 'He' ('He ha's no Children') not Macbeth at all, but Malcolm? He, the man who tells me ('Be comforted') that I can make a medicine of 'our' great revenge to cure this deadly grief, he has no children – how else could he believe in such a medicine? This would be an acknowledgement of the depths of incomprehension plumbed in this scene. An actor, or reader, need have no difficulty in issuing those words, 'He ha's no Children', so as to make unmistakably clear who 'He' is, and whether the energies of the words are frustratedly embittered, or appalled in their belated comprehension of a murderer's root-bitterness, or deeply saddened by the shallowness of unthinkingly inexperienced political consolation. But an actor or a reader must have difficulty, of a salutary and illuminating kind, in deciding, in choosing. And upon such a choice a great deal will hang, in this play which gives such salience to choosing. In responses begin responsibilities, and the ultimate responsibility is to damnation and salvation.

It was in furtherance of this truth within the double principle, this conviction that in a play or in the dramatic element the words might present a proper impassivity, at least on initial acquaintance, that Eliot gave vent to his dismay at the state of the acting profession. He never reprinted his sharp essay on a production of *The Duchess of Malfi* in 1919. Of the actress Miss Nesbitt, Eliot says that she

> continued to make the part, and ruined the lines. We required only that she should transmit the lines, but to transmit lines is beyond the self-control of a modern actor, and so she did what the modern actor does: she 'interpreted' them.[1]

The self-control of this is real, and itself dramatically tense, on the edge of fury. The ensuing overstatement is therefore understandable.

> As *Hamlet* is performed, only the plot is Shakespeare's; and the words might as well be the flattest prose. For poetry is something which the actor cannot improve or 'interpret'; there is no such thing as the interpretation of poetry; poetry can only be transmitted; in consequence, the ideal actor for a poetic drama is the actor *with no personal vanity*.

Perfectly edged and level, those italics of Eliot's. The thought of an actor with no personal vanity remains to this day as thrilling as that of men whose heads do grow beneath their shoulders.

'There is no such thing as the interpretation of poetry; poetry can only be transmitted': this goes too far, though as Eliot said 'Of course one can "go too far" and except in directions in which we can go too far there is no interest in going at all; and only those who will risk going too far can possibly find out just how far one can go'.[2] Eliot's provocations about transmission and interpretation remain in touch with his even better-grounded understanding of the two oppositely valuable ways in which the dramatic element may be realized, may be both transmitted and interpreted.

---

1 – *Arts & Letters*, iii (1919–20), 36–9.
2 – Preface to Harry Crosby, *Transit of Venus* (1931), p. ix. This itself goes further than Eliot was later prepared to go ('but it is often true that only by going too far can we find out how far we can go'; 'The Music of Poetry', *On Poetry and Poets*, p. 36).

The master of the vacuum

In 1955 Eliot praised Wyndham Lewis as 'the greatest prose master of style of my generation', and then turned to a favourite resource and recourse, brackets: '(James Joyce was the greatest *non*-stylist, the master of the vacuum of personal style into which all things rush.)'[1] The brackets, functioning here as a vacuum flask, seal the compliment to Joyce so that it does not cool the compliment to Wyndham Lewis. Eliot's insight, though it is not bringing to bear specifically upon tone the concept of a vacuum, gives warrant for the critical conjunction of a vacuum and a style, and it affiliates a respect for Joyce to much else of crucial importance to Eliot. As in spiritual discipline, something negative is found to be deeply positive.[2] But then that is just what is emphasized by the stylistic device of italicizing, of all prefixes, *non*-, effecting a relation of a tone to a vacuum. 'The master of the vacuum of personal style into which all things rush' had moved Eliot more than thirty years earlier, in 1923, to a re-formulation of Matthew Arnold's awe at Wordsworth, 'He has no style':

In this book [*Ulysses*] Joyce has arrived at a very singular and perhaps unique literary distinction: the distinction of having, not in a negative but a very positive sense, no style at all. I mean that every sentence Mr. Joyce writes is peculiarly and absolutely his own, that his work is not a pastiche; but that nevertheless, it has none of the marks by which a 'style' may be distinguished.

'No art, and particularly and especially no literary art, can exist in a vacuum':[3] true, but the unexpected truth is that a vacuum can exist in art.

1 – *Hudson Review*, vii (1955), 526.
2 – See Eloise Knapp Hay, *T. S. Eliot's Negative Way* (1982), throughout; and Cleo McNelly Kearns, *T. S. Eliot and Indic Traditions* (1987), pp. 82–4, 237: 'The approach through negation, erasure, cancellation appeals to Eliot in part because it allows him to avoid or at least to reframe a philosophically and culturally questionable language of presence. Both negative and positive ways, however, have their uses for poetry and for meditation, and within both are various degrees and oppositions of negativity and affirmation.'
3 – *The Bookman*, lxx (1930), 598.

In Eliot, as in all great poets and critics, the literary matter is more than literary.

> But when we would have grasped for him, there was only a
> vacuum
> Surrounded by whispering aunts.
>
> (*The Family Reunion*, II, i)

> But waiting, simply waiting,
> With no desire to act, yet a loathing of inaction.
> A fear of the vacuum, and no desire to fill it.
>
> (*The Elder Statesman*, I)

In the crucial review-article on Henry Adams in 1919, Eliot had refashioned Matthew Arnold's lamenting of Shelley: Adams 'was seeking for education, with the wings of a beautiful but ineffectual conscience beating vainly in a vacuum jar'.[1] Instead of Arnold's angel, a conscience; instead of Arnold's void, a vacuum jar.

Three times the word 'void', which is not vacuum but is its sibling in craving, tolls in a letter to Paul Elmer More dated 'Shrove Tuesday, 1928'; it is a shriving letter. Of 'certain persons for whom religion is wholly unnecessary', Eliot says:

They may be very good, or very happy, they simply seem to miss nothing, to be unconscious of any void – the void that I find in the middle of all human happiness and all human relations, and which there is only one thing to fill. I am one whom this sense of void tends to drive towards asceticism or sensuality, and only Christianity helps to reconcile me to life, which is otherwise disgusting.[2]

The play upon 'miss nothing' is entirely grave: far from missing nothing, such people do not enough miss (feel the absence of) the true salutary nothing that is the void. 'And only Christianity': but then even Christianity only 'helps to reconcile' Eliot to life. It is the chastened insufficiency of 'helps to' there which might reconcile to Eliot even those unsympathetic to his beliefs.

1 – *The Athenaeum*, 23 May 1919.
2 – Quoted in John D. Margolis, *T. S. Eliot's Intellectual Development 1922–1939* (1972), p. 142.

The void and the vacuum can be positive in their very negativity. Nature abhors a vacuum. So does the religious supernatural, which yet loves to convert the human abhorrence of a vacuum into a spiritual incitement, driven by this sense of void.

'Not in a negative but a very positive sense': 'this sense of void'. The enactment of such a sense, which is a main enterprise of *The Waste Land*, has been apprehended by Michael Edwards:

There is one moment in *The Waste Land*, in the first section, which seems to escape the toils of language, by looking to a possibility beyond speech:

> I could not
> Speak, and my eyes failed, I was neither
> Living nor dead, and I knew nothing,
> Looking into the heart of light, the silence.

'Silence' at the end of its line rhymes semantically with negatives at the end of the three previous lines. And 'I knew nothing' isn't the same as 'I didn't know anything': like silence, 'nothing' is positive, as in Mallarmé (or Lewis Carroll).[1]

'I was neither / Living nor dead': the weighty moment has its lighter counterpart in the nickname, Old Possum, which Eliot invited by saying in the preface to *For Lancelot Andrewes* (1928) that he had united the essays 'to refute any accusation of playing 'possum'.

The Waste Land is a congregation of voids. The 'dead sound' of a church clock;[2] the tarot card 'Which is blank'; 'the violet hour' which issues in a 'throbbing between two lives': all of these are fostered by the encompassing vacuum of silence or rather silences. There is the wounded malignant silence of the woman and her hair which 'Glowed into words, then would be savagely still'; and the painful benignant silence that is 'the heart

---

1 – *Eliot/Language* (1975), p. 19.
2 – Eliot wrote of George Wyndham's sense of North's Plutarch: 'He appreciates the battles, the torchlight, the "dead sound" of drums, the white, worn face of Cicero in his flight peering from his litter' ('A Romantic Aristocrat', 1919; *The Sacred Wood*, p. 28); this fostered in *The Waste Land* both the 'dead sound' and 'the torchlight red on sweaty faces'.

of light, the silence', *Heart of Darkness* astonishingly flooded with light. There is 'the frosty silence in the gardens'; and the horror which is at once heraldic and animal: 'The jungle crouched, humped in silence.' But perhaps even this last is not the worst. 'There is not even silence in the mountains'. Almost all of Paul Goodman's kinds of silence may be heard in *The Waste Land*:

Not speaking and speaking are both human ways of being in the world, and there are kinds and grades of each. There is the dumb silence of slumber or apathy; the sober silence that goes with a solemn animal face; the fertile silence of awareness, pasturing the soul, whence emerge new thoughts; the alive silence of alert perception, ready to say, 'This . . . this . . .'; the musical silence that accompanies absorbed activity; the silence of listening to another speak, catching the drift and helping him be clear; the noisy silence of resentment and self-recrimination, loud with subvocal speech but sullen to say it; baffled silence; the silence of peaceful accord with other persons or communion with the cosmos.[1]

Such of those kinds and grades of silence as are not to be found in *The Waste Land* were to surface in *Four Quartets*.

A relation of the sound of sense to the sense of void is intimated in the opening words of *The Waste Land*, perfectly clear in their meaning but with an elemental simplicity of doubt as to just what word is to be stressed, what exactly is the posture proper to the opening.

> April is the cruellest month, breeding
> Lilacs out of the dead land, mixing
> Memory and desire, stirring
> Dull roots with spring rain.

Manifestly the first five words are a disagreement with – even a courteous rebuke to – something which it is believed that you sentimentally believe. The speaker reveals a preconception, or a prejudice, as to a preconception or prejudice of yours. But is this fixed upon April or upon the cruelty of months? If you stress

1 – *Speaking and Language* (1971), p. 15.

'April', then the meaning is: 'April – and not as you will have thought, November – is the cruellest month.' If you stress 'cruellest', the meaning is: 'April is the cruellest – and not as you will have thought, the kindest – month.' These two intonations are more likely contestants than, for instance, 'April *is* the cruellest month', though this is not impossible: it would convey to a listener an insistence that the grim fact be admitted: 'April is – come on, admit that you really know this to be so, despite the usual romanticizing of April – the cruellest month.' Or it would convey someone bringing home this acknowledgement fully to himself: 'April is – I really do have to admit it, odd though this be – the cruellest month.'

The force of this opening, its unforgettability, is in its combination of unmistakable directness with all these lurking possibilities of mistaking its direction. On the one hand, the gist and pith of the opening words are not in doubt; on the other, much might hang upon the exact discrimination of what we are being disagreed with about, or of the prevailing presupposition about our presupposition.

It is often said that the opening lines of the General Prologue to the *Canterbury Tales* settle the matter. But they don't. Hugh Kenner may say of *The Waste Land* that it 'opens with a denial of Chaucer',[1] and Cairns Craig speak of 'Eliot's inversion of Chaucer in the first line of *The Waste Land*'.[2] But Chaucer's lines are less unequivocal than this would suggest, for they do not present April as the kindest month; the energies of April, of its weather and of its incitements to a longing which will not be entirely fulfilled, are not sentimentalized by Chaucer. Moreover, for every poem about April which can be offered (so that the preconception here be one about April), a counter-poem about say November can be offered (so that the preconception be about cruel months). And since the words are the very opening, we lack that sufficiency of established context which will often secure us.

What we are thought to think is related to what we may be expected to know, and often the intonation (and the sound of

1 – *The Invisible Poet*, p. 135.
2 – *Yeats, Eliot, Pound and the Politics of Poetry* (1982), p. 233.

sense) of a poem may be affected profoundly by some prior piece of knowledge invoked, such as gives a particular dramatic embodiment to the words. I once chose Edmund Blunden's finest poem, 'Report on Experience', for a BBC anthology; the intelligent actor read the opening lines straight, as if their sense were naked and spontaneous:

> I have been young, and now am not too old;
> And I have seen the righteous forsaken,
> His health, his honour and his quality taken.
>   This is not what we were formerly told.

But the actor stood in need of intelligence in the old sense too, news from somewhere; in this case, news of the allusion to Psalm xxxvii: 'I have been young, and now am old; yet have I not seen the righteous forsaken, nor his seed begging bread.' Blunden reports a different experience from the Psalmist's. 'This is not what we were formerly told.' So the tones of Blunden's lines must be something like this:

> '*I* have been young, and now am' *not too* 'old';
> And I *have* 'seen the righteous forsaken'.

What we were formerly told can no longer simply be believed – though it is the poem's triumph, as it moves on, that this is something very different from saying that what we were formerly told can simply no longer be believed. Here the sound of sense is the refraction of some earlier words. Or of thoughts in a head, met by a counter-thought. 'April is the cruellest month'.

Or take the opening not of the first but of the last section of *The Waste Land*.

> After the torchlight red on sweaty faces
> After the frosty silence in the gardens
> After the agony in stony places
> The shouting and the crying
> Prison and palace and reverberation
> Of thunder of spring over distant mountains
> He who was living is now dead

> We who were living are now dying
> With a little patience

The first three lines announce their sound of sense, their intonation an incantation. But it is not at first clear, and it is never at last clarified, in exactly what way the ensuing fourth line comes 'after' those three premonitions. Is it: After A, after B, after C: then D? Or is the fourth line too another After, simply no longer needing to reiterate After since by now the word can tacitly govern the lines? After A, after B, after C, [after] D – and so into what would be the same syntactical dubiety of the fifth and sixth lines. The sequence is clear as to each unit of meaning but not as to its articulate energy. Is it a series of lines that stretches out to the crack of doom, the doom finally arrived at as 'He who was living is now dead'? Then the voice, an Atlas, will have to hold up everything from 'After the torchlight' through to the distant words 'distant mountains', only then coming upon the painful thought it has been painfully seeking. Or is the voice to arrive earlier? After that, and that, and that, then this, this, this. What is being asked in the reading is what is being creatively contemplated in the writing, something finally though only equivocally arrived at: patience.

We don't have a word for such a sequence as Eliot variously creates, and this is to the point; we are not to say 'stanza', but 'verse paragraph' is not quite it, being too prose-based as a term. The last three lines of the sequence end not only with a white space at the end of the line but with a white space after the lines, so that there is doubly no termination, 'No end to the withering of withered flowers' or of withered men, no end to this evocation of the most important form of ending:

> He who was living is now dead
> We who were living are now dying
> With a little patience

And here the art consummates the uncertainties which had earlier been schooling us – by a spiritual discipline – for finality, for the disappointment of finality. The parallelism of the 'He who . . .' / 'We who . . .' lines is very strong but not conclusive;

it does not reveal whether the next line – a conclusion in which nothing is concluded? – is the end of the old thought or the beginning of a new one. Is the antithesis finished at 'dying'? But then 'dying' has not arrived at the endedness of 'dead'.

> Think at last
> We have not reached conclusion, when I
> Stiffen in a rented house.
>
> ('Gerontion')

You are at a loss to give your voice the posture proper to the sentence about dying, since the sequence would not necessarily be: 'We who were living are now dying with a little patience.' It might be:

> We who were living are now dying.
> With a little patience

Lacuna indeed. The former sense of meaning, 'Now that we talk of dying', would have a 'dying fall'; the latter, open-mouthed at the newly beginning end, would suggest 'lips parted, the hope'.

Is 'With a little patience' a retrospect or a prospect? The effect depends upon there being no punctuation supplied such as would placate our impatience and settle the matter: no full stop after 'dying' or after 'patience'.[1] Eliot effected a characteristic insight by means of a characteristic punctuation (brackets again) when, speaking of his recorded reading of *Four Quartets*, he remarked on 'the punctuation (which includes the absence of punctuation marks, when they are omitted where the reader would expect them)'.

---

1 – Since sentences end with full stops or an equivalent punctuation, this is to dissent from Calvin Bedient's 'crafted' assurance (*He Do the Police in Different Voices*, p. 167) that 'the sentence ends . . .', and from his graph:

Crafted for suspense, surprise, and pathos, the sentence ends with the word "patience" as if with the faintest last rumble of the thunder struck into the sky so many centuries ago, a quiver now past all expectancy, exhausting itself quickly in two syllables . . . Toward the end we find a figure of repetition-and-variation, one aligned with anaphora, a graph of what has been twisted awry:

> He who was living   is now dead
> We who are living   are now dying with a little patience

The variation of course jars.

So does the twisting of 'We who were living' to 'We who are living'.

And to what end, all this? The realization of patience, the incarnating of what it is to possess one's soul in patience. For patience is itself a relation of past to future here in the present. To be patient is to relate a future to a past here and now.

> Think
> Neither fear nor courage saves us.
>
> ('Gerontion')

Yet patience may save us. For whereas courage presupposes no such relation of past to future, patience does, like its companions endurance, fortitude and perseverance. All of these are virtues especially important to Eliot in their kinship to tradition, the literary and cultural embodiment of a relation of past to future such as is in the best sense living in the present. In patience, retrospect and prospect meet in a re-affirmation, just as retrospect and prospect meet in the play of Eliot's syntax against his line-endings and his punctuation or lack of it – yet not a complete lack of it, since, as Eliot said, 'verse, whatever else it may or may not be, is itself a system of *punctuation*; the usual marks of punctuation themselves are differently employed.'[1]

It may have been mildly perverse of Eliot to agree to read his poems aloud for recording. For one thing, such a poem as *The Waste Land* is created for the printed page: no actor could voice the spacings, the indentings, the unforeseen capitalizings, or the different effect to the eye of having some French words be in italics and others not. For another thing, many of Eliot's most characteristically powerful effects (the power released by arching a tonal reservation against the sound of sense at other points in the poem) derive from this sense of void, this tonal recognition, implicit in the expression of every experience, of other kinds of experience which are possible. Among them there might be the experience of looking primarily backward as against forward within patience, the more delicate as decision because some combination of the two is always entailed.

In reading his poem for recording, Eliot is obliged to settle for intonations, and so for sounds of sense, which the printed page

1 – *Times Literary Supplement*, 27 September 1928.

can leave as invitations to the exercise of various responsive responsibilities. This necessity in utterance is partly a consequence of the different intimations which the distinct notations of writing and of speaking make inevitable.[1] It is next a consequence of the particular kinds of poems which Eliot mostly writes, poems which are often consciously at a remove from the directly speakable and which therefore confront the sacrifice-acknowledging truth that 'any form of poetry restricts one's liberty'.[2] 'We do not take kindly to the thought that, in order to gain one thing, we may have to give up something else of value.'[3] But a price is always paid; there is no such thing as a free verse. Eliot on the page seeks to profit from the very ineffabilities enforced by print, since print (like everything in life) cannot but entail sacrifice – the only question being whether we can learn how to avail ourselves of sacrifice. Lastly, the limitations of utterance's decisions are a consequence of Eliot's particular powers and convictions, deeply suspicious of the histrionic. 'A very small part of acting is that which takes place on the stage!'[4] Of the greatest actors it may be necessary to say, as was said of David Garrick:

> On the stage he was natural, simple, affecting:
> 'Twas only that, when he was off, he was acting.
> (Goldsmith, 'Retaliation')

Aware that he neither wished nor was cut out to be a great actor, Eliot settled for not being an actor at all, or for being what he judged the least corrupted kind of actor. 'So far as possible, the reciter should not dramatize.'[5] He did not act his poems, he simply read them aloud. He sought only to transmit the lines. Not for him the greatness of Olivier, able to utter Coriolanus's words to Virgilia, 'My gracious silence, hayle', in the spirit of utmost gentleness (since Virgilia's silence has its graciousness

1 – See Eric Griffiths, *The Printed Voice of Victorian Poetry* (1988).
2 – *The Criterion*, xv (1936), 709.
3 – 'Johnson as Critic and Poet', *On Poetry and Poets*, p. 165.
4 – '"Rhetoric" and Poetic Drama', *Selected Essays*, p. 41.
5 – Eliot, as reported in *John O'London's Weekly*, 19 August 1949. I owe my knowledge of this to Ronald Bush, *T. S. Eliot*, p. 270.

when set against the vulgar mobbing of Coriolanus at his victorious return), while at the same time intimating how easily Coriolanus might have been angered by such silence, so that the very same words – 'My gracious silence, hayle' – might have been said acerbly: *Is* it gracious to withhold your welcome? Is it for me to hail you, Virgilia, on such an occasion?

Eliot merely reads. He uses his voice with a studied blankness; this card, which is blank, is something he is forbidden to say, or forbidden to say with the assurance that it could legitimately be said in no other way.

F. R. Leavis was dismayed by Eliot's recorded voice and performance of *Four Quartets*, and attributed the deficiencies (darkly) to there being something wrong with Mr Eliot, something wrong with his relation to his body. The phrase 'lacking in body' has its insinuating power.

It brings home to us, indeed, how good the verse is; but it does so not by teaching us anything about the rhythms – anything we didn't know already from the printed page. The printed page tells us how they go: the verse is so marvellously exact.

Mr Eliot, if a great composer, is not a great, or good, or even a tolerable executant. His voice, as he uses it, is disconcertingly lacking in body. One wouldn't wish him to elocute in the manner of Mr Robert Speaight (whose *actor's* declamation of Mr Eliot's verse empties it), but a capacity for some strength of tone is clearly desirable. Mr Eliot's reading is of course not unintelligent and insensitive in the actor's way, but it is not positively intelligent and sensitive in the way one would have expected of the poet himself. Judged by that standard, it *is* unintelligent. His command of inflexion, intonation and tempo – his *intention*, as performer, under these heads – is astonishingly inadequate. He seems to be governed by a mechanical routine – to be unable to reduce his *clichés* (which suggest the reading of the Lessons) to a sensitive responsiveness.[1]

Such strong criticism lives up to its belief that a capacity for some strength of tone is clearly desirable. But Leavis is signally uninterested in interrogating his own responses, and this makes him both very appropriate and very inappropriate to Eliot's double art of 'sensitive responsiveness', of responses continually responded to. Leavis himself believed in telling people how

1 – *Scrutiny*, xv (1947), 80.

things go; being all of a piece, he accepted that this meant believing that the words of a poem should tell him. There must be no doubt about the rhythms: 'The printed page tells us how they go: the verse is so marvellously exact.' But sometimes the printed page will tacitly acknowledge that both its glory and its peril may reside in its right *not* to tell us how the rhythms or cadences or tones go; glory, because of how uniquely responsive it can be to delegate responsibility, as even God divinely did; peril, because this can so easily become not delegation but evasion of responsibility. When Leavis poises the two halves of his sentence with a colon, 'The printed page tells us how they go: the verse is so marvellously exact', he makes the second half a concomitant of the first. But what if some of the marvellous exactness of the verse in Eliot had been bent not upon telling us how they go but upon declining, in a principled way, so to tell us? There is such a thing as an exactness of reservation or of delegation. Marvell's dry withholdings were a great gift to Eliot:

> I yet my silent judgment keep,
> Disputing not what they believe:
> But sure as oft as women weep,
> It is to be supposed they grieve.
>
> ('Mourning')

Leavis's passionate argument is underdescribed; just *why* is a capacity for some strength of tone (in reading aloud) clearly desirable? Or rather, what might someone achieve, that he or she could not otherwise achieve, by forgoing such strength of tone? What might thereby be seen and shown that would otherwise not be realized? Leavis is markedly unastonished when he says that Eliot's 'command of inflexion, intonation and tempo . . . is astonishingly inadequate'. This response to a poet as great as Eliot (for in 1947 Leavis still unreservedly acknowledged Eliot a great poet) ought to issue in an immediate responsibility: to ask oneself at least what Eliot's intention – 'his *intention*, as performer, under these heads' – *might* conceivably have been, even if a critic were then to hold that the poet misconceived it.

Leavis animates a tissue of prejudices; a living tissue, then, and one very germane to Eliot's enterprise. Notice the merely prejudicial appeal when Leavis accommodates 'the reading of the Lessons' both to '*clichés*' and to 'a mechanical routine'. Perhaps the reading of the Lessons is more to the point than just to furnish a biased snub. The man who had suggested that the ideal form of drama was the Mass would have been happy to accept that one type of an ideal actor (there are others, such as the ballet dancer) might be the priest whose self-abnegation is the negation of personal vanity. Of a vain modern priest, Eliot might have said: 'We asked only that he should transmit the lines, but to transmit lines is beyond the self-control of a modern priest, and so he did what the modern priest does: he "interpreted" them.' At which point it would become clear that one might do worse than render poems aloud as if one were reading the Lessons, especially if they are religious poems, as both *The Waste Land* and *Four Quartets* are. The routine slight to the reading of the Lessons may show only that it is the critic who is 'governed by a mechanical routine'.

Eliot's reading 'is not positively intelligent and sensitive in the way one would have expected of the poet himself'. But finding such expectations balked, one should first of all ask exactly why one had them. 'Not positively intelligent'? Then perhaps negatively intelligent. For the negative and the positive, like a great writer, also have a serious skill at balking expectations: 'the distinction of having, not in a negative but a very positive sense, no style at all'. Or the distinction of having, not in a negative but a very positive sense, no 'sound of sense', but instead a depth which is to be, in both senses, sounded by the person without whom Eliot's sense of void would be merely void: the reader.

Leavis (this thought would have vexed him) promulgated a muscular counterpart to Helen Gardner's more melting idiom. 'The printed page tells us how they go'; or,

As I read I feel myself being directed or played on by a master who obtains his effects without any hesitation or fumbling, who asks only that I should let my heart beat in accordance with his controlling hands.[1]

1 – *The Waste Land* 1972 (1972), p. 20.

Only? Abnegation dissolves here into abdication. And such dissolution is the odd consequence of both Leavis's and Helen Gardner's being too obdurate as to a poet's control, especially in their underestimating the insights of remission. 'And that is flat', announced Frost, in another of his thrillingly one-sided accounts of the sound of sense:

There are tones of voice that mean more than words. Sentences may be so shaped as definitely to indicate these tones. Only when we are making sentences so shaped are we really writing. And that is flat. A sentence *must* convey a meaning by tone of voice and it must be the particular meaning the writer intended. The reader must have no choice in the matter. The tone of voice and its meaning must be in black and white on the page.[1]

Four times, the word 'must', and the first time italicized, just to make sure that we have no choice in the matter. But then the reader of Eliot may offer to the reader of Frost the words uttered in *The Waste Land*: 'Others can pick and choose if you can't.'

Dear Mrs. Equitone

Dr Leavis ought to have felt foxed by Madame Sosostris. For in giving voice to her, Eliot's printed page keeps its cards very close to its chest, among them the card which is blank which she is forbidden to see. If the point about effective verse rhythms really is that then 'the printed page *tells* us how they go', the rhythms with which Eliot endows Madame Sosostris would have to be judged far from effective. But then telling is exactly what her closing lines are, at the same time as telling is what they explicitly speak of. Their movement is so gingerly, itself 'so careful', as to feel like, yes, walking – but on egg-shells, or are they hot coals?

> I see crowds of people, walking round in a ring.
> Thank you. If you see dear Mrs. Equitone,
> Tell her I bring the horoscope myself:

1 – 30 May 1916 (*Selected Letters*, p. 204).

One must be so careful these days.

(*The Waste Land*)

The rhythmical vacuum of the last line, its collusive sucking of us into a paralysing consciousness of any number of possible emphases, inflections or nuances, the way in which it so delicately lays its finger alongside its nose, being a canny word to the wise from someone known to be the wisest woman in Europe, she with pride and cunning availing herself of the dark decorum of 'One': all of this, in its refusal to come clean rhythmically, shows you fear in a hand of cards. It is even something of a relief, after such studiedly sinister caution, such giving away so little except the intimation that much is at stake, to come upon the hallucinatory clarity of the lines which then follow, their rhythms at least looming clear through the fog:

> Unreal City,
> Under the brown fog of a winter dawn,
> A crowd flowed over London Bridge, so many,
> I had not thought death had undone so many.

Mrs. Equitone sounds as if she is a match for Madame Sosostris, and indeed more than a match socially. The name Mrs. Equitone is finely judged in its suggestion of the class-based courteous suasions of such equanimity of tone as Madame Sosostris is either mocking or creepily apeing, such resolutely unemphatic cadences. So gloved. There is something at once naive and vulgar, it is implied, about the usual assumption that *emphasis* constitutes strength. On the contrary, nothing could be stronger than the limp handshake or the freedom from *stress* of the assuredly class-confident.

Attention to Mrs. Equitone can draw out four strands; these are related not as following the one from the other, but as plaited within Eliot's poetry though not only there. First, there are the facts of a particular life and the interpretation of a particular character and social being (Eliot's, here). Second, there is tone as socially constituted and as exercising class pressures. Third, there is the implication of tone in national identity and therefore in national power, such as in the difficulty of mastering (from without) 'the delicious social hints and evasive claims-by-mumble of spoken English'[1] or the difficulty of hearing, let alone voicing, that multiplicity of tones which makes Chinese so courteously resistant to the foreigner. Fourth, there is the involvement of tone in the internationality which is expatriation or transplantation, James's or Conrad's, Eliot's or Beckett's, where the relocation from one subspecies of a language to another (from, say, American English to British English) will have as many intricacies as the move, say, from Polish to English or from English to French. Given all these pitfalls, a willed tonelessness comes to have its attractions. But this can so easily play into the hands of a class or a culture. Tonelessness is often itself an activity of tone, as one may have an expressionless expression on one's face.[2] Once again the vacuum will exert its pull. 'One must be so careful these days.'

Eliot himself, a master at beating the English at their own social games, came to perfect his equitones, which were altogether equable and yet hinted (or was one unjustly imagining it?) something inequitable, something only pretending to be even-handed. Hugh Kenner, fascinated by Eliot's so acting the Englishman, has a comical dossier of these performances.

> Eliot at the Garrick, leaning upon a stick, with an undertaker's demeanor; to whom an old friend, Dr. Bard,
> 'Now do not pretend you are suffering from rheumatism.' And Possum:
> 'I am not pretending that I am suffering from rheumatism. [*con fuoco*] I no longer pretend that I am learned. [*molto con brio*] I no longer pretend I am pretending.'

---

1 – William Empson, *Argufying*, p. 156; it is on the previous page of this lecture on 'Rhythm and Imagery in English Poetry' (1961) that Empson says: 'I should guess that Miss Marianne Moore really talks without stress, and only could be scanned by counting syllables, so that she was quite right to make her innovation.'

2 – Robert Lowell, 'The Quaker Graveyard in Nantucket: VI Our Lady of Walsingham':

> There's no comeliness
> At all or charm in that expressionless
> Face with its heavy eyelids. As before,
> This face, for centuries a memory,
> *Non est species, neque decor*,
> Expressionless, expresses God.

Then: 'And what makes you so pleased with life?'

[Should *you* be italicized? To a shipboard acquaintance who thought the white cliffs of Dover scarcely real, Eliot once replied, 'Oh, they're real enough', a statement to which four meanings may be attached according as each of the four words in turn is stressed.][1]

Kenner, insinuating his square brackets, makes an excellent impresario, as he does too for a later scene at the Garrick Club where Eliot is both being and playing the cheese-connoisseur host. ' "That is a rather fine Red Cheshire . . . which you might enjoy." It was accepted; the decision was not enquired into, nor the intonation of *you* assessed.'[2]

You especially lent itself to Eliot's polished polite disconcertions. Its air of casualness can so easily turn out to be not air at all but the vacuum again. To Kenner's compilation might be added Eliot's exquisite letter of thanks to someone who had written in praise of his work: 'I don't think you could have done it better.' Put the emphasis lightly upon 'better', and there could be no better praise; but put it lightly upon 'you' and there could be no graver pity for the limits of someone's critical powers. What Eliot avails himself of on these occasions is clearly a traditional repertoire of wit's vacancies; there is Shaw thanking someone for an unsolicited book, 'which I shall waste no time in reading', or there is the strong letter of recommendation: 'The Department will be fortunate indeed that gets Dr MacCabe to work for it.' But Eliot gave his own turn to these traditional possibilities of assassination by intonation. He took dextrous advantage of the national colouring (English or American?) which might affect how you found your way through these turns of phrase, their wit then involving a recognition, implicit in the expression of every national experience, of other kinds of national experience which are possible.

The matter of Eliot's nationality was literally settled, or re-settled, in 1927 when he became an Englishman, but the extent to which Englishness became him: this remained both a question and a hiding-place of his power. There is a memoir by

1 – *The Pound Era* (1972), p. 437.
2 – *The Pound Era*, p. 441. The ellipsis is Kenner's.

Brigid O'Donovan, not quite convincingly entitled 'The Love Song of T. S. Eliot's Secretary', which lets us in on how it struck a contemporary at Faber and Faber:

Eliot – he was called Tom by his friends and T.S.E. behind his back – was a big bear-like man in his mid-forties, soberly dressed, with neat back and sides. He moved slowly, turned his head slowly, and lit up his face with a slow smile. He was never cross, was mostly gentle and kind, and usually had some amusing and sarcastic comment to make about every incident or individual who came our way, not excluding members of the firm. Nevertheless, he was a warmhearted and affectionate man, and everyone was very fond of him.[1]

So far so good, including the odd flash, asking to be italicized, within 'some amusing *and sarcastic* comment'; 'nevertheless', too, is a fine touch and might have caused the creator of Madame Sosostris ('Had a bad cold, nevertheless', in a supreme moment of Eliot's rhythm and lineation) to light up his face with a slow smile. But it was not Eliot's face that was his most remarkable physical characteristic.

His most remarkable physical characteristic was his extraordinarily flat voice. He had acquired a perfect educated English accent – I don't think any Englishman, nor an American either, could have guessed he was American by birth and childhood education, but he had overlooked the rise and fall that is particularly typical of English English speech. It may have been that he was confused by speaking French before changing over to an English accent.

This is brightly unmisgiving about the poet who was so alert to misgivings; there is a real charm in the thought that the great poet 'had *overlooked* the rise and fall . . .', and then in the kindly explanation which comes to mind or to hand: 'It may have been that he was confused by speaking French . . .' But goodnaturedly preposterous though the memoir is, it witnesses to some things that are central to Eliot: his voice's being a remarkable physical characteristic (one knows what she means but this is a strange way of putting it, and much to the point in suggesting the way in which a voice, and particularly Eliot's,

1 – *Confrontation*, Fall/Winter 1975, pp. 3–4.

both is and is not physical), and his voice's being extraordinarily flat. 'And that is flat': Frost's insistence on the sound of sense was opposed by a voice of which they say 'this is flat'. The flatness, as Brigid O'Donovan recognized, issues from some inner acknowledgement, not to be made explicit, of a necessary accommodation within English English of something American and something French.

Difficulties of tone and problems of preconception or prejudice have a conjunction in foreignness. An informed preconception may facilitate understanding as powerfully as a misinformed prejudice may impede it. The tone of a foreign language, or of a foreigner using one's native language, is notoriously elusive. Frost's manifesto was therefore altogether bleak about any poetry written in that extremity of foreignness a 'dead language', Frost insisting not that we have little chance of ever being inward enough with the language but that we have no chance.

The living part of a poem is the intonation entangled somehow in the syntax idiom and meaning of a sentence. It is only there for those who have heard it previously in conversation. It is not for us in any Greek or Latin poem because our ears have not been filled with the tones of Greek and Roman talk. It is the most volatile and at the same time important part of poetry. It goes and the language becomes a dead language, the poetry dead poetry. With it go the accents and stresses the delays that are not the property of vowels and syllables but that are shifted at will with the sense. Vowels have length there is no denying. But the accent of sense supercedes all other accent overrides and sweeps it away. I will find you the word 'come' variously used in various passages as a whole, half, third, fourth, fifth, and sixth note. It is as long as the sense makes it. When men no longer know the intonation on which we string our words they will fall back on what I may call the absolute length of our syllables which is the length we would give them in passages that meant nothing. The psychologist can actually measure this with a what-do-you-call-it. English poetry would then be read as Latin poetry is now read and as of course Latin poetry was never read by Romans. Bridges would like to read so now for the sake of scientific exactness. Because our poetry must sometime be as dead as our language must, Bridges would like it treated as if it were dead already.

I say you cant read a single good sentence with the salt in it unless you have previously heard it spoken. Neither can you with the help of all the characters and diacritical marks pronounce a single word unless you have previously heard it actually pronounced. Words exist in the mouth not in books. You can't fix them and you dont want to fix them. You want them to adapt their sounds to persons and places and times.[1]

This catches the wonders of writing, exuberantly overriding caveats as it overrides the protocols of punctuation, for 'the accent of sense supercedes all other accent overrides and sweeps it away'. Its fervour is an affirmation of freedom, since it resists scientistic fixity; and yet, as in all the best freedom-fighting, Milton's *Areopagitica* for instance, there has to be a line drawn. Frost is authentically in favour of freedom for words: 'You want them to adapt their sounds to persons and places and times'; but for him the liberty/licence line is that though a word may sound how it chooses, a word must choose how it sounds. Words are clearly free to take any decision they wish – except that of not making clear their decision. The negative insistence of the passage – upon the truth, unpalatable to classicists, that since words live in the cave of the palate and the shell of the ear, they cannot truly live for us in caves and shells where we ourselves have never lived – is oddly more magnanimous than is the positive insistence that the tone must always be positively indicated.

The tonal recesses of foreignness echo before even the first line of *The Waste Land*, since the epigraph from Petronius does not simply give us both Latin and Greek, it gives us Latin within which Greek is spoken. How confident can we be of tone within such vistas? There is an instability even in the signal difference of the alphabets, which we see with our own eyes.

Nam Sibyllam quidem Cumis ego ipse oculis meis vidi in ampulla pendere, et cum illi pueri dicerent: Σίβυλλα τί θέλεις; respondebat illa: ἀποθανεῖν θέλω.

He may have seen the Sibyl with his own eyes, but can we hear with our own ears what the boys say and what she replies? So much of the life of tone is efficacy of feeling, and Eliot pointed out that 'it is easier to think in a foreign language than it is to feel in it'; what then of feeling in a foreign language which is

1 – 19 January 1914 (*Selected Letters*, pp. 107–8).

ensconced within another foreign language? And both of them dead languages here, in one of which someone says, but not then in our living language, 'I want to die.'

Or what of the tone within the first foreign words of the poem proper, words which are not only foreign but are about the complications of foreignness and whether a Lithuanian be Russian or German or even perhaps simply Lithuanian?

> we stopped in the colonnade,
> And went on in sunlight, into the Hofgarten,
> And drank coffee, and talked for an hour.
> Bin gar keine Russin, stamm' aus Litauen, echt deutsch.

Helen Gardner summons the era:

In the little vignette of a party drinking coffee in the Hofgarten of the Residenz at Munich before the war, the lady who declares so proudly that she isn't Russian but a true-blue German, though she comes from Lithuania, must have made some of the poem's first readers wonder what had happened to her in the confusions out of which the now defunct Baltic States emerged at Versailles.[1]

But how can Helen Gardner declare so confidently that the lady declares this so proudly? For it is not only that the single line of German gives us so little context, but that the snatch which is all that comes to our ear is not of our tongue. The odds are that Helen Gardner is right, but she has not herself 'talked for an hour' there, and has not overheard for an hour. A further kind of wondering is invited by the lines than the one about what had since happened to the woman from Lithuania. Wondering about the tone; not about what her words meant exactly but about what exactly she meant by them. For one marked feature of the foreign eruptions within *The Waste Land* is their initiating themselves as not only foreign but about foreignness: first a Lithuanian speaking German about not being Russian, and then, twenty lines later, someone singing in German about his Irish girl, '*Mein Irisch Kind*'.

What the Lithuanian said is finally overtaken by 'What the

1 – *The Waste Land* 1972, p. 7.

Thunder said'. What the Thunder said is massively clear: DA. What the Thunder meant is massively unclear, or rather is categorically clear since the meaning is a consequence of the category to which the listener belongs. DA is heard differently by each group. This bespoken hearing is prejudgement or prejudice pushed to both unanimity and dissent, unanimity within the group and dissent from the other groups. It is the interpretative community raised to divine heights.

The most straightforward elucidation of DA is this:

Three groups – gods, demons, men – approach the creator Parajapti and each in turn asks him to speak. To each group he answers 'DA'. Each group interprets this reply differently. According to the fable, 'This is what the divine voice, the Thunder, repeats when he says DA, DA, DA: "Control yourselves; give alms; be compassionate."'[1]

But, bringing this home, Eliot reinterprets this foreign parable of interpretation and its categorial inevitabilities. The re-ordering of the sequence may remind us that here too prejudice is sequential. In the words of B. Rajan:

The Thunder's single seed-word, DA, is apprehended in three ways by three orders of experience. The Gods hear it as *Damyata*, man as *Datta* and the Asuras as *Dayadhvam*. This is the sequence in the Sanskrit, and it has the obvious advantage of providing us with an orderly descent through the scale of existence as well as with an indication of the main shortcoming of each of the three orders. Eliot begins with man, and it can be argued that he does so not because of reckless egocentricity but because all three imperatives are heard in the poem as addressed to the human condition.

A further and more important justification of the sequence is that it enables Eliot to put 'control' (*Damyata*) at the end, and it is precisely control which the poem has failed to achieve in contemplating and ransacking its contents and in administering to them the vestigial rites of renewal.[2]

---

1 – B. C. Southam, *A Student's Guide to the Selected Poems of T. S. Eliot* (1968), p. 90.
2 – *The Waste Land in Different Voices*, edited by A. D. Moody (1974), p. 11. For a stealing of Eliot's Thunder, see Calvin Bedient, *He Do the Police in Different Voices*, pp. 195–201: 'Then Spoke the Thunder (Heteromodality, Heteroglossia, Diegesis, Mimesis)'. Cleo McNelly Kearns, *T. S. Eliot and Indic Traditions*, pp. 219–24, is distinctly informative.

But what Eliot then puts at the very end, in his final act both of control and of surrender, is the movement into the other word or words of Sanskrit:

> Why then Ile fit you. Hieronymo's mad againe.
> Datta. Dayadhvam. Damyata.
>
> Shantih   shantih   shantih

The very end, and yet not, since after as many as five full-stops within the antepenultimate and penultimate lines, perfect peace asks no punctuation. Here is no formal ending.[1]

Eliot had two tries at explaining what he had effected with 'Shantih', and neither of them will quite do. The note as originally published reads:

Shantih. Repeated as here, a formal ending to an Upanishad. 'The Peace which passeth understanding' is a feeble translation of the content of this word.

The note as revised in later editions reads: '. . . "The Peace which passeth understanding" is our equivalent to this word.' But neither was quite it. Eliot did well to repudiate the slight to such wording as is a glory of Christianity in English, 'The Peace which passeth understanding'; to call this a feeble translation of the content of the Sanskrit word is not only the wrong kind of surrender but also questionable in itself, for strictly speaking 'The Peace which passeth understanding' is not a *translation* of the content of the Sanskrit. But in remedying this slight, Eliot played into the hands of those who would accuse him of ostentatious pretension in having recourse to Sanskrit, for if 'The Peace which passeth understanding' really is 'our equivalent to this word', why not simply use our equivalent? The thought of an equivalent is both unavoidable and misguided. What Eliot achieves in the words of the poem, and does not

---

1 – A. D. Moody suggested that the early printings of the poem deserve textual consideration (*Thomas Stearns Eliot: Poet*, p. 308), and Cleo McNelly Kearns, *T. S. Eliot and Indic Traditions*, p. 226, persuasively argued that, as in the first edition, there should be a blank line before the last line of the poem; my text therefore departs here from that of 1963.

quite find words for in the notes, is something else: the poignant admission that even so perfect a phrase as 'The Peace which passeth understanding' can no longer effect within our culture what 'Shantih' can effect within its culture. There should be no surprise that this word of Sanskrit which – until Eliot gave it such currency – was itself likely in the most literal sense to pass understanding should mean 'The Peace which passeth understanding'.[1]

Eliot could bring this about as art, though he could not bring it out in commentary. The critics' commentaries take all the tension out of the matter. Lyndall Gordon says: 'Eliot again uses Sanskrit for its novelty, but his explanatory note shows that he thinks in traditional Christian terms: "And the peace of God, which passeth all understanding, shall keep your hearts and minds through Christ Jesus."'[2] But Eliot does not quote the whole of the verse in his note, offering only 'The Peace which passeth understanding';[3] and 'for novelty' is shallow (as if Eliot set great store by novelty in itself). Though there is a sense in which Eliot is indeed thinking in traditional Christian terms, one of his saddened thoughts is that such thinking and feeling have become enfeebled ('a feeble translation . . .'). The poem's pain is in the acknowledgement that it is only outside our own traditional terms that we can now even conceive of the peace which passeth understanding, while at the same time the fact that this is outside our own culture means that we can do no more than conceive of it, cannot enter into and possess it. Eliot was once asked why he had not continued his early studies in Indian philosophy. 'He answered that in order to do so he would have had to learn to use an alien language; as a man of the Western civilization his terms must be found within the

1 – Kearns adduces 'the full context of *shantih* in Hindu tradition, where it is, as anyone raised in that tradition would know at once, simultaneously a mantra, a closing prayer for many ritual occasions, and one of the most prestigious terms in the Sanskrit language for the goal of meditative truth' (*T. S. Eliot and Indic Traditions*, pp. 228–9).

2 – *Eliot's Early Years*, p. 115.

3 – This moves Bedient to say that 'this somewhat brusque paraphrase, however, with its omission of any reference to Christ, virtually reifies "Peace" and thus faces it in the direction of the Orient' (*He Do the Police in Different Voices*, p. 220).

Christian tradition.'[1] This has its discursive dignity, personal and professional, but it is not wiser than the artistic decision taken within *The Waste Land*, where Eliot did truly 'learn to *use* an alien language' – use, because the alienness was not masked or elided, and because the acknowledgement that no such terms could any longer 'be found within the Christian tradition' was the uncompromising gist.

'And the peace of God, which passeth all understanding, shall keep your hearts and minds through Christ Jesus.' But what if, in our Waste Land, our hearts and minds do not any longer keep 'the peace which passeth understanding'?

If such chastened losses and chastening ungainabilities are Eliot's admonitory art here, then Conrad Aiken mistook the poet's purpose:

Why, again, Datta, Dayadhvam, Damyata? Or Shantih? Do they not say a good deal less for us than 'Give: sympathize: control' or 'Peace'? Of course; but Mr Eliot replies that he wants them not merely to mean those particular things, but also to mean them in a particular way – that is, to be remembered in connexion with a Upanishad. Unfortunately, we have none of us this memory, nor can he give it to us; and in the upshot he gives us only a series of agreeable sounds which might as well have been nonsense.[2]

There can be no doubt that Eliot wants the Sanskrit words to mean in a particular way, but '*remembered* in connexion with a Upanishad' is too uninterested in the difference in the depth of 'remembered'. To remember it as a surface item of information is one thing, but to have it alive within a deeper memory is quite another. Aiken sees fit to remind Eliot that 'Unfortunately, we have none of us this memory, nor can he give it to us' – as if Eliot were so stupid and so out of touch as ever to have supposed otherwise. The inaccessibility, except to merely schooled memory, of 'Shantih' is Eliot's piercing point. 'The Peace which passeth understanding' has passed from our memory; 'Shantih' can never be part of *our* memory. There is little peace in the

---

1 – Recorded by Kathleen Raine, in *Yeats and the Occult*, edited by George Mills Harper (1976), p. 82.
2 – (1923); *T. S. Eliot: The Man and His Work*, ed. Tate, p. 201.

thought, but there is much more thought than is suggested by 'only a series of agreeable sounds which might as well have been nonsense'.

Just how unexpectedly wide Eliot's sympathies were in these ethnic and religious contexts (not his empathies, admittedly, but then there is a good unsentimental and unappropriating side to that) can be felt when someone attacks him in exactly the terms within which Eliot himself has often been felt to be aggressively armoured. A letter about Eliot to Eliot's friend and mentor Paul Elmer More on 23 May 1935, from Eliot's fellow-Christian C. S. Lewis, is remarkable not only for its violent vivacity but for the number of points at which it suggests the matters of Eliot's own art without ever inquiring into why this should be so. Fifty years after it was written, the letter asks notice not only because it touches upon some central questions about Eliot's poetry, but because it brings blisteredly alive the profound vexation which Eliot pristinely inspired. All this is in Lewis's letter, plus its being a scarred tissue of prejudicial incitements and excitements.

There may be many reasons why you do not share my dislike of Eliot, but I hardly know why you should be surprised at it. On p. 154 of the article on Joyce you yourself refer to him as 'a great genius expending itself on the propagation of irresponsibility.' To me the 'great genius' is not apparent: the other thing is. Surely it is natural that I should regard Eliot's work as a very great evil. He is the very spearhead of that attack on πέρας which you deplore. His constant profession of humanism and his claim to be 'classicist' may not be consciously insincere, but they are erroneous. The plea that his poems of disintegration are all satiric, are intended as awful warnings, is the common plea of all these literary traitors to humanity. So Juvenal, Wycherley, Byron excuse their pornography: so Eliot himself excuses Joyce. His intention only God knows: I must be content to judge his work by its fruits, and I contend that no man is fortified against chaos by reading the Waste Land, but that most men are by it infected with chaos. The opposite plea rests on a very elementary confusion between poetry that represents disintegration and disintegrated poetry. The Inferno is not infernal poetry: the Waste Land is. His criticism tells the same tale. He may say he is a classicist, but his sympathy with depraved poets (Marlowe, Jonson, Webster) is apparent: but he shows no real love of any disciplined and magnanimous writer save Dante. Of Homer, Sophocles, Virgil, Milton, Racine he has nothing to say. Assuredly he is one of the enemy: and all the more dangerous because he is sometimes disguised as a friend. And this offence is exaggerated by attendant circumstances, such as his arrogance. And (you will forgive me) it is further aggravated for an Englishman by the recollection that Eliot stole upon us, a foreigner and a neutral, while we were at war – obtained, I have my wonders how, a job in the Bank of England – and became (am I wrong) the advance guard of the invasion since carried out by his natural friends and allies, the Steins and Pounds and *hoc genus omne*, the Parisian riff-raff of denationalised Irishmen and Americans who have perhaps given Western Europe her death wound.[1]

Give? Sympathize? Control? Ungenerous, uncompassionate, and uncontrollable, this is itself so wounded and so infected with chaos that one does not even have to leave Eliot to fend for himself: the other great writers blackguarded here will fend for him – Juvenal, Byron, Joyce . . . The idea that Jonson was a depraved and undisciplined poet is depraved and undisciplined. There is comedy in Lewis's untimely belief that Eliot had nothing to say of Milton; next year Eliot was to issue an indictment of Milton innocently entitled 'A Note on the Verse of John Milton'. There is farce in Lewis's indignation about the Bank of *England*. (Wrong bank.) There is burlesque in Lewis's not being able to bring himself to emit a question-mark for his bracketed cry '(am I wrong)'. And as Lewis's yeasty animus rises, there is the pathology of rhetoric and of prejudice, the swerving rage at Eliot as 'the advance guard of the invasion since carried out by his natural friends and allies, the Steins and Pounds and *hoc genus omne*, the Parisian riff-raff of denationalised Irishmen' – at which point his petard hoists Lewis. For what was Lewis but that doubly denationalized Irishman, the Ulsterman who lives in England? It is the old fury, Henry Adams chafing at the Americans let loose in London, Lewis exploding at the denationalized Irishmen who have perhaps given Europe her death wound. Lewis's rhetoric is madly unmisgiving, whereas Eliot's art is lucidly fraught, yet both begin in pain at foreignness and at denationalized disintegration.[2]

1 – This letter is quoted by courtesy of the Rare Book Room, Firestone Library, Princeton University, and used by permission of the Estate of C. S. Lewis.
2 – Derek Brewer gives a happy sketch of Lewis ten years later, reconciled (it would seem) to – though not perhaps with – Eliot, and very Irish: 'T. S. Eliot's work he greatly admired. He was once on a committee with Eliot to revise the translation of

Parisian riff-raff: Eliot's mother had feared for him, yet only in the motherly way of 1910: 'I cannot bear to think of your being alone in Paris, the very words give me a chill. English-speaking countries seem so different from foreign. I do not admire the French nation, and have less confidence in indivi-duals of that race than in English.'[1] But to Eliot it was clear that there were English-speaking countries that were foreign. England, for one. In 1917, an expatriate American in England and to remain so for another ten years, he wrote about Turgenev in a way which combines strength with wistfulness. Of course Eliot was thinking of himself too, and hoping, but there are no sidelong glances, only a direct admiring contemplation of Tur-genev's exemplary achievement:

Turgenev was, in fact, a perfect example of the benefits of transplantation; there was nothing lost by it; he understood at once how to take Paris, how to make use of it. A position which for a smaller man may be merely a compromise, or a means of disappearance, was for Turgenev (who knew how to maintain the role of foreigner with integrity) a source of authority, in addressing either Russian or European; authority but also isolation.[2]

This is the prose of a man steeling himself, there in the wit and penetration of the parenthesis – '(who knew how to maintain the role of foreigner with integrity)' – a parenthesis itself exiled, authoritative, and isolated; guarding its integrity, whereas most brackets are compromises or means of disappearance. How perfectly the poise is maintained in the dubitability admitted by *role*, an acknowledgement of the actorly that must be made one with integrity. Of Byron, Eliot wrote: 'He was an actor who devoted immense trouble to *becoming* a role that he

—

the Psalms and referred to himself, in comparison with Eliot, as a "whippersnapper" – pronounced very Irish, with aspirated initial *hw* and strongly rolled *r*'s' (*C. S. Lewis at the Breakfast Table*, edited by James T. Como, 1979, p. 50). There is a complex comedy in the anecdote (1952) told by William Turner Levy (*Affection-ately, T. S. Eliot*, p. 28): 'At the conclusion of the service, I led Eliot directly across the aisle to meet the rector's wife, who had been alerted that Eliot was coming. She proceeded to introduce each of her three children in turn to "Mr. C. S. Lewis", adding that it was a day they would all remember! I could see that Eliot was vastly amused.'

1 – 3 April 1910; Gordon, *Eliot's Early Years*, p. 33.
2 – *The Egoist*, December 1917.

adopted';[1] complementarily, he saw 'the advantages which both Turgenev and James enjoyed': 'Since Byron and Landor, no Englishman appears to have profited much from living abroad.'[2] Here was an American who had profited much from living abroad, and had devoted immense trouble to *becoming* a role that he adopted, the Englishman.

Eliot later decided not fully to maintain the role of foreigner with integrity. He did not forfeit integrity, but he forfeited foreignness. Or rather, he played down his foreignness in much of his public life (perhaps in his private life too), and in much of his literary and cultural criticism. But he maintained the role of foreigner with integrity in the place where it really mattered: his poetry. Eliot in 1941 wrote of the 'prejudice against patriotic verse', and denied that Kipling's patriotism was 'merely the nostalgia of a man without a country':

To explain away his patriotic feeling in this way is only necessary for those who consider that such feeling is not a proper theme for verse. There are perhaps those who will admit to expression in poetry patriotism on the defensive.[3]

'Defence of the Islands', verses by Eliot to accompany an exhibition of photographs of the war effort, had been distributed in 1940 and published within *Britain At War* (1941). Eliot said that the verses 'cannot pretend to be verse'. His 'patriotism on the defensive' (literally so, not 'defensive' patriotism) issued, in those years, in *Four Quartets*. *Four Quartets*, whose patriotism for England at war is more like Henry James's than Winston Churchill's, remains as occupied with the ways in which its author is not an Englishman as with the ways in which he is, and this in the texture and cadence of the verse as much as in the memories of earlier shores, the rocky Massachusetts sea of 'The Dry Salvages' and 'Its hints of earlier and other creation'. Like the Turgenev he drew, Eliot 'recognized, in practice at least, that a writer's art must be racial – which means, in plain

1 – 'Byron', *On Poetry and Poets*, p. 205.
2 – *Little Review*, August 1918.
3 – *On Poetry and Poets*, p. 243.

words, that it must be based on the accumulated sensations of the first twenty-one years'.

When he wrote that, Eliot was on the eve of thirty. He became an Englishman on the eve of forty. The next year, he dated one of his letters 'St. George's Day', 1928:

Some day I want to write an essay about the point of view of an American who wasn't an American, because he was born in the South and went to school in New England as a small boy with a nigger drawl, but who wasn't a southerner in the South because his people were northerners in a border state and looked down on all southerners and Virginians, and who so was never anything anywhere and who therefore felt himself to be more a Frenchman than an American and more an Englishman than a Frenchman and yet felt that the U.S.A. up to a hundred years ago was a family extension. It is almost too difficult even for H.J. who for that matter wasn't an American at all, in that sense.[1]

The letter has comedy, pathos, resilience, and – because of the rueful third-person and the movement of it all (no pause after 'and who so was never anything anywhere') – an entire absence of self-pity. The sequence of nationalities ('more a Frenchman than an American and more an Englishman than a Frenchman') has a history behind it. Matthew Arnold, consciously uncompromising, had written to Clough about *The Bothie* and the Zeit Geist: 'More English than European, I said finally, more American than English'.[2] Nearer to hand there had been Pound's warning in 1913:

If a man's work require him to live in exile, let him suffer, or enjoy, his exile gladly. But it would be about as easy for an American to become a Chinaman or a Hindoo as for him to acquire an Englishness, or a Frenchness, or a European-ness that is more than half a skin deep.[3]

And the young Eliot, aware of the depth of his own skin, had written of James Huneker in 1909: 'In fact, he is far too alert to be an American; in his style and in his temper he is French.'[4]

1 – To Herbert Read; *T. S. Eliot: The Man and His Work*, ed. Tate, p. 20.
2 – November 1848; *The Letters of Arnold to Clough*, edited by Howard Foster Lowry (1932), p. 95.
3 – *Patria Mia*, p. 47.
4 – *Harvard Advocate*, 5 October 1909.

The tone of the fine letter to Herbert Read can be judged if one sets it beside the preface which Eliot published five months later in 1928, the preface to E. A. Mowrer's *This American World* in which Eliot felt obliged to preclude any personal revelation even while telling the same personal story. There is no self-pity here either, but that is because we are granted little more than a rehearsing of the facts, starched with the publicness of 'I perceived that I . . .' and with clichés such as 'guarded jealously' or 'years of maturity':

My family were New Englanders, who had been settled – my branch of it – for two generations in the South West – which was, in my own time, rapidly becoming merely the Middle West. The family guarded jealously its connexions with New England; but it was not until years of maturity that I perceived that I myself had always been a New Englander in the South West, and a South Westerner in New England; when I was sent to school in New England I lost my southern accent without ever acquiring the accent of the native Bostonian.[1]

'It may have been that he was confused by speaking French before changing over to an English accent.' The man who felt himself to be more a Frenchman than an American had a mother whose words might give him her chill: 'I do not admire the French nation, and have less confidence in individuals of that race than in English'; so it was as well that Eliot felt himself to be more an Englishman than a Frenchman. Since tone (under one aspect) is the expression on the face of the words, and since it is possible though risky to wear an expressionless expression, there is relevance in one of Eliot's warnings against a faceless accentless internationalism. Of the great European writers (Dante, Shakespeare, Goethe), Eliot wrote:

They are local because of their concreteness: to be human is to belong to a particular region of the earth, and men of such genius are more conscious than other human beings. The European who belonged to no one country would be an abstract man – a blank face speaking every language with neither a native nor a foreign accent. And the poet is the least abstract of men, because he is the most bound by his own language: he cannot even

1 – Preface to Edgar Ansel Mowrer, *This American World* (1928), pp. xiii–xiv.

afford to know another language equally well, because it is, for the poet, a lifetime's work to explore the resources of his own.[1]

These days one hears of teachers who grumblingly insist that a student is not permitted to have *two* 'second languages'; Eliot believed that the poet, of all people, is not allowed to have two 'first languages' either.

One of the reasons for learning at least one language well is that we acquire a kind of supplementary personality; one of the reasons for not acquiring a new language *instead* of our own is that most of us do not want to become a different person.[2]

An expatriate must face the fact that he or she will become a different person, and when Eliot moved from the United States of America to England he acquired to some degree a new language instead of his own. He aged, and 'as we age we both live in a different world, and become different men in the same world'.[3] But these complex painful feelings of his about nations and transplantation were responsible for his triumphing over the feeling which writhes in the words 'and who so was never anything anywhere'. That in 1928 was a grim vacuum, there where a worthy sense of place, and of nationality, ought to be. But far from being never anything anywhere, a blank face speaking some language with neither a native nor a foreign accent, Eliot was moved to continue to be a great poet. 'Now and in England'.

1 – 'Goethe as the Sage', *On Poetry and Poets*, p. 216.
2 – 'The Social Function of Poetry', *On Poetry and Poets*, p. 19.
3 – 'Rudyard Kipling', *On Poetry and Poets*, p. 237, within a discussion of Kipling, complicated as he was of nation and of place.

VI

MEDIATION

Between season and season

In 1922 Eliot needed to compare English and American poetry. This involved him in comparing the English language as it was in the two countries; and this in turn meant invoking a third term, French, in order to get purchase on the other two. In his 'London Letter' to *The Dial* in New York, Eliot wrote:

> The English language is of course badly written in both countries. In England it is not ungrammatical, but common; it is not in bad taste, but rather tasteless. English imposes less upon the writer than French, but demands more from him. It demands greater and more constant variation; every word must be charged afresh with energy every time it is used; the language demands an *animosity* which is singularly lacking in those authors who are most publicly glorified for their style.[1]

That the distinctions go very deep for Eliot is clear from the fact that what he says here of words – 'English imposes less upon the writer than French, but demands more from him' – he was later to echo when thinking of the word of God: Eliot affirms 'the Christian view, which demands more, and expects less of human nature, than any other'; 'the Catholic should be too dissatisfied with the world as it is to be afraid of change in itself; nor does he *expect* a great deal of the world at any time, though his *demands* be severe.'[2]

'The language demands an *animosity*': Eliot italicized *animosity* here, just as there he italicized *expect* and *demands*. In

1 – *The Dial*, lxxii (1922), 510–13. I draw here on a page of my essay on American English, in *The Force of Poetry* .
2 – *Time and Tide*, 12 January 1935; *Christian Register*, 19 October 1933.

italicizing, he actualized energies of emphasis which are necessarily pre-emptive and frequently prejudicial. His prose practices are here very different from his poetic ones. As a poet he is marked by refusing to avail himself of those applied emphases which had been available to the less stringent Victorian poets, who often affect an emphasis which they have not effected. Such lines often prove vacuous without these fillings-in, and, since the poets were not sensitive to the positive uses of a tonal vacuum, they ordered their servants, italics, to authorize the words. This, even within good poems.

> Yes! in the sea of life enisled,
> With echoing straits between us thrown,
> Dotting the shoreless watery wild,
> We mortal millions live *alone*.
>   (Arnold, 'To Marguerite – Continued')

'Thou hadst *one* aim, *one* business, *one* desire': the italics betray that although Arnold may have had faith in the Scholar-Gipsy, he did not have faith in 'The Scholar-Gipsy'. If Eliot can be said to have had one aim, one business, one desire, it was to achieve a poetry which would not call upon such demeaning auxiliaries. In the whole of *Prufrock and Other Observations*, there are only two words italicized, both in 'Portrait of a Lady':

> How much it means that I say this to you—
> Without these friendships – life, what *cauchemar*!

And:

> 'Perhaps you can write to me.'
> My self-possession flares up for a second;
> *This* is as I had reckoned.

The former instance keeps its counsel as to whether *cauchemar* is in italics as being emphasized by its oppressive speaker or as not being English (for elsewhere in the volume French goes unitalicized, and in *The Waste Land* French is both italicized and not); and the latter instance flares as protestation and vindictive self-justification.

As a poet, then, Eliot eschewed italics, or reserved them for a seldom pleasure. As a prose-writer, especially when he was in the vicinity of prejudice or animosity or vacuum, he often had recourse to them, with a sense that they were both appropriate and inappropriate to the tricky matter. Italics will set limits to our response; they assist conveniently and dangerously, therefore, when one is considering the propensity to be 'terribly *limited* by prejudice and self-conceit'.[1] Italics are a way of declining to argue, as in Eliot's characterization of Belloc: 'His peculiar function is to attack, not arguments, but *prejudices*; and prejudices are attacked, not with arguments, but with *convictions*.'[2] Agreement is not hereby arrived at, it is set out from, for these are personal elements and 'they appear to us, when we disagree, as *prejudice*, and when we agree, as *wisdom*'.[3] Such italics are an open animus, an emphasis and a tone. 'And that is flat.'

Animus is distinguishable from but is not distinct from prejudice. Like animosity, animus does not have a verb form, or an adjective form, and this gives it an ugly monolithic power different in kind from the variously powerful insinuations of *prejudice*, *prejudicing* and *prejudicial*. The OED definition is a reminder that though animus may be death-dealing, it is itself an impulse of life, extinguishable only in death: 'Actuating feeling, disposition in a particular direction, animating spirit or temper, usually of a hostile character, *hence*, animosity.' The dictionary's instance from 1863 is psychologically and morally subtle: 'an intense feeling, or, as we say, animus; this is the word we use when a speaker or writer, who is labouring to substantiate a defamation, finds it more than he can do to repress emotions, that are not of the most amiable sort, and which he does not choose to avow.'

Animus, then, is a sibling of prejudice. The relation of animus to animation, incarnate in the life of the words, constitutes an aegis of Eliot's development. In the early poems, those in the volumes of 1917 to 1922, the animation of the language is at one with – though not conterminous with – animosity and

1 – *After Strange Gods*, p. 63.
2 – *English Review*, liii (1931), 245.
3 – *Theology*, xlvi (1943), 103.

animus. Animosities are not simply given in to, but they are not given up. Their incitements are continuous with the poems' excitements, even though one of the things which Eliot wishes to excite is a principled concern about how such reflexes are effected, a double warning. Yet for the later Eliot, the Christian Eliot and in particular the Eliot of *Four Quartets*, an essential quest becomes where and how to discover an animation, in the very words, which would not have its deepest source in animosity.

There have since 1942 been readers of *Four Quartets* who have felt that Eliot's poetry lessened its life once it deemed unworthy the earlier insights of animosity; and readers who have felt that, in losing his life of animosity, Eliot found other and deeper sources of life and of animation for his words; and readers (Leavis the most passionate) sure that *Four Quartets* is damaged by an animosity that is unacknowledged and unjustified – against the human, against time, and against the supreme achievement of the human within time: our daily language.

Within the terms of prejudice, then (terms which constitute one aspect under which Eliot's poetry may be seen), the story may be elementarily told as this: early Eliot is characterized by incitements both to prejudice and to not being sentimentally prejudiced against prejudice; late Eliot forgoes these incitements, though necessarily with a sufficient sense of their reality for the word *forgoes* to mean something. But where then, in the terms of such a story, does this leave the poems that come between *The Waste Land* and *Four Quartets*? It leaves them where it finds them: between.

This is neither a derogation from them nor a description of what happens to be their place on the graph of Eliot's development. For it is not their plight or their position merely, this being between, it is their occupation and their element. In the 1920s in which he became forty, Eliot must have hoped, must have trusted, that these poems were not to be his last words but rather a stage in his patient achievement. 'The Love Song of J. Alfred Prufrock' had proved not to be what he had once feared, his swan song; the same hope (barely prayable) must have been invested in 'The Hollow Men', itself a creaking croaking death-song about singing. As always, the more-than-difficulty for the artist is to create something which is both true in and of itself and also true to subsequence, a stage yet not merely a stage. Eliot's preoccupation with the lifetime of an artist, which made him the first critic to insist that it was Shakespeare's whole *oeuvre* which constituted Shakespeare's greatest work, came to coincide with his preoccupation with 'a lifetime burning in every moment'.

When Eliot wrote 'The Hollow Men' (1925) and *Ash-Wednesday* (1930), he was not between poems, as a poet might turn humbly to translation, knowing himself between poems. Eliot was writing poems which were themselves between-poems. They are, for instance, transitional poems, not only as transitions for Eliot, but as meditations on the nature of transitions. Or of transit, 'Journey of the Magi' (1927) and 'A Song for Simeon' (1928) being different comprehensions of what it is to be between two worlds, one dead, the other anything but powerless to be born.

'Between' had been needed for a void in *The Waste Land* ('throbbing between two lives'), as it was to be for a reconsideration of a related void ('Being between two lives') in 'Little Gidding':

> There are three conditions which often look alike
> Yet differ completely, flourish in the same hedgerow:
> Attachment to self and to things and to persons,
>   detachment
> From self and from things and from persons; and,
>   growing between them, indifference
> Which resembles the others as death resembles life,
> Being between two lives – unflowering, between
> The live and the dead nettle.[1]

1 – Eliot wrote to John Hayward, who had difficulty with these lines which had at this stage 'between / The live and dead nettle': 'You know as well as I do that the dead nettle is the family of flowering plant of which the White Archangel is one of the commonest and closely resembles the stinging nettle and is found in its company. If I wrote "the live nettle and the dead" it would tend to suggest a dead stinging nettle instead of a quite different plant, so I don't see that anything can be done about that.' Helen Gardner comments: 'I suspect that Hayward, along with many readers of the poem, was ignorant of "the White Archangel" and had taken it that the "unflowering" plant of "indifference" grew between a live and a dead specimen of the same

But the preposition 'between' comes to flower as nowhere else in the poems which come between *The Waste Land* and *Four Quartets*. Twenty successive lines of 'The Hollow Men' are swayed by it:

> Between the idea
> And the reality
> Between the motion
> And the act
> Falls the Shadow
>
> *For Thine is the Kingdom*

There are three such chantings, always with a spectral voice at the margin coming between the obduracies of 'Between'.

'Between' constitutes a crux for Eliot for two reasons. First, that it is an intersection of these three, and only these three, prepositional functions: Space, Time, and Relation.[1] Though 'at', 'in' and 'on' apply to Space and to Time Position (not the same as Time), and 'by' applies to Space and Time, 'between' is apparently unique among English prepositions in incarnating this trinity of Time, Space and Relation.

> If space and time, as sages say,
> Are things that cannot be,
>
> ('Song')[2]

space and time are nevertheless things that cannot be ignored, and this means that 'between' will have particular

—

plant. The image is very apt, when explained: indifference, that neither stings nor bears a flower, being between selfish love that stings and unselfish that bears a white flower. Eliot did do something about it, by inserting "the" before "dead nettle", although I doubt if this protected readers from misapprehension' (*The Composition of Four Quartets*, p. 200).

1 – See Randolph Quirk, Sidney Greenbaum, Geoffrey Leech, and Jan Svartvik, *A Comprehensive Grammar of the English Language* (1985), Chapter 9, on prepositions, and especially 9.7. All prepositions deal in relations but not in the particular sense given by grammarians to Relation, 'relative position → abstract relation between participants: a fight/match *between* X and Y; relationship/contrast/affinity *between* two things' (9.32). On *The Waste Land* and 'in-betweenness', see Maud Ellmann, *The Poetics of Impersonality* (1987), pp. 95–8.

2 – Published 1905, revised 1907 (*Poems Written in Early Youth*).

reponsibilities, especially in poems which undertake the cross-
ings which mark these middle poems of Eliot's.

The second feature of 'between' which makes it indispensable
to these athwart poems is its antithetical nature, unusual for a
preposition and perhaps unique. For 'between' has the force
which Freud attributes to the antithetical sense of primal
words,[1] the force of meaning opposite things, or, here, of
serving opposite functions. Freud's insight, which is related to
his conviction that in dreams the category of contraries and
contradictories is disregarded, is famously applicable to such
verbs as 'cleave' (stick together or cut apart) and 'unbend' ('He
was a stiff and unbending man, but he could unbend on
occasion'), or to such an adjective as 'certain', the duplicity of
which we have grown used to ignoring or using:

> And evening newspapers, and eyes
> Assured of certain certainties,
>
> ('Preludes')

– 'certain' as left unspecifiedly uncertain, or as making assurance doubly sure? But a preposition is a part of speech which we
are unaccustomed to considering as antithetical, as not a direction but an axis. 'Between', though, is at once a joining and a
separation, disconcertingly accommodating itself both to acts of
mediation or meeting and to acts of obstruction or disjuncture.

In the space which separates two points; in the direct line which joins two
points.

Expressing the relation of the continuous space, or distance, which extends
from one point to another, and separates them, or of a line which passes
from one to the other and unites them.

Of the lines in *Ash-Wednesday* VI beginning

> And the lost heart stiffens and rejoices
> In the lost lilac and the lost sea voices
> And the weak spirit quickens to rebel

1 – 1910; reprinted in *Collected Papers* (1925), vol. iv.

Hugh Kenner has written: 'Here every noun, verb and adjective pulls two ways.'[1] *Ash-Wednesday* has constant recourse to the preposition which pulls two ways, 'between'. Twenty times, 'between' constitutes the relations within *Ash-Wednesday*. *Ash-Wednesday* is the only poem by Eliot which has a hyphen in its title; some of Eliot's best commentators have failed to transmit the hyphen,[2] yet it matters because it is a quintessence of 'between', at once joining and separating what it compounds.

Ash-Wednesday practises the dispositions of 'between'. There is, for instance, the balance which has on either side of the 'between' not just equipollence but identity, a balance, though, which is itself antithetical in that it may be the face of hope or of despair, the blessing of mercy or the curse of justice. Mercy can levelly begin a section of the poem (IV), against all syntactical odds, with an uninterrogative 'Who', leading into a line which settles 'between' securely by its twin pair:

> Who walked between the violet and the violet

Yet mercy is not complaisant, and is moved at once by its knowledge of eternal dolour to variegate its cadence and its 'between', moving the preposition now to the brink of the line and then reassuring us by the happiness of the variegation which ensues, so that the perfect match of the violet and the violet is not threatened but made strong by the asymmetry of the various ranks of varied green:

> Who walked between the violet and the violet
> Who walked between
> The various ranks of varied green
> Going in white and blue, in Mary's colour,
> Talking of trivial things
> In ignorance and in knowledge of eternal dolour
> Who moved among the others as they walked,
> Who then made strong the fountains and made
>   fresh the springs

1 – *The Invisible Poet*, p. 226.
2 – Helen Gardner, Lyndall Gordon and Ronald Bush among them.

This is the benign counterpart to the malign equipollence in the next section of the poem, where the symmetry is anything but reassuring, and where 'between', again at first within the line and then at the line-ending, contains no comfort although the sufferers are not debarred from prayer implored:

> Will the veiled sister pray for
> Those who walked in darkness, who chose thee and
>   oppose thee,
> Those who are torn on the horn between season and
>   season, time and time, between
> Hour and hour, word and word, power and power, those
>   who wait
> In darkness?

The extreme equivocating power of 'between', its serviceable lending of itself to the tender or the punitive, which is extendedly alive in these lines from *Ash-Wednesday*, had crystallized for 'A Game of Chess' in *The Waste Land*: 'The ivory men make company between us'. 'This line was omitted at Vivien Eliot's request. The author restored it, from memory, when he made a fair copy of the poem for the sale in aid of the London Library in June 1960.'[1] What makes the line so cutting is the dark double-edgedness of 'between'. What is it, to *make company between* two people? It is not the same as keeping them company, or as making a bond between them. 'Between' becomes an impediment admitted in the marriage of untrue minds.

'Between' in *Ash-Wednesday* may be a state, or a hinge, or a fearful responsibility, 'Wavering between the profit and the loss'. 'This is the time of tension between dying and birth'. And there is the moment which returns to the earlier between-poem, when *Ash-Wednesday* crosses to 'The Hollow Men', to its dream-crossing to the twilight kingdom, along the line 'The dreamcrossed twilight between birth and dying'.

Eliot's Ariel poems grasp the word: the simplest childlike physicality of it in 'Animula', with the infant 'Moving between

1 – *The Waste Land: A Facsimile and Transcript*, p. 126.

the legs of tables and of chairs,' or the old man's tentative idiosyncrasy of it in 'Marina', turning his hard-of-hearing head for 'Whispers and small laughter between leaves and hurrying feet'.[1] And, coming between these Ariel poems and *Four Quartets*, there will be the sequence of 'Landscapes' (1934–6), being between and contemplating it:

> Children's voices in the orchard
> Between the blossom- and the fruit-time:
> Golden head, crimson head,
> Between the green tip and the root.
>
>   ('I. New Hampshire')

Here the essence of 'between' is incarnate in the two hyphens, both joining and separating, with the first one waiting patiently to be consummated by time: 'Between the blossom- and the fruit-time'. The tone is unmistakable and yet the minutiae are ineffable; the voice cannot say a hyphen, and the syntax of the line 'Between the blossom- and the fruit-time' is such that 'the blossom-' could well be construed or heard as 'the blossom'.[2] The difference is miniature but substantial, since instead of the quite separated seasons ('between season and season') or manifestations (blossom and fruit) there is the seasonal continuity through 'between' in the filament trustingly thrown forward by the hyphen, 'the blossom-', waiting with patient confidence to be fulfilled in and by 'time'. It is such a continuity as exists more robustly, though as mysteriously, in the thought and the wording of 'Between the green tip and the root'.

---

1 – 'The phrases "small laughter *between* leaves" and "*under* sleep" introduce a deeper mystery, arising from the way the prepositions of place promise a kind of concreteness, a location for the laughter, which the nouns at once withdraw' (Graham Martin, *Eliot in Perspective*, p. 114). In the manuscript now in the Bodleian Library, the draft of this line of 'Marina' does not have 'between'.

2 – It is true that Eliot reluctantly turned down a suggestion of John Hayward's for 'Little Gidding' II: 'I am afraid that "down-cast", that is, with a hyphen between "down" and "cast", would hardly do because the word will be spoken much the same whether there is a hyphen or not' (Gardner, *The Composition of Four Quartets*, p. 176). But this is a different case, both in that Eliot was resisting the unwanted 'downcast' and in that this is not a counterpart to the expectant hyphen of 'Between the blossom- and the fruit-time'.

Eliot makes differently much of 'between' in another of the 'Landscapes':

> Here the crow starves, here the patient stag
> Breeds for the rifle. Between the soft moor
> And the soft sky, scarcely room
> To leap or soar.
>
> ('IV. Rannoch, by Glencoe')

'Scarcely room': no more than there is room for a main verb in the second sentence. Room only for a word to re-arrange itself, as 'moor' turns to occupy the space of 'room', the perfectly fitting and patient anagram, or re-tracing of the steps, as a type of rhyme.

The relation of these aspects of 'between' to prejudice in these between-poems of Eliot's is triangular, and is a matter of mediation. 'Between' is mediation; Christ, variously craved in these poems, is the Mediator; prejudice or prejudication is what mediates for us all, whether individually or socially, between the multifariousness of impressions and the organization of the ideal, or between experience and knowledge.[1] Prejudice comes between experience and knowledge, this with the inevitable doubleness of what it is to come between, either as protectively mediating or as threateningly impeding. Here the necessary term, kin to prejudice, is generalization. To generalize is to be an idiot, said a poet who was no idiot and who was generalizing; Blake's version of the Cretan Liar paradox is analogous to the difficulties presented by an unprejudiced consideration of prejudice. 'Ethnic prejudice is an antipathy based upon a faulty and inflexible generalization.'[2]

The price paid for generalization was apparent to Eliot, so he

---

1 – For some of the philosophical implications of the immediate and the mediate, see Bradley: 'It is matter of the most ordinary experience that the mediated and complex should appear immediate and simple' (*Collected Essays*, i, 15); and Eliot: 'And if anyone assert that immediate experience, at either the beginning or end of our journey, is annihilation and utter night, I cordially agree'; 'On the other hand, as we need to be reminded, we have no direct (immediate) knowledge of anything: the "immediately given" is the bag of gold at the end of the rainbow' (*Knowledge and Experience in the Philosophy of F. H. Bradley*, pp. 31, 151).
2 – Allport, *The Nature of Prejudice*, p. 10.

could unequivocally praise Charles-Louis Philippe even though the terms had to be equivocal: 'He had a gift which is rare enough: the ability not to think, not to generalize.'[1] But not all generalization is to be eluded, and Eliot set himself to the other half of the truth:

The true generalization is not something superposed upon an accumulation of perceptions; the perceptions do not, in a really appreciative mind, accumulate as a mass, but form themselves as a structure; and criticism is the statement in language of this structure; it is a development of sensibility.[2]

This, as Eliot would have agreed, is more easily said than done, given the old entanglement of perception with preception. Eliot is therefore at his most persuasive when he resorts not to exposition but to a paradox compacted in the very wording: 'It is difficult – it is perhaps the supreme difficulty of criticism – to make the facts generalize themselves.'[3] This offers neither a permissive thought, 'let the facts generalize themselves', nor a coercive one, 'generalize the facts', but a teasing contrariety of difficulty: 'It is difficult – it is perhaps the supreme difficulty of criticism – to make the facts generalize themselves.' Here responsibility meets delegation in such an arch as sustains the tonal achievements of great poetry. Eliot's taut apophthegm has its creative relation to the cunning arts of society, as with a lady knowledgeable about Shakespeare and about Chopin:

> Among the smoke and fog of a December afternoon
> You have the scene arrange itself – as it will seem to do –
> With 'I have saved this afternoon for you';
> And four wax candles in the darkened room,
> Four rings of light upon the ceiling overhead,
> An atmosphere of Juliet's tomb
> Prepared for all the things to be said, or left unsaid.
>
> ('Portrait of a Lady')

1 – Preface to *Bubu of Montparnasse*, p. 11.
2 – 'The Perfect Critic', *The Sacred Wood*, p. 15.
3 – 'Philip Massinger', *Selected Essays*, p. 205.

Negative capability

'The Hollow Men' comes between *The Waste Land* and the rescuing of Eliot, five years later, from his anguish at the waste land. The title 'The Hollow Men', since it was formed (Eliot says) by combining Kipling's 'The Broken Men' with Morris's 'The Hollow Land', has thereby a subterranean continuity with *The Waste Land* which goes deeper than the manifest syntactical shaping of *The Waste Land* / 'The Hollow Men'. Gone from 'The Hollow Men' are all the incitements to and of prejudice: the names which invite, the stereotypes which solicit.

The vacuum abides, and its conflux with prejudice is what it always was. In the terms of Fontenelle's exchange between Strato and Raphael, and of Pound's exchange with Fontenelle and with Eliot: 'We should root out all prejudice': 'But reason would hunt out all our old notions and leave nothing else in their place. She would create a species of vacuum. And how could one bear this?'[1] This impinged on Eliot: on a particular page of *After Strange Gods* (p. 41), he writes of Pound in terms of prejudice ('His powerful and narrow post-Protestant prejudice peeps out from the most unexpected places'), after having just written of a vacuum: 'Confucius was not born into a vacuum; and a network of rites and customs, even if regarded by philosophers in a spirit of benign scepticism, make a world of difference.'

In 'The Hollow Men', it is not that a vacuum has been filled, rather that a hollowness has been admitted. If there are no incitements to prejudice, it is because there are no incitements to anything except the pallidly appalled. The poem is affecting as a triumph of affectlessness, a movement away from wrong feeling but into a feeling of feelinglessness, of 'Paralysed force, gesture without motion'. In its extirpation of prejudice, reason 'would create a species of vacuum. And how could one bear this?' One could bear it by passing into a limbo-world where feeling is powerless to be borne. 'Here is a place of disaffection', in the words of 'Burnt Norton', 'Filled with fancies and empty of meaning'. Hollow. The hollow men have no dangerous lean-

1 – *The Egoist*, May 1917.

ings, because their malaise has passed beyond danger (as a man with terminal cancer is not in *danger* of dying); a leaning is for them nothing but a slackening, an indifference, a plaintive acquiescence:

> We are the hollow men
> We are the stuffed men
> Leaning together
> Headpiece filled with straw. Alas!

A lassitude: it is impossible to imagine Alas! uttered with less likelihood of wringing the heart, except at the thought of this very fact. The exclamation, with its limp exclamation-mark, is at once full of effect and empty of affect. It has a tonelessness which is a bitter travesty of that creative abstention from decisive tone which accompanies the living dramatic power of Ah or Oh. Where in dramatic writing, whether for the stage or not, there is a multiplicity of possibilities as to tone, the impossibility being only the choosing once and for all from such an *embarras de richesses*, here there is abject poverty of spirit, of will, and of being; here there is the impossibility of any living tone. Instead of competition and solicitation, there is a dead sound.

> We are the hollow men
> We are the stuffed men
> Leaning together
> Headpiece filled with straw. Alas!
> Our dried voices, when
> We whisper together
> Are quiet and meaningless
> As wind in dry grass
> Or rats' feet over broken glass
> In our dry cellar

Meaningless, not rising even to meaning Death, though being the shape of it. 'Shape without form, shade without colour' –

> If shape it might be call'd that shape had none
> Distinguishable in member, joynt, or limb,

> Or substance might be call'd that shadow seem'd,
>> (*Paradise Lost*, II, 667–9)

Eliot's cue, '*A penny for the Old Guy*', hovers between a subtitle and an epigraph.[1] It calls up the old energies of prejudicial animosities: Catholic against Protestant, Protestant against Catholic, terrorism attempted and then terror executed upon a man, and upon his faith, both doomed to be execrated every year – a ritual hateful in the prejudicial power which it once possessed, and yet scarcely less hateful (only differently so) in the hollow affectlessness of the bonfires of November the Fifth, Guy Fawkes' Day.[2]

> Please to remember
> The Fifth of November,
>> Gunpowder treason and plot;
> We know no reason
> Why gunpowder treason
>> Should ever be forgot.

They might be honourably forgotten if they had been forgiven. Or they might be remembered, valuable to some degree if only

1 – In the *Collected Poems*, the poem is given a title-page: 'The Hollow Men / 1925 / *Mistah Kurtz – he dead*'; and then has at the head of the poem itself: 'The Hollow Men / *A penny for the Old Guy*'. This is not the same as having simply two epigraphs as is the case with *Sweeney Agonistes* or with 'Burnt Norton'. Bush says: 'When he affixed the Guy Fawkes Day epigraph to "We are the hollow men" . . .', but the poem as published has '*A penny for the Old Guy*' before, not after, the section-numbering 'I' ('We are the hollow men'), which makes it speak to the whole poem, though it does not do so exactly as does '*Mistah Kurtz – he dead*' since the Conrad epigraph commands the title-page. 'His very last act [of composition and ordering] was to append the epigraph "Mistah Kurtz – he dead" ' (Bush, *T. S. Eliot*, pp. 95–6), but neither 'the epigraph' nor 'an epigraph' will quite catch what Eliot is elusively doing here with the two premonitions.

2 – Bush takes the Guy Fawkes ritual as still genuinely alive: 'The English people do not simply remember the fate of Guy Fawkes, they re-enact it every year. And the forms of their re-enactment partake of that primitive vitality of rhythm and style which, Eliot said in 1923, was the source of "*all* art", especially poetry' (*T. S. Eliot*, p. 97). But vitality is what the hollow men neither have nor want, and Eliot seems to me to have chosen Guy Fawkes' Day for the opposite reason from Bush's, for its being essentially extinct and hollow, a mere travesty of that primitive vitality which he valued in, say, the music hall of Marie Lloyd. Guy Fawkes' Day is to ritual what the hollow men's nullity is to the *via negativa*.

because alive in a living world of angers and judgements and prejudices and convictions, a world in which men gave their lives for their faiths. But to the hollow men the 'gunpowder treason and plot' are neither remembered nor forgotten, they are straw that fills the headpiece. Eliot remembers gunpowder treason and plot when he buttonholes the passer-by with his children's cadging cry 'A penny for the Old Guy', but he also takes care not to include the remembrance within the poem itself (a poem evoking a deadness beyond animosity), reserving the atavistic folk-memory for the differently prejudicial pressure of his subtitle-epigraph.

'The language demands an *animosity*': the extraordinary art of 'The Hollow Men' is its evocation of a catatonic spiritual state which is the worse for lacking animosity even of an evil kind.

> *Here we go round the prickly pear*
> *Prickly pear prickly pear*
> *Here we go round the prickly pear*
> *At five o'clock in the morning.*

The effect here is disturbing because the lines are so lacking in affect; the horror of them is not the pointed pain that invades the nursery world of 'Here we go round the mulberry bush' but the differently horrible feeling that, paralysed within this hollow-ness, it makes not the faintest difference whether we go round the mulberry bush or a prickly pear. 'If you pricke us doe we not bleede?' If Jews, yes; if the hollow men, no. The laceration of the prickly pear lines is not that they feel like a laceration but that they are so without feeling. Not callous, not sadistic, but drained of all affect. Their being without any feeling except that of feelinglessness is a particular challenge to a poet convinced that an important function of intelligence is 'the discernment of exactly what, and how much, we feel in any given situation'.[1] For what if 'we feel' were to meet 'We are the hollow men'? The hollow men may not just deny but elude intelligence. Kenner misguidedly seeks to bring them back within the orbit of Eliot's

1 – *The Egoist*, November 1917.

powers, rather than leaving Eliot as working with impotence; Kenner accommodates the hollow men to social satire or political disparagement when he says that they 'epiphanize the flaccid forbearance of an upper-middleclass twentieth-century community, where no one speaks loudly, and where the possession of an impeccably tailored uniform marks one as unlikely to disturb the silence'.[1] But the poet who rejected 'a Hell for the *other people*' would not have busied himself with a limbo for the other people.

'So far as we are human, what we do must be either evil or good; so far as we do evil or good, we are human; and it is better, in a paradoxical way, to do evil than to do nothing: at least, we exist.'[2] The hollow men are not human, or they do not exist, or they exist only as eternally suffering (in Hardy's word) 'exist-lessness'.

Eliot remarked of a character in a play by Marston: 'Balurdo, like the others, is so unreal that to deny his reality is to lend him too much existence'.[3] Balurdo is one of the hollow men, as his name suggests (stupid or stupefied, senseless or sense-less) and as Eliot appreciated: he said of Marston's minor characters here that they

are as completely lifeless as the major characters. Whether decent or indecent, their drollery is as far from mirth-provoking as can be: a continuous and tedious rattle of dried peas. And yet something is conveyed, after a time, by the very emptiness and irrelevance of this empty and irrelevant gabble; there is a kind of significant lifelessness in this shadow-show. There is no more unarticulated scarecrow in the whole of Elizabethan drama than Sir Jeffrey Balurdo. Yet Act V, Sc. i. of *Antonio's Revenge* leaves some impression upon the mind, though what it is we may not be able to say.

What Eliot says here may leave upon our minds the impression that 'The Hollow Men' was the inspired turning to effect of what in Marston had proved so bafflingly ineffectual: an utter affectlessness. 'We can say of the scene, as of the play, that

1 – *The Invisible Poet*, pp. 161–2.
2 – 'Baudelaire', *Selected Essays*, p. 429.
3 – 'John Marston', *Selected Essays*, pp. 225–6.

however bad it is no one but Marston could have written it.' The play evokes (Eliot quoted this) 'the numb'd earth'. Lifeless, the tedious rattle of dried peas; lifeless, the hollow men's 'dried voices'. Empty, 'this empty and irrelevant gabble', as are the 'empty men' of the poem. 'There is a kind of significant lifelessness in this shadow-show':

> Between the emotion
> And the response
> Falls the Shadow

There may have been 'no more unarticulated scarecrow in the whole of Elizabethan drama than Sir Jeffrey Balurdo', but in 'The Hollow Men' Eliot articulated an even greater degree of unarticulated gangling:

> We are the hollow men
> We are the stuffed men
> Leaning together
> Headpiece filled with straw. Alas!

The hollow men do not acknowledge the vacuum or the void, even while they enjoy none of the complacency or happiness which Eliot sensed in his acquaintances: 'They may be very good, or very happy, they simply seem to miss nothing, to be unconscious of any void – the void that I find in the middle of all human happiness and all human relations, and which there is only one thing to fill.'[1] The hollow men, possessing and possessed by hollowness, not vacuum or void, are at once filled and hollow:

> We are the hollow men
> We are the stuffed men

In their deprivation of affections and of affect, they have arrived only at a lethal travesty of spiritual mortification. Defending St John of the Cross, and himself, to Bonamy Dobrée, Eliot urged that the epigraph chosen for *Sweeney Agonistes* ('Hence the soul

1 – To Paul Elmer More (Margolis, *T. S. Eliot's Intellectual Development 1922–1939*, p. 142).

cannot be possessed of the divine union, until it has divested itself of the love of created beings') had to be understood in relation to the Way of Contemplation: 'merely to kill one's human affections will get one nowhere, it would be only to become rather more a completely living corpse than most people are.'[1]

'At least, we exist': Eliot's essay on Baudelaire judged him 'man enough for damnation', and it located Baudelaire's accessibility to religious experience within the fertile negativity of *ennui*, that deathliness which has a positive possibility denied to or denied by the hollow men. Accidie, etymologically 'the non-caring state', can at least be evil, since it is the cardinal sin of torpor; this is more than the hollow men can be, though it might have been the saving of them as it may have been of Baudelaire.

His *ennui* may of course be explained, as everything can be explained, in psychological or pathological terms; but it is also, from the opposite point of view, a true form of *acedia*, arising from the unsuccessful struggle towards the spiritual life.[2]

'Not in a negative but a very positive sense': this (which was said by Eliot of a vacuum of style, the year after 'The Hollow Men') is beyond the spiritual reach of the forms peopling – though that is scarcely the word – this the first of Eliot's between-poems, 'The Hollow Men'. But the positive sense of something negative is what was achieved in the consummation of the between-poems, *Ash-Wednesday*.

Instead of a headpiece unceremoniously filled with straw, a forehead ceremonially marked with ashes. Instead of the way the world ends, the way Lent begins. Instead of 'Please to remember / The Fifth of November', this: 'Remember, man, that thou art ashes, and to ashes thou shalt return.' And yet the bonfire had turned the Guy Fawkes effigy to ashes; the bonfire is in its origins a bonfire, and our harmless bonfire-nights were once in deadly earnest. *Bonfire*: 'a fire in which heretics, bibles, or proscribed books were burnt.'

The differences between *Ash-Wednesday* and 'The Hollow

1 – *T. S. Eliot: The Man and His Work*, ed. Tate, p. 84.
2 – *Selected Essays*, p. 423.

Men' are immense, and yet we are invited to try to measure them, since the later poem so sets itself to redeem the earlier one, not by rescinding it but by seeking the benign form of the energies which were there so malignly cauterizing as to leave the hollow men unable to muster even the perilous energies of malignancy. The accents of *Ash-Wednesday* are from the beginning at once poignantly like and unlike the accents with which 'The Hollow Men' begins. For at this stage of spiritual discipline the alternative to negative hollowness is something which is strangely close to the affectless, not in a negative but a very positive sense: something which neither stiffens towards conclusion (as Gerontion does) nor goes limp, 'leaning together' (as the hollow men do). 'Teach us to care and not to care': this aspires to a Christian paradox at once spiritual and corporeal like yoga, a paradox of disciplined relaxation, of an effort towards effortlessness, an effort to be unforced, yet once more to possess its soul in patience.

Because I do not hope to turn again
Because I do not hope
Because I do not hope to turn
Desiring this man's gift and that man's scope
I no longer strive to strive towards such things
(Why should the agèd eagle stretch its wings?)
Why should I mourn
The vanished power of the usual reign?

Because I do not hope to know again
The infirm glory of the positive hour
Because I do not think
Because I know I shall not know
The one veritable transitory power
Because I cannot drink
There, where trees flower, and springs flow, for there
    is nothing again

This so yearns for repose as to undertake not to repine. The allusion to Shakespeare's Sonnets, which might once have been a flash of justified pride, has been subdued to an admission of how easy it is for envy (the subject of this Sonnet 29) to be at work in alluding. Better the flat fatigue of 'Desiring this man's gift and that man's scope', where all desire to be ostentatious, to catch a new light, has gone from this dulled and humble turn, this admission: 'Desiring this mans art, and that mans skope'. Shakespeare's art and scope are humbly acknowledged to be much greater than anything striven for in *Ash-Wednesday* – and yet the spiritual paradox of the poem's prayer is that one may be granted such things exactly because one no longer strives to strive towards such things. 'Though I do not wish to wish these things': not 'though', *because*. Shakespeare's 'art' has been replaced by 'gift', both as a talent (still, as yet, seeking consummation in achievement, in art), and as something given not only to Shakespeare but as given by him to a later poet who might avail himself of allusion. Then there is the further allusion, by which Shakespeare's glorious line, 'The uncertaine glory of an Aprill day',[1] is clouded and lessened to 'The infirm glory of the positive hour'. *Positive*, as too assured, too knowing, too confident; and yet there is something truly positive about the negativity of the uncompetitive unstriving dealings with Shakespeare here. The glory of the positive hour is infirm, just because of its being so positive ('Assured of certain certainties'), in comparison with 'negative capability':

Several things dovetailed in my mind, & at once it struck me, what quality went to form a Man of Achievement especially in Literature & which Shakespeare possessed so enormously – I mean *Negative Capability*, that is when man is capable of being in uncertainties, Mysteries, doubts, without any irritable reaching after fact & reason.[2]

To this profoundly secular sense in Keats, Eliot sought the religious equivalent.

The judgement

'May the judgement not be too heavy upon us': it is not only the sentiment here which is incompatible with the prompt practical-

1 – *Two Gentlemen of Verona*, I, iii.
2 – Keats, 21, 27(?) December 1817 (*Letters*, ed. Rollins, i, 193).

ities of prejudice, but the cadence. *Ash-Wednesday* recoils from both prejudice and prejudgement; the art has come to judge these things differently, and is no longer bent upon social judgement (albeit of spiritual failings) but is instead bending before divine judgement. Judgement is mine, saith the Lord. 'And pray to God to have mercy upon us': again 'upon us', not only in abjection rather than in subjecting, but 'us' as other than the 'you' ('the *other people*') upon whom prejudice traditionally exercises its justice or its mercy. Yet the Christianity of the poem is not sentimentalized, since the matter of God's eternal pre-judgement is not burked: it is not only Calvinists who must attend to election and reprobation, to the painful inconceiv-ability either of God's predestining or of his not doing so.

> Struggling with the devil of the stairs who wears
> The deceitful face of hope and of despair.
>
> (III)

Not 'or' but 'and'. Tone is the expression on the face of the words, and a reader may often be uncertain whether a counte-nance is shining upon him. Here in these lines, the two faces become one, no longer mutually exclusive but turning their exclusion outward. Among the stairs which lead into Eliot's 'devil of the stairs' are those which were divinely and diaboli-cally tempting, God's judgement cruelly readied to deceive the very devil with the face of hope and with the stairs of Heaven:

> The Stairs were then let down, whether to dare
> The Fiend by easie ascent, or aggravate
> His sad exclusion from the dores of Bliss.
>
> (*Paradise Lost*, III, 523–5)[1]

'Easie ascent' is a hideous retort upon Satan. *Facilis ascensus Averni* . . .

It is only with some sense of the mystery of God's judgement, and of whether the Last Judgement can honestly be conceived of

---

1 – It is not only the conjunction of the devil and the stairs which suggests this, but the aggravated internal rhyming, Milton's *Stairs / dare* prompting Eliot's *stairs / wears / despair*.

by man as anything more than God's Pre-Judgement finalized, that everything in the poem which speaks mercy – 'And pray to God to have mercy upon us' – could ever be felt as substantially expressed:

> Beyond compare the Son of God was seen
> Most glorious, in him all his Father shon
> Substantially express'd, and in his face
> Divine compassion visibly appeerd,
> Love without end, and without measure Grace,
> Which uttering thus he to his Father spake.
>   (*Paradise Lost*, III, 138–42)

> No place of grace for those who avoid the face
> No time to rejoice for those who walk among noise and
>   deny the voice
>   (*Ash-Wednesday* V)

There are faces but no names. The prejudicial power of names is not invoked in *Ash-Wednesday*, a poem which nevertheless evokes a naming power whenever it capitalizes: not only God and Lord, but Lady, the Virgin, Mother, the Rose, the Garden, and – supremely the poem's word – the Word. Only one name, in its dailiness yet uniqueness, is admitted by the poem: the name of Mary; and this then is coloured by the chastened receding with which it makes its two appearances: 'Going in white and blue, in Mary's colour,' and 'In blue of larkspur, blue of Mary's colour'.

Yet the colour of the poem (alive in its 'varied green' and white and blue) requires a ground against which it may figure, and just before the centre of the poem – as in the related shaping of 'Marina' in the same year – there comes the darkness which must be left behind.

> At the second turning of the second stair
> I left them twisting, turning below;
> There were no more faces and the stair was dark,
> Damp, jaggèd, like an old man's mouth drivelling,
>   beyond repair,

Or the toothed gullet of an agèd shark.

(III)

The predatory is not denied, only escaped, and the poem which so often says 'pray' is here thinking *prey*. The leopards of the previous section (II) were beasts of prey too, but they visited upon the bones an ultimate serenity:

> Under a juniper-tree the bones sang, scattered and shining
> We are glad to be scattered, we did little good to each other,
> Under a tree in the cool of the day, with the blessing of sand,
> Forgetting themselves and each other, united
> In the quiet of the desert.

How lucidly cool, this entire freedom from animosity. In 'Rhapsody on a Windy Night', the young Eliot had brought home the foreign thought that 'La lune ne garde aucune rancune'; but with these shining bones of *Ash-Wednesday*, the question of bearing a grudge never even arises; the bones never had a grudge to bear, a grudge never entered the hollow round of their skull. The ensuing Section III is a new start and reversion, for only a few lines separate the leopards' cleanly fastidiousness, the bones' whiteness, from the ensuing counter-vision which will always lurk, 'the toothed gullet of an agèd shark'.

The two visions, though, needed to be crisply separated. Eliot's original printing of Section II in 1927 and 1928, independently as 'Salutation', had brought to life within the bones' song some elements of revulsion which disturbed the clarity of internal equilibrium:

> Lady of silences
> Calm and distressed
> Torn and most whole
> Rose of memory
> Rose of forgetfulness
> Spattered and worshipped
> Exhausted and life-giving
> Worried reposeful

> The single Rose
> With worm eaten petals
> Is now the Garden[1]

It is not that this song needed to eschew tension, but that the needed tension was that of distance not distaste. Which is why *Ash-Wednesday* does not accommodate 'Spattered and worshipped'. Or 'With worm eaten petals'. 'In a society like ours, worm-eaten with Liberalism, the only thing possible for a person with strong convictions is to state a point of view and leave it at that':[2] but in *Ash-Wednesday*, a poem not bent upon society, let alone upon 'a society like ours', such a line as 'With worm eaten petals' would feel worm-eaten with illiberalism. With animosity.

For, succeeding the vacuum of the early poems which had craved the animations of animosity even while suspecting them, and succeeding the dreary numbness of the hollow men addicted to their emptiness, *Ash-Wednesday* aspires to the spiritual void which may with grace issue in spiritual life: a void which is a benign and waiting vacancy like that which Eliot imagines in *Ash-Wednesday* when he tacitly suggests to Keats's Grecian Urn that there are better ways of being breathless:

> The silent sister veiled in white and blue
> Between the yews, behind the garden god,
> Whose flute is breathless, bent her head and signed but
>   spoke no word

(IV)

'Breathless', 'spoke' and 'word' all put their pressure on 'signed' to be 'sighed', but – in this unreal garden, unlike in the Unreal City – nothing is here for sighs.

'The language demands an *animosity*': the art now demanded an 'Animula'. This poem's words, contemplating the soul's withering, are withering but not contemptuous:

> Issues from the hand of time the simple soul
> Irresolute and selfish, misshapen, lame,

1 – *The Criterion*, vii (1928), 31–2.
2 – *After Strange Gods*, p. 13.

Unable to fare forward or retreat,
Fearing the warm reality, the offered good,
Denying the importunity of the blood,
Shadow of its own shadows, spectre in its own gloom,
Leaving disordered papers in a dusty room;
Living first in the silence after the viaticum.

More than a decade before he became a Christian, Eliot had written: 'As a matter of fact, the human soul – *l'anima semplicetta* – is neither good nor bad; but in order to be good, in order to be human, requires *discipline*.'[1] It had been required of Eliot that he discipline himself in new ways to achieve the unprejudicial gravity of 'Animula'; its levelling generality fosters a bleak generosity.

'The warm reality' was to be a phrase which Eliot would need again, when in 1933 he characterized the poems of Harold Monro:

Inanimate objects take on animation of a kind; his old houses are not so much haunted by ghosts as they are ghosts themselves haunting the folk who briefly visit them. Under the influence of this sincere and tormented introspection, the warm reality dissolves: both that for which we hold out our arms, and that at which we strike vain blows.[2]

'Animation of a kind', in relation to 'inanimate objects', is what characterizes the soul of 'Animula'. But in the poem of 1929 it was not the real known name of Harold Monro that was brought to light but rather the names of more-than-total strangers, eternally undiscoverable, strange suggestive names that are felt in the poem – in a way which is new in Eliot – not as prompting any reflexes of prejudicial animosity but as proposing the waiving of human judgement even while couched as what could so easily have been judgement – 'avid of speed and power'.

'Animula', which has (among its many ways of speaking) an Augustan weight of generality, is Eliot's *Vanity of Human Wishes*, a poem to which Eliot published an Introduction in the next year, 1930; but whereas Johnson summoned his real names

1 – *New Statesman*, 24 June 1916.
2 – Critical Note to Harold Monro, *Collected Poems* (1933), p. xvi.

(Wolsey and Charles XII), themselves summoning the earlier real names in Juvenal (Sejanus and Hannibal), Eliot presents at first a poem quite without names, the story of the generic soul, and then, after the space after the line 'Living first in the silence after the viaticum', ends the poem amazingly by blowing this generality to pieces in a firework display of night-names. 'They mount, they shine, evaporate, and fall.'

> Pray for Guiterriez, avid of speed and power,
> For Boudin, blown to pieces,
> For this one who made a great fortune,
> And that one who went his own way.
> Pray for Floret, by the boarhound slain between the
>   yew trees,
> Pray for us now and at the hour of our birth.

This abstains from judgement and asks mercy. It asks mercy through the two mediators, those who in the loving way come between: Christ the Mediator, and the woman who mediated the Mediator to humankind and who intercedes. The name of Mary is signed but unspoken. For it is she who is prayed to pray for us now and at the hour of our death. The spoken names in 'Animula' are those of the dead stationed beyond any judgement that we might pass. Whether they are damned 'is, of course, another question', and as with Baudelaire 'we are not prevented from praying for his repose'.[1]

'Mary's colour' warms *Ash-Wednesday*. Mary's name, unvoiced, colours 'Animula'. Mary suffers a sea-change, into something rich and strange: 'Marina'. Of the between-poems it is 'Marina' which most centrally raises the question of a demanded *animosity*. The poem begins with a sequence

> What seas what shores what grey rocks and what islands

which neither asks (in the mood of the interrogative epigraph from Seneca) 'What seas are these?', nor exclaims, 'What seas these are!', nor states, 'What seas the sirens sang in, is a puzzling question.' The sequence is affecting in its being at once so clear

---

1 – *Selected Essays*, p. 429.

and so hazed, the power of sight being restored, the fog lifting. And then there erupt the ugly clarities of all that threatens true life and that had threatened Pericles' recovery of Marina and of himself.

What seas what shores what grey rocks and what islands
What water lapping the bow
And scent of pine and the woodthrush singing through the fog
What images return
O my daughter.

Those who sharpen the tooth of the dog, meaning
Death
Those who glitter with the glory of the hummingbird, meaning
Death
Those who sit in the sty of contentment, meaning
Death
Those who suffer the ecstasy of the animals, meaning
Death

The litany of horror is the sounding of deep lethal animosities. The masque of the Seven Deadly Sins has been reduced to Four (we moderns are busy men), and the first of these is aggression, not only flaunting its own cruelty but staging the dog-fighting which makes a change from cock-fighting and bear-baiting:[1]

Those who sharpen the tooth of the dog, meaning
Death

Against the benign uncertainty of the poem's opening lines is set the malign indubitability of this chant. Under one aspect, the chant is an authoritative authoritarian exegesis of an allegory: 'meaning Death', with Death truly capital if you take the line-beginning as not conventional here but as unusually lethal with

1 – I take this to be the answer to Graham Martin's objection: 'the individual images carry little conviction. Thus, of the first, why "dog"? why not wolf or hyena, or any fierce, traditionally contemptible carnivore?' (*Eliot in Perspective*, p. 118). On the humming bird, Eliot's change from the manuscript's 'peacock', and the relation to Eliot's youthful reading of Mayne Reid, see Crawford, *The Savage and the City in the Work of T. S. Eliot*, pp. 21–2.

meaning. But under another aspect the chant is an insistence upon the darkness of all obdurate significance: to mean death (the capital a poetic convention only) is uglily to intend it, as with to mean mischief or to mean business. This would be casting a grim religious light upon

> Those who sharpen the tooth of the dog, meaning
> Death

For it is not just that they emblematize or allegorize Death but that they mean Death as aggressive seethers mean trouble, and as the stagers of dog-fights mean blood. Not that overt aggression has a monopoly of meaning Death in this glowering way. Histrionic vanity will second aggression:

> Those who glitter with the glory of the hummingbird,
> meaning
> Death

As will flaccid sloth:

> Those who sit in the sty of contentment, meaning
> Death

And delusive lust:

> Those who suffer the ecstasy of the animals, meaning
> Death

Animals cannot be charged with behaving like animals, nor beasts with bestiality. In early Eliot there had been the animalizing of particular men (seized, though, as particular men may have to be seized, by prejudicial categorizing):

> Apeneck Sweeney spreads his knees
> Letting his arms hang down to laugh,
> The zebra stripes along his jaw
> Swelling to maculate giraffe.
> > ('Sweeney Among the Nightingales')

But in 'Marina' this has become the animalizing of man, a judgement so universal as to be without prejudice. The Deadly Sins are not 'a Hell for the *other people*'. The dog-teeth lovingly filed for the dog-pit; the preening of the hummingbird; the sedentary piggishness; the drug-shudder: these mean Death, and they are great levellers.

This litany has been deplored for its animosity. David Ward has spoken of Eliot's 'warping (if only momentarily) a beautiful poem by a harsh puritanical grumbling':

In a poem so full of delicate uncertainty this kind of emphasis destroys the finely attuned poise so rudely that its dramatic and emotional rightness of purpose must be absolutely secure.

But dramatically it is wrong. It is far too deliberate and heavy a rhetoric for the imagined situation; too plainly it is an elaborate embroidery of the words 'sensuality', 'pride', 'sloth' and 'lust' because by themselves those words would sit too baldly. And it is emotionally wrong: the assertive negative morality doesn't fit with the air of tentative discovery. And, most important of all, the failure of tone here may seed some doubts about the validity of the rest of the poem.[1]

But Ward fails to attend to the way in which the unfittingness is the point, as does Graham Martin when he leaves it at saying that the tone of these lines is 'moralistic, denunciatory and strangely out of key with the occasion'. Strangely and richly. For what do we find becomes of the 'assertive negative' animosities, not only those of the Deadly Sins themselves but those which righteously anathematize?

> Those who suffer the ecstasy of the animals, meaning Death
>
> Are become unsubstantial, reduced by a wind,
> A breath of pine, and the woodsong fog
> By this grace dissolved in place

The Sins, in themselves and as gratifications of the punitive, are dissolved; they are not denied but they become without

1 – *T. S. Eliot: Between Two Worlds* (1973), pp. 91, 171.

substance in the graced air of the poem. The white space (the non-temporal pause, a potent embodiment of the 'between') before the new start that is 'Are become unsubstantial' is a judged contemplation of a judgement; and it is compounded by the minute indenting of those words (despite their syntactical continuity), intimating a fresh phase, secure though breath-based:

> Are become unsubstantial, reduced by a wind,
> A breath of pine, and the woodsong fog
> By this grace dissolved in place

Usually things are held in place, not dissolved in place; and the word here is 'unsubstantial', not 'insubstantial' (a crucial vigilance); and the blockish Sins are not 'reduced' *to* anything, to a wind or a breath, but are reduced by a wind and a breath.

Far from its being destroyed, as Ward thinks, poise is what 'Marina' possesses; poised between early and late Eliot, it is the greatest of the between-poems, being the one where the energies of animosity are at once acknowledged to be substantial and believed to be so transcendable that they can 'become unsubstantial'. The best criticism it has received was the succinct review by the twenty-four-year-old William Empson:

The dramatic power of his symbolism is here in full strength, and the ideas involved have almost the range of interest, the full orchestra, of *The Waste Land*. One main reason for this is the balance maintained between otherworldliness and humanism; the essence of the poem is the vision of an order, a spiritual state, which he can conceive and cannot enter, but it is not made clear whether he conceives an order in this world to be known by a later generation (like Moses on Pisgah) or the life in heaven which is to be obtained after death (like Dante). One might at first think the second only was meant, but Marina, after all, was a real daughter; is now at sea, like himself, rather than already in the Promised Land; and is to live 'in a world of time beyond me', which can scarcely be a description of Heaven. At any rate, the humanist meaning is used at every point as a symbol of the otherworldly one; this seems the main point to insist on in a brief notice because it is the main cause of the richness of the total effect. In either case the theme is the peril and brevity of such vision.[1]

1 – 1931 (*Argufying*, p. 356).

Eliot believed that humanism mistook itself when it arrogated the primacy of religion, but he deplored those who believed that religion did not stand in need of humanism. Such matters were the dual preoccupation of his essays in these years, in 'The Humanism of Irving Babbitt' (1928), 'Second Thoughts about Humanism' (1929), and 'Religion without Humanism' (1930). Eliot would have resisted the terms of Empson's antithesis, otherworldliness and religion, yet 'Marina' is a poem which does not utter religion but breathes it.

Yet in 1917 the question as Eliot phrased it had been one which accorded to religion respect but not worship: 'And might it not be maintained that religion, however poor our lives would be without it, is only one form of satisfaction among others, rather than the culminating satisfaction of all satisfactions?'[1] This question had been couched to solicit Yes, and it answers to the presence which religion has in such early poems as 'Preludes':

> I am moved by fancies that are curled
> Around these images, and cling:
> The notion of some infinitely gentle
> Infinitely suffering thing.
>
> Wipe your hand across your mouth, and laugh;
> The worlds revolve like ancient women
> Gathering fuel in vacant lots.

But in the passionately perturbed poems of 1925 to 1930, the convert's poems, the question is always seeking to rephrase itself as this: 'Might it not be maintained that religion is not one form of satisfaction among others but the only form of satisfaction?' And is not Christ's Satisfaction the only satisfaction? So desperate was the craving for relief from life's vile meaninglessness (a craving which had sprouted in The Waste Land, and which had gnawed the hollow men) that it needed all of Eliot's powers of resistance not to succumb to a mis-estimation (not

1 – *International Journal of Ethics*, July 1917.

over-estimation) of religion as the only satisfaction, rather than as at once the foundation and the capstone of all satisfactions.

The conflict can be heard in the painful obduracy with which 'between' becomes charged. There is the severity of severance: 'The division between those who accept, and those who deny, Christian revelation I take to be the most profound division between human beings.' This severity, though, is not limited to 'the *other people*', since this same essay exempts no one from an excruciating 'between': 'The human mind is perpetually driven between two desires, between two dreams each of which may be either a vision or a nightmare: the vision and nightmare of the material world, and the vision and nightmare of the immaterial.'[1] Eliot, finding incarnation indispensable (and not only as the Incarnation), was moved to speak of 'the culture of a people as an *incarnation* of its religion', because this word could 'avoid the two alternative errors: that of regarding religion and culture as two separate things between which there is a *relation*, and that of *identifying* religion and culture'.[2] Eliot's purposes required the italicizing of *relation* and *identifying*; my smaller ones would italicize *between*.

Eliot succeeded in exercising his resistance, in one direction, by making religious subject-matter itself the manifest aegis of the poems so that the particular way in which they are religious would not claim more than it should. In his essay 'Religion and Literature', Eliot was to grant that it is not simply wrong of a reader to think of religious poetry as a 'department of poetry':

He believes, not always explicitly, that when you qualify poetry as 'religious' you are indicating very clear limitations. For the great majority of people who love poetry, '*religious* poetry' is a variety of *minor* poetry: the religious poet is not a poet who is treating the whole subject matter of poetry in a religious spirit, but a poet who is dealing with a confined part of this subject matter.[3]

It is this intense acknowledged circumscription (that of devotional poetry, as when one writes religious poems instead

1 – *Revelation*, edited by John Baillie and Hugh Martin (1937), pp. 2, 31.
2 – *Notes towards the Definition of Culture*, p. 33.
3 – *Selected Essays*, p. 390.

of writing poems religiously) which creates 'Journey of the Magi', 'A Song for Simeon', and 'Animula'. It even sets the limits within which *Ash-Wednesday*, though much wider in its art and its scope, is offered for our crediting.

But Eliot also exercised a different resistance to the wrong kind of religious supremacy when he incarnated within a poem of this time a sense of those satisfactions that are other than religion's. 'Marina' is invested with a joy that has not 'divested itself of the love of created beings', and supremely of the supreme created being, one's child. The poem is the work of a man whose childlessness is necessarily near the heart of his relation to his artistic creation. Eliot created this, his most loving poem, by grace of a story in which the great reconciliation scene is not only between a parent and a child but between a parent and a child (who is no longer a child) who are strangers to each other, this to the point at which the very word 'reconciliation' is dissolved in place.

Such are the satisfactions of 'Marina', and they witness to the last rephrasing of Eliot's question of 1917: 'Might it not be maintained that religion is neither one form of satisfaction among others nor the only form of satisfaction, but the culminating satisfaction of all satisfactions?' Religion can be this only if the other satisfactions are real and realized. In establishing this as more than

> an abstraction
> Remaining a perpetual possibility
> Only in a world of speculation
> > ('Burnt Norton')

'Marina' made possible the even larger (it could not be purer) air of *Four Quartets*.

VII

THE USE OF MEMORY

The unfamiliar Name

Eliot opened *Four Quartets* by contemplating possibilities and impossibilities: those of time, those of redemption. 'Burnt Norton' did not, in the epic manner, haste into the midst of things, but it did at once move there:

> Time present and time past
> Are both perhaps present in time future,
> And time future contained in time past.
> If all time is eternally present
> All time is unredeemable.

Six years before 'Burnt Norton', Eliot had sung in *Ash-Wednesday* (through a bird, as he so often sang, in *The Waste Land* as in *Four Quartets*) 'Redeem the time, redeem the dream'.

Four Quartets is devoted to acts of redemption, for Eliot knew that the poem had to gather in as much as was more than humanly possible of his life's work. 'Little Gidding' was to be his conclusive enterprise as a poet, and his first notes for this last poem summoned the individuals who vanish yet who 'emerge / in another pattern & recreated & / reconciled / redeemed'.[1] At the heart of 'Little Gidding', in awe of Dante, is the meeting with the 'familiar compound ghost'. The climax of this sequence is the rendering of

> the gifts reserved for age
> To set a crown upon your lifetime's effort

and the last of the gifts is this:

1 – Gardner, *The Composition of Four Quartets*, p. 157.

> And last, the rending pain of re-enactment
> > Of all that you have done, and been; the shame
> > Of motives late revealed, and the awareness
> Of things ill done and done to others' harm
> > Which once you took for exercise of virtue.

You: both Eliot, admonished by the ghost, and we, admonished by Eliot; not you 'the *other people*'.

Eliot attempted no rescinding of his early poems, or rewriting of them. The voice sent forth can never be recalled, and anyway most rescindings and rewritings make for melodrama: the comic melodrama of W. H. Auden or the caricatural melodrama of Robert Lowell. But the new and final enterprise for Eliot was to show how much had remained to be said – how much had not been accessible to the early awareness which had derived its animation from prejudicial animosity insistent and resisted. The crux of the lines on 'things ill done and done to others' harm' is their freedom from animosity, including animosity directed at self; it is a different freedom from that of the shining bones in *Ash-Wednesday*, because it is in pain.

Eliot had been dissatisfied with his incomplete draft of 'Little Gidding':

The defect of the whole poem, I feel, is the lack of some acute personal reminiscence (never to be explicated, of course, but to give power from well below the surface) and I can *perhaps* supply this in Part II.[1]

The 'acute personal reminiscence' was to give power from well below the surface because of an acute personal and impersonal *dis*satisfaction with Eliot's earlier achievement. Not the repudiation of it, but an aching to be free from its stringencies of animosity, freed into the stringencies of charity or loving-kindness.

This necessitated a change of weighting which was much more than a change of mind while never constituting that suspect thing, a change of heart. ('New styles of architecture, a change of heart': Auden snuffed the bogus there.) The young

1 – Gardner, *The Composition of Four Quartets*, p. 24.

Eliot had dwelt upon humiliation. In 1918 he had praised Wyndham Lewis's *Tarr*:

Here there is another point of contact with Dostoevsky, in a variation on one of Dostoevsky's best themes: Humiliation. This is one of the most important elements in human life, and one little exploited. Kreisler is a study in humiliation.[1]

And in one of his deepest statements of principle (going to the heart of his judgements on humankind, on contemporary civilization and on its art) he had in 1919 praised Stendhal:

Stendhal's scenes, some of them, and some of his phrases, read like cutting one's own throat; they are a terrible humiliation to read, in the understanding of human feelings and human illusions of feeling that they force upon the reader.[2]

> For varying forms, one definition's right:
> Unreal emotions, and real appetite.[3]

Human illusions of feeling were in danger of becoming Eliot's obsession or even his forte, especially as the current illusions of feeling were then more often liberal self-deception than conservative self-deception. In the name of pity, crimes were committed. Eliot praised Charles-Louis Philippe: 'the love and the pity are so obviously towards real people, so obviously real emotions and not literary confections, that they elicit love and pity from us.' Yet even Philippe could not always judge this aright: 'But in attempting something more like a novel, more impersonal, he seems to me to give less of himself, and instead of pity, we are aware rather of an atmosphere of moral putrefaction.'[4] But in his late work Eliot was able to dwell less upon human illusions of feeling and more upon human feelings – for instance, the feeling of humility, as well as the feeling for it ('for' both as sympathy with it, and as tentatively seeking it).

Humility stands to humiliation as at once intimate and remote, 'more distant than stars and nearer than the eye'.

1 – *The Egoist*, September 1918.
2 – *The Athenaeum*, 30 May 1919.
3 – *The Waste Land: A Facsimile and Transcript*, 'The Fire Sermon', p. 41.
4 – Preface to *Bubu of Montparnasse*, pp. 12–13.

Humiliation may foster humility or may nurse a hurt pride. In these straits, a sensitive navigation becomes all-important. So Eliot may quietly maintain that 'humility is endless', and this is a double truth: humility must never propose to itself an ulterior end, and humility must ever acknowledge the regression which lies in wait for it, for humility must not be proud of being humble, or proud of not being proud of being humble, or . . . 'Humility is endless': but Eliot, resisting the temptation of a proud apophthegm about humility, does not end there:

> The only wisdom we can hope to acquire
> Is the wisdom of humility: humility is endless.
>
> The houses are all gone under the sea.
>
> The dancers are all gone under the hill.

So ends 'East Coker' II, suddenly banking and veering like a great aeroplane. It is a counterpart, on a huge scale, to a fine turn in Hopkins, where the notebook entry for his sermon of 5 December 1879 ends:

(Some words on humility, which I had not time to write)

We can estimate the poem's tact, its wisdom about humility, if we place it by the honourable but less felicitous ending which Eliot shaped for his lecture 'To Criticize the Critic':

But I hope that what I have said today may suggest reasons why, as the critic grows older, his critical writings may be less fired by enthusiasm, but informed by wider interest and, one hopes, by greater wisdom and humility.[1]

This is too settled in the presence of humility's mystery, too trusting as to what can be effected by the movement from 'I hope' to 'one hopes', too clearly having the last word of 'humility'. But what was not perfected in the lecture of 1961 had been so in the poem of 1940.

The 'we' of 'The only wisdom we can hope to acquire' is not open to being named, unlike the 'I' of 'I hope'. Names are no

1 – *To Criticize the Critic*, p. 26.

longer salient, and in their prejudicial focusing are now looked upon with a differently suspicious and interrogating eye. Think back to the earliest Eliot, the Eliot who fashioned 'J. Alfred Prufrock', the Eliot of whom Virginia Woolf recorded in her diary on 15 November 1918:

> I was interrupted somewhere on this page by the arrival of Mr Eliot. Mr Eliot is well expressed by his name – a polished, cultivated, elaborate young American, talking so slow, that each word seems to have special finish allotted it. But beneath the surface, it is fairly evident that he is very intellectual, intolerant, with strong views of his own, & a poetic creed.[1]

The energies of this young American had been diversely fired by names. There were his fabricated correspondence columns in *The Egoist* in December 1917, with the acutely hilarious contributions from J. A. D. Spence (Thridlington Grammar School), Helen B. Trundlett (Batton, Kent), Charles James Grimble (The Vicarage, Leays), Charles Augustus Conybeare (The Carlton Club, Liverpool), and Muriel A. Schwarz (60 Alexandra Gardens, Hampstead, N.W.) There was Eliot's pleasure in Edith Wharton's *Summer*, in 1918: 'She even allows herself to be detected in just the slight smile of an inhabitant of Boston (where the type of novel in question is read) at the name of the Honorius Hatchard Memorial Library, 1838, in the village of North Dormer.'[2] There was his persistent, even obsessive, making play and making free with names. On occasion, the name will need to be his own, as in 'Mr. Eliot's Sunday Morning Service',[3] or in his lugubrious gratitude to Edward Lear:

> How unpleasant to meet Mr. Eliot!
> With his features of clerical cut,
> And his brow so grim
> And his mouth so prim
> And his conversation, so nicely

---

1 – *The Diary of Virginia Woolf*, edited by Anne Olivier Bell (1977; 1979 edition), i, 218–19.
2 – *The Egoist*, January 1918.
3 – Lyndall Gordon most interestingly notes the family feeling here: 'In particular he evidently resented Sunday morning services conducted by his cousin, Fred Eliot, who became a Unitarian minister' (*Eliot's Early Years*, p. 70). How pleasant to distinguish the Messrs Eliot.

> Restricted to What Precisely
> And If and Perhaps and But.
>> ('Five-Finger Exercises' v)

This concurs with that dark remark of Virginia Woolf's, 'Mr Eliot is well expressed by his name'. For Mr Eliot, people were well expressed by their names, whether imaginary people for his poems like Mrs Cammel and Professor Channing-Cheetah and Miss Nancy Ellicott, or real people like Mr Polack who had written a letter to *The Athenaeum* in 1920: 'I feel that Mr. Polack's feelings have run away with him. (So look'd he once, when in an angry parle He smote . . .).'[1] Or like Mr J. Beaumont Pease, at the British Bankers' Association: 'Then, after pease porridge hot, came pease porridge cold.'[2]

But such onomastic *trouvailles*, not left as casual slights, had once moved Alexander Pope to be grateful to the gods for having named his enemy Curll:

> Or that where on her Curls the Public pours,
> All-bounteous, fragrant Grains and Golden show'rs
>> (*The Dunciad*, II, 3–4)

Matthew Arnold had dwelt upon Mr Roebuck (who had vociferated 'I pray that our unrivalled happiness may last') and upon the lopped victim of callousness ('Wragg is in custody'). Such *trouvailles* could be disputatiously offered as findings, but they would not have to minister to the punitive or the complacent, as the creator of Prufrock and of Hakagawa knew.

Nomen est omen. There is a happiness in the fact that the poet, the maker, who so engraved upon our culture the words *il miglior fabbro* should have made his living at Faber and Faber; there is even a happy irony in its being, of all the great publishing houses, Faber and Faber which Eliot joined and graced, given that the name Faber and Faber is a gentlemanly confidence trick, necessitated by the disbanding of Faber and Gwyer in 1929 and by the instinct that 'Faber' alone would not carry quite the weight: hence the businesslike fantasizing of a second Faber. Geoffrey Faber must have felt twice the man.

1 – *The Athenaeum*, 25 June 1920.
2 – *The Criterion*, x (1931), 709.

Eliot's first book, *Prufrock and Other Observations*, con-sisted of twelve poems, of which four had a person's name in the title, and three had a name in the first line; plus the chillingly unnaming 'Portrait of a Lady'. His second book,[1] *Poems* (1920), had almost exactly the same: twelve poems, of which four had a person's name in the title, and four a name in the first line; plus the chillingly unnaming 'Gerontion' or Portrait of a Little Old Man. If someone were to do what no one ever does – that is, read straight through all of Eliot's poems, having never previously read any of them – the single most striking impres-sion would be the vanishing of names from them.

Four Quartets is resolutely, markedly, unnaming – or rather, unnaming of *persons*. The sequence-title, *Four Quartets*, names no names, unlike Eliot's earlier candidate for the honour, *Kensington Quartets*.[2] Each of the four poems is famously named after a not-especially famous place (Burnt Norton, East Coker, the Dry Salvages, and Little Gidding), and this all the more brings home the absence of persons' names. Only Adam, in 'East Coker', and Krishna and Arjuna in 'The Dry Salvages', are permitted to breach the veil of unnaming. Apart from the name of 'England', which comes three times in 'Little Gidding' and not elsewhere in *Four Quartets*, and which consummates the patriotism of a sequence of poems which had begun in peacetime but ended in mid-war, there is in 'Little Gidding' no place's or person's name at all.

Eliot's principled practice has now become to stave off names, in the interest of slowing down or even precluding any rush to judgement. *The Waste Land* had said

> Only at nightfall, aethereal rumours
> Revive for a moment a broken Coriolanus

where the name Coriolanus is alive with animosity and anima-tion, not only because of everything about the man and his caste

---

1 – I exempt the two limited printings, the pamphlet *Poems* (Hogarth Press, 1919), and *Ara Vos Prec* (John Rodker, 1920).
2 – See Valerie Eliot, quoting a letter of Eliot's, 3 September 1942, in the *Times Literary Supplement*, 16 July 1971; and Gardner, *The Composition of Four Quartets*, pp. 26–7.

and his story, the animosities which he aroused and which he acted out, but because this person's name is a wrested place-name: Corioles, the town seized in battle and flaunted in a victor's name, Corioles to which Coriolanus later dedicated himself fanatically and half-heartedly. But what happens when 'at nightfall' and 'a broken Coriolanus' are revived for a moment in 'Little Gidding'? There we hear 'If you came at night like a broken king', and again:

> If I think of a king at nightfall,
> Of three men, and more, on the scaffold
> And a few who died forgotten
> In other places, here and abroad,
> And of one who died blind and quiet,
> Why should we celebrate
> These dead men more than the dying?

Quiet, yes, with no names cried out. We may overhear the unspoken or underspoken names of Charles I, Archbishop Laud, and the Earl of Strafford (and more).[1] We may even wonder whether we hear, or are only imagining, in the line 'Of three men, and more, on the scaffold', the name of St Thomas More, here in a poem so dedicated to the relation of Church and State in desperately troubled times; for Wordsworth had cele-brated these dead men:

> and, therefore, to the tomb
> Pass, some through fire – and by the scaffold some –
> Like saintly Fisher, and unbending More.
> ('Ecclesiastical Sonnets', Part II, XXVI)[2]

---

1 – John Hayward, in the notes to Pierre Leyris's translation *Quatre Quatuors* (1950), gives these names to the 'three men'; Hayward's notes, because of Eliot's friendship and overseeing, are reliable.

2 – Wordsworth's also praising 'More's gay genius' in this sonnet may enter into Eliot's twice referring to 'genius' just before the line which has 'and more'. Eliot wrote about St Thomas More in the *Times Literary Supplement*, 2 December 1926, where he referred drily (and anonymously) to 'Sir Thomas Elyot, whose association with More laid him for a time under suspicion of excessive orthodoxy.' Such a suspicion, centuries later, attached to this collateral descendant of Sir Thomas Elyot who introduced his forebear into 'East Coker'.

Could Eliot's 'scaffold' stand within three words of 'more' and not revive for a moment Thomas More, so pertinent to the poem's central attention?[1] Yet such a name, like those which are accorded the respectful privacy of 'a few who . . .' and of 'one who . . .', remains spectral, distant, without antagonism though the subject be civil war. 'We cannot revive old factions', as would happen if we really did 'revive for a moment a broken Coriolanus'. The poem has no wish to 'follow an antique drum'. Names can too easily stir the old hatreds.

Even family can become the good old cause of faction. The poet's name both is and is not that of his famous ancestor; so instead of such a gambit as 'Mr. Eliot's Sunday Morning Service', the impulse now is to quote Sir Thomas Elyot (in 'East Coker', the ancestral place) without quotation marks and without naming him. Likewise to be reticent about the Eliot/Elyot family while nevertheless seeing that it is woven into the poem:

> there is a time for building
> And a time for living and for generation
> And a time for the wind to break the loosened pane
> And to shake the wainscot where the field-mouse trots
> And to shake the tattered arras woven with a silent motto.

The private allusion in the last line follows upon the delicate twofold allusion, of a different kind, to Tennyson, 'Mariana' and *Maud*.[2] The 'silent motto' is private but not secret or exclusive; it is strange but not strangerly; and as an allusion it is a triumph because of its esteeming one invaluable principle in allusion: that the poet should, in everybody's interest, see to it that the line offers itself whether or not a reader takes the allusion. 'And to shake the tattered arras woven with a silent motto': the undulation, wind-shaken, is haunting.

---

1 – Eliot's prose summary included: 'If I think of three men on the scaffold'; the poetic manuscript had 'Of three men in turn on the scaffold'; Eliot then wrote – above 'in turn' – ', and more,'. Between this and the final text there was 'Of three men, or more, on the scaffold' (Gardner, *The Composition of Four Quartets*, pp. 201–2).

2 – 'The mouse / Behind the mouldering wainscot shrieked' ('Mariana'). 'And the shrieking rush of the wainscot mouse' (*Maud*).

And then, if we know and care, the private or family allusion brings its further sense of time and of building and living and generation. For the Eliot family motto enjoined action not words: *Tace et Fac*. The dedication of *The Sacred Wood* had been to the memory of Eliot's father, Henry Ware Eliot:

FOR
H. W. E.
'TACUIT ET FECIT'

Yet how can a poet live up to such a family motto, since a poet has to do with words? Perhaps the family motto spurred Eliot towards the conviction for which he had other less personal grounds, the conviction which would reconcile *Tace et Fac* with the poet's calling by valuing supremely 'that intensity at which language strives to become silence'.[1]

> Words, after speech, reach
> Into the silence.
>
> ('Burnt Norton')

'And to shake the tattered arras woven with a silent motto': the motto is silent for so many reasons and yet the reasons are not in competition: because any motto woven upon an arras is silent; because in the old decaying house there is no one to hear ('My house is a decayed house', though not now possessed by Gerontion's prejudicial animosity); because the motto is not revealed here in the poem, the line itself keeping silent; because, if you do know the motto, it is in a dead language, in Latin, not in our speaking language; and because it is a silent motto as enjoining silence. *Tace et Fac*.

This is an art of actively fending off, working both with and against names, but fending off names is not new to Eliot, only this peace of mind in the doing of it. 'The hot gates' of 'Gerontion' had embroiled the battle of Thermopylae, unnamed but not peacefully so. The 'fletchers' and 'smiths' of 'Coriolan: II. Difficulties of a Statesman' had been warringly not pacifically

1 – *The Athenaeum*, 14 May 1920. Elizabeth Drew first noted the hint at the family motto in 'East Coker'.

uncapitalized, being anachronistic English names unheard among the warring parties of the Romans and the Volscians:[1]

> A commission is appointed
> To confer with a Volscian commission
> About perpetual peace: the fletchers and javelin-makers and smiths
> Have appointed a joint committee to protest against the reduction of orders.

This way of putting things was hostile to more than just the arms race. But the 'silent motto' is shaken by no hostility.

The unnaming power of *Four Quartets* is at work in Eliot's crucial decision to replace the manuscript-reading 'Are you here, Ser Brunetto?' with 'What! are *you* here?' ('Little Gidding' II), while retaining 'the brown baked features' which all but name Brunetto. The unnaming power is at work too in the new relation to Conan Doyle's way with names. The younger Eliot had delighted in the insinuating power of the names in the Sherlock Holmes stories. (The name Sherlock Holmes is itself a triumph, and *The Hound of the Baskervilles* is no less great a title than *Tess of the d'Urbervilles*.) Eliot regretted Conan Doyle's lapses into easy prejudiciality, and deplored *The Mazarin Stone* where ' "Count Negretto Sylvius" is a name unworthy of the inventor of Dr. Roylott of Stoke Moran, as the personage is unworthy of the inventor of Professor Moriarty.'[2] That was in 1929; by 1940, the creative movement in Eliot is towards reducing Conan Doyle's proper names to nouns.

> In the middle, not only in the middle of the way
> But all the way, in a dark wood, in a bramble,
> On the edge of a grimpen, where is no secure foothold,
>   ('East Coker')

Donald Davie saw into the life of this: 'we all know what a grimpen is, yet we shall look in vain for any dictionary to

1 – Geoffrey Hill elicits his own comedy and pathos from the name, in the 'Fresh dynasties of smiths' in *Mercian Hymns* XX.
2 – *The Criterion*, viii (1929), 555.

confirm us in our knowledge. For "Grimpen" occurs elsewhere only once, as a place-name in Arthur Conan Doyle's *Hound of the Baskervilles*.[1] In due course, the Supplement to the *Oxford English Dictionary* rose to the challenge, and there is now a dictionary in which we shall not look in vain for 'grimpen'.

Grimpen was paid by Eliot the high compliment of being sunk to lower case. And Eliot engaged in what is a complementary, albeit antithetical, activity when he gave to *name* an upper-case N.

IV

> The dove descending breaks the air
> With flame of incandescent terror
> Of which the tongues declare
> The one discharge from sin and error.
> The only hope, or else despair
>   Lies in the choice of pyre or pyre—
>   To be redeemed from fire by fire.
>
> Who then devised the torment? Love.
> Love is the unfamiliar Name
> Behind the hands that wove
> The intolerable shirt of flame
> Which human power cannot remove.
>   We only live, only suspire
>   Consumed by either fire or fire.
>
> ('Little Gidding')

The *Love / wove / remove* sequence, uniquely in this lyric, refuses us the satisfactions of true rhyme, 'Of love satisfied' (in the words of *Ash-Wednesday*). 'Love' is a word which we may yearn to capitalize; here in 'Little Gidding', Eliot neither grants nor denies this, since he stations the word so that we shall never know whether or not it is personified to the Absolute here. The

1 – *Eliot in Perspective*, ed. Martin, p. 70.

first occurrence has to be, for syntactical reasons, 'Love', not 'love'; and the second occurrence, for reasons of poetic lineation. Whether we can be confident of the high abstraction is something on which the poem keeps its silent judgement, while indubitably believing in love's mystery.

'Love is the unfamiliar Name': the capital on Name, a capital which had not been in the manuscripts, turns it from a noun into a name, and it should incite us (but not this time prejudicially) to wonder about the capital that is at once plain and unascertainable in the poem's 'Love', and to inquire into just what we understand by love.

'Love is the unfamiliar Name': this is a strangely loving rebuke to a sentiment of yours. Because it too is a quiet challenge to a preconception or prejudice, it constitutes a profoundly unexpected complement to Eliot's earlier challenge: 'April is the cruellest month'. The earlier counterthought had gained its disconcerting force, first, from its being the scarcely contextualized inaugurative utterance of a poem, and, second, from its combining a direct unexpected sense with an unsettled stress. This later counterthought seeks a greater calmness in the presence of a greater awe. What we are to contemplate is not now the opening of a poem, or a decision as to how to hear its words, but the thought itself, assured of its meaning, sure of its intonation, and yet thereby an undistracted challenge. April may seem not to be cruel but is: from this we ascend, from a month to an eternity, but we also descend lower: pain may seem not to be love or Love but is. It has become an unfamiliar thought, that the name of the supreme agency of pain (the agency behind agency, the Name behind the hands) is love or Love. Can you call the shirt of flame love, leave alone Love? If not, you will be defeated by the immitigably eternal flames of Hell, for if the thought is now unfamiliar to us, it was not unfamiliar to Dante and his world of rooted Christian paradox.

We cannot understand the inscription at Hell Gate:

> *Giustizia mosse il mio alto Fattore;*
> *fecemi la divina Potestate,*
> *la somma Sapienza e il primo Amore.*

Justice moved my high Maker; what made me were the divine Power, the supreme Wisdom, and the primal Love. [Eliot's emphatic non-italics]

until we have ascended to the highest Heaven and returned.[1]

But the turning of 'name' into a Name in 'Little Gidding' IV is paired with an act of positive unnaming, a vacuum to be filled. Unspoken and unignorable, there is a name alluded to, a name which (like the capitalized Name) begins with N. For it is the shirt of Nessus, that murderous token of animosity's lethal life-blood, which cleaves to Eliot's lines:

> The intolerable shirt of flame
> Which human power cannot remove.

Names had been familiar properties and propensities in early Eliot. In *Four Quartets*, we are to become familiar with the absence of names, 'not in a negative but a very positive sense'. But what then of the names which do win admittance to the poem? Why Adam, and Krishna and Arjuna? Adam enters 'East Coker' IV because he is the entrance of us all, in his uniqueness the first of men, the first named of humankind, and the namer of the animals. Krishna is granted audience at the beginning and ending of 'The Dry Salvages' III, which embarks from a state of mind unanxious, equable, and musing:

> I sometimes wonder if that is what Krishna meant –
> Among other things—or one way of putting the same thing:
> That the future is a faded song, a Royal Rose or a lavender
>   spray
> Of wistful regret for those who are not yet here to regret,
> Pressed between yellow leaves of a book that has never
>   been opened.[2]

This sympathizes with wistfulness, and is touched not only by it but with it. By the end of the section, though, the poem has reached admonishment:

> At the moment which is not of action or inaction
> You can receive this: "on whatever sphere of being

1 – 'Dante', *Selected Essays*, pp. 244–5.
2 – On Eliot's fusion of many verses from the *Gita*, see Kearns, *T. S. Eliot and Indic Traditions*, pp. 248–50.

The mind of a man may be intent
At the time of death"—that is the one action
(And the time of death is every moment)
Which shall fructify in the lives of others:
And do not think of the fruit of action.
Fare forward.

        O voyagers, O seamen,
You who come to port, and you whose bodies
Will suffer the trial and judgement of the sea,
Or whatever event, this is your real destination.'
So Krishna, as when he admonished Arjuna
On the field of battle.

           Not fare well,
But fare forward, voyagers.

The mind turns round as with the might of waters. The judgement of the sea, though it is smaller than the judgement of God, is immensely larger than the judgements of men, and especially than their prejudices. Four years before 'The Dry Salvages', Eliot had made clear what it was that he so valued in Arjuna. The year was 1937, the prompting was the Spanish Civil War, and the point of entry was the thought of 'an ideally unprejudiced person':

Now an ideally unprejudiced person, with an intimate knowledge of Spain, its history, its racial characteristics, and its contemporary personalities, might be in a position to come to the conclusion that he should, in the longest view that could be seen, support one side rather than the other. But so long as we are not compelled in our interest to take sides, I do not see why we should do so on insufficient knowledge: and even any eventual partisanship should be held with reservations, humility and misgiving. That balance of mind which a few highly-civilized individuals, such as Arjuna, the hero of the *Bhagavad Gita*, can maintain in action, is difficult for most of us even as observers.[1]

This deserves respect even from those who believe that Eliot misjudged the Spanish Civil War. Yet another of Eliot's

1 – *The Criterion*, xvi (1937), 289–90. The allusion to Arjuna here has often been brought into persuasive relation to that in 'The Dry Salvages' but not, I think, with a particular attention to prejudice and 'an ideally unprejudiced person'.

attempts to redefine and reapply Keats's 'negative capability', it bears witness to one form which conviction may legitimately though unexpectedly take. Such balance of mind can be distinguished both from the unmisgiving fervour that is partisanship and from the unperturbed tolerance that is indifference. It must not be mistaken for the easy equability which Hazlitt had in mind when he remarked that the scales of the mind are pretty sure to remain even when there is nothing in them. In this explicit meeting of Arjuna with Eliot's imaginative attention to prejudice and to humility, the commentary from 1937 shows what kind of continuing life and what kind of new spirit the matter of prejudice has in the sequence of Eliot's great last poems which had begun in the previous year.

The return

'We cannot say', Eliot says, 'at what point "technique" begins or where it ends.'[1] We can say, though, that technique does not inherently possess a direction but is instead an axis. The very same turn, or device or resource, which on one occasion will exert its pressure in this direction may on another occasion press the other way. Eliot had always, even in his most acerb phase, resisted the demands of animosity while insisting that they were unignorable; when he came to resist the demand *for* animosity, and to make this form of resistance not only an impulse but an occupation of his poetry, he therefore did not seek other techniques or resources, but duly re-directed his previous steps, and this the more purposefully in that by doing so he was able to remind his reader of that old animosity which indeed had a substantial existence but could blessedly become unsubstantial.

Clichés, for instance, have a strong affinity with prejudice, for they can move us to immediate assent or dissent as being themselves ready-made units, forms of prejudication, prejudgement or prejudice. So cliché had once been for Eliot the occasion for a sardonic turn, a retort; as in 'Gerontion':

1 – *The Sacred Wood*, p. ix.

> What will the spider do,
> Suspend its operations, will the weevil
> Delay?

As if a spider could do anything else, as if a spider did not conduct its operations precisely by suspending them: the cliché has the animated animosity of a web.

> The spider's touch, how exquisitely fine!
> Feels at each thread, and lives along the line.
>   (*An Essay on Man*, I, 217–18)

But the spider's feeling at each thread and its living along the line are exquisite death to its victim who will soon neither feel nor live. In 'Gerontion' the weevil joins forces with the spider, for the weevil has its etymological filaments back to the web and to weaving, as well as to the root, 'to move about briskly': not much point then in trusting gullibly that the weevil will delay.

Eliot's, or rather Gerontion's, grim play with the name and nature of these forms of life is a soured counterpart to the miracle which Milton celebrated in *Paradise Regained*:

> Him thought, he by the Brook of *Cherith* stood
> And saw the Ravens with their horny beaks
> Food to *Elijah* bringing Even and Morn,
> Though ravenous, taught to abstain from what
>   they brought:
>
>   (II, 266–9)

It will take no less a miracle than unravenous ravens for the weevil to delay or for the spider trustworthily to suspend its operations.

But by the war-time of *Four Quartets*, Eliot's operations have come to require a suspension of such hostilities. Eliot has no wish, as poet or as citizen, to acquiesce in the merely clichéd, but no longer is the impulse primarily to arm clichés. Something more pacific is now hoped for. Eliot seeks to negotiate. A cliché like 'field of action' is left peacefully to lie fallow; there is no intention of rousing it into being a battlefield, though the battlefields of the English Civil War and of other wars (including the one being waged as Eliot wrote) necessarily put some pressure upon the phrase, especially as the battlefield potentiality of 'field' is paired with the military-action potentiality of 'action'.

First there is the phrase 'love of a country', invoking both the national and the rural in a conviction that the countryside – with its just-mentioned hedgerows – is the only lasting ground of national and patriotic feeling, 'love of a country' being crucially different from 'love of country'. And there follows the phrase 'field of action'.[1] Whereupon the two come to terms:

> Thus, love of a country
> Begins as attachment to our own field of action
> And comes to find that action of little importance
> Though never indifferent.

> ('Little Gidding')

Antagonism to clichés – like the expression of antagonism through clichés – has been succeeded by confidence in their good sense, in their generous common humanity. Donald Davie, who did so much to awaken critical intelligence about the renovating of clichés (in *Purity of Diction in English Verse*), was by the same token the critic who warned against the exacerbated impulse to let no dead metaphor rest in peace; if every dead metaphor had to be resurrected or galvanized, Davie observed, the result would be an intolerable fidget.

In 'Little Gidding', 'love of a country' and 'field of action' propose a composition, a compromise, a making peace. The two phrases play into each other's hands, they do not contend for the upper hand in the way which Eliot now sees as meaning Death:

> There are flood and drouth
> Over the eyes and in the mouth,
> Dead water and dead sand
> Contending for the upper hand.
> The parched eviscerate soil
> Gapes at the vanity of toil,
> Laughs without mirth.

1 – The earliest draft had: 'So love of a country / Begins in love of our own activities' (Gardner, *The Composition of Four Quartets*, p. 198).

> This is the death of earth.
>> ('Little Gidding')

The lines are appalled by the travesty of life which they con-template, with the dead phrase, 'Contending for the upper hand', annulling itself: try to imagine water and sand as each having a hand and these hands contending. It is an ultimate evocation of dearth, as if *dearth* were the crushing of 'death of earth'.

We are being made aware that the organisation of society on the principle of private profit, as well as public destruction, is leading both to the deformation of humanity by unregulated industrialism, and to the exhaustion of natural resources, and that a good deal of our material progress is a progress for which succeeding generations may have to pay dearly. I need only mention, as an instance now very much before the public eye, the results of 'soil-erosion' – the exploitation of the earth, on a vast scale for two generations, for commercial profit: immediate benefits leading to dearth and desert.[1]

The exploitation of the earth leading to dearth and desert: 'Dead water and dead sand'; 'This is the death of earth.' The judge-ment is itself 'on a vast scale', and in being so it is something quite other than prejudice.

The compacted obduracy of these lines from 'Little Gidding' avails itself of cliché but finds no pleasurable glint in the fact. This is not the dryness of a delectably dry wit but of drouth, which 'laughs without mirth'. It constitutes a warning not to sentimentalize the Eliot of *Four Quartets*, or to suppose that his only way with clichés is now to be relaxed about them. Yet such relaxation prospers. There is, for instance, a very strange and entirely unsardonic humour about the way in which the opening of 'Burnt Norton' pits the abstract against the concrete. The word 'abstraction' and the word 'concrete' are both openly put before us. 'Abstraction' here:

> What might have been is an abstraction
> Remaining a perpetual possibility
> Only in a world of speculation.

1 – *The Idea of a Christian Society*, p. 61.

'Concrete' here:

> So we moved, and they, in a formal pattern,
> Along the empty alley, into the box circle,
> To look down into the drained pool.
> Dry the pool, dry concrete, brown edged,

Nothing could better bring out the difference between the abstract and the concrete than to have the abstract noun 'abstraction' in the vicinity of the most indisputably concrete sense of 'concrete'.[1] But what is scarcely less remarkable is Eliot's having been so good-natured in his dealings as to remove all possibility of strife from this opposition. The contrast might be with the way in which Dr Leavis's pugnacious insistence on the 'concrete' was countered by his critics; there was F. W. Bateson's roguish question, 'What could be more abstract than Leavis's use of the word "concrete"?', and there was Davie's impish question:

I have been puzzled by Dr. Leavis' description of Johnson as 'weighty'. Not that I would disagree; but I cannot decide whether the critic is aware of his own puns. For instance, he quotes:

> 'For why did Wolsey near the steeps of fate,
> On weak foundations raise th' enormous weight?'

And I find something comical in the comment: 'The effect of that is massive; the images are both generalized, and unevadably concrete'. Must I think that Dr. Leavis is being impish?[2]

Eliot's new reconciliatory ways with diction are at one with his allusive practice. Early Eliot would convey by sabotage that there was a war on: adopting Oliver Goldsmith's line 'When lovely woman stoops to folly' and then undoing it by adding the innocuous little word 'and':

> When lovely woman stoops to folly and
> Paces about her room again, alone,

1 – On 'the abstract style in criticism': 'The confused distinction which exists in most heads between "abstract" and "concrete" is due not so much to a manifest fact of the existence of two types of mind, an abstract and a concrete, as to the existence of another type of mind, the verbal, or philosophic' (*The Sacred Wood*, p. 8).
2 – *Purity of Diction in English Verse* (1952), p. 38.

> She smoothes her hair with automatic hand,
> And puts a record on the gramophone.
>
> (*The Waste Land*)

In 'Little Gidding', Eliot takes up one aspect of this same device, of *and* at the end of the line, involving a quotation; but the effect now is not of doubt but of blessed indubitability:

> Sin is Behovely, but
> All shall be well, and
> All manner of thing shall be well.

The quotation from Dame Julian of Norwich is saved from complacency by the tentativeness, the tremulousness even (though within this sheer faith), in the *but* and the *and* at the ends of the lines. What had been in *The Waste Land* an act of hostility, demanding surrender from the enemy, has become an act of self-surrender. But it is not to sin that the self surrenders itself here, only to sin's inescapability.

There had once been the contemptuous haling-in of second-rate Tennyson: Eliot came together with Tennyson ('They were together, and she fell') so that Tennyson might fall ('They were together, and he fell'). But now when Tennyson is admitted to the poems, it is the great Tennyson: *In Memoriam* VII, for instance, which Eliot quoted in full and praised to the full in his essay:

> He is not here; but far away
> The noise of life begins again,
> And ghastly through the drizzling rain
> On the bald street breaks the blank day.

>   *

> The day was breaking. In the disfigured street
> He left me, with a kind of valediction,
> And faded on the blowing of the horn.
>
> ('Little Gidding')

Unlike a great deal of allusion (allusion is always needing to rise above envy, converting gall to manna), this in no way disfigures Tennyson; what we hear is no kind of malediction. There are, too, the lines in 'The Dry Salvages' which re-engage with *In Memoriam*'s contemplation of death by water. Eliot ends 'The Dry Salvages' IV:

> Also pray for those who were in ships, and
> Ended their voyage on the sand, in the sea's lips
> Or in the dark throat which will not reject them
> Or wherever cannot reach them the sound of the sea bell's
> Perpetual angelus.

This starts from the prayer of the *In Memoriam* stanza, *a b b a* or *abba*, a form within which on one occasion Tennyson himself had enfolded – in the second couplet – a poignant reprise:

> And bless thee, for thy lips are bland,
>   And bright the friendship of thine eye;
>   *And* in my thoughts with scarce a *sigh*
> *I* take the pressure of thine *hand*.

> (CXIX)

Eliot re-created the 'perpetual angelus' of the *In Memoriam* stanza in those first two lines:

> Also pray for those who were in ships, and
> Ended their voyage on the sand, in the sea's lips

> Also pray for those who were in ships,
>   And
>   Ended their voyage on the sand,
> In the sea's lips

The remoteness can nevertheless reach them.

>   In that open field
> If you do not come too close, if you do not come too close,
> On a summer midnight, you can hear the music
> Of the weak pipe and the little drum

>   ('East Coker')

'Perhaps, if it is a great play, and you do not try too hard to hear them, you may discern the other voices too.'[1]

Allusion is always a return, and the word 'return' within an allusion will align the use of poetry with the use of memory. Nothing in *Four Quartets* is more of an accomplishment than the return of 'Little Gidding' III in section V. From this:

---

1 – 'The Three Voices of Poetry', *On Poetry and Poets*, p. 102.

> This is the use of memory:
> For liberation – not less of love but expanding
> Of love beyond desire, and so liberation
> From the future as well as the past. Thus, love of a
>   country
> Begins as attachment to our own field of action
> And comes to find that action of little importance
> Though never indifferent. History may be servitude,
> History may be freedom. See, now they vanish,
> The faces and places, with the self which, as it could,
>   loved them,
> To become renewed, transfigured, in another pattern.

To this:

> We die with the dying:
> See, they depart, and we go with them.
> We are born with the dead:
> See, they return, and bring us with them.

This graced return is not only within the poem but to Ezra Pound, whose poem 'The Return' (1912) Eliot had quoted in his short book on Pound in 1917:

> See, they return; ah, see the tentative
>   Movements, and the slow feet,
>   The trouble in the pace and the uncertain
>   Wavering!
>
> See, they return, one, and by one,
>   With fear, as half-awakened;

'These were the souls of blood': Pound too had become for Eliot one such soul, 'of blood' both as close kin to Eliot and as set against him during this war. In 1942 Pound was not a man of tentative movements, not a man to be moved by uncertain wavering. There is poignancy in Eliot's return to Pound, Eliot during the Second World War musing back to the poem he had celebrated during the Great War; the unsentimentality of the poignancy is in the sense of alienation from what Pound had turned to and now seemed likely never to return from. This sequence from 'Little Gidding' III and V might seem remote from prejudice, but a pitying judgement is being passed upon Pound and his extremity of prejudice there.

> This is the use of memory:
> For liberation – not less of love but expanding
> Of love beyond desire, and so liberation
> From the future as well as the past.

We think of prejudice as enthralling us to the past (to perceive is to read the present in terms of the past to predict and control the future), but Eliot repeatedly warned that this was only a backward half-look, since we suffer 'the enchainment of past and future'. Three passages on the prejudicial pressures of the future show this movement of mind.

Instead of the sophistication of the man [Anatole France] who knows all about the past, who has understood all philosophies and faiths and seen through them, infinitely learned, infinitely 'intelligent' (magic word), and infinitely weary, weary; instead of that kind of humbug he [André Gide] offered us the sophistication of the daring mind, freed from all prejudices and inhibitions (how that word fatigues one!), exploring all possibilities, willing to try anything – the slave, not of the past, but of the future.[1]

More [Paul Elmer More], like Babbitt, seems almost to have been born in a state of emancipation from the prejudices of his time and place. Many people give the appearance of progress by shedding the prejudices and irrational postulates of one generation only to acquire those of the next: by 'keeping up to date'.[2]

But the spectacle of the individual in conflict with the dominant tendencies and prejudices of his time, and consequently that of the individual in conflict with the dominant prejudices and tendencies of the coming time, does not influence critics like Mr. Calverton in favour of the individual.[3]

Plainly the political judgement is important to Eliot; among 'the fundamental beliefs of an intellectual conservatism', he had long ago stipulated 'distrust of the promises of the future and

1 – *The Criterion*, xii (1933), 470.
2 – *Princeton Alumni Weekly*, 5 February 1937.
3 – *The Criterion*, xii (1933), 248, on V. F. Calverton's Marxist study, *The Liberation of American Literature*.

conviction that the future, if there is to be any, must be built upon the wisdom of the past'.[1] Later he deprecated 'the kind of political theory which has arisen in quite modern times': 'It too often inculcates a belief in a future inflexibly determined and at the same time in a future which we are wholly free to shape as we like.'[2] Yet Eliot's point is not limited to the political application or to the times when, as he drily put it, revolution is in vogue. It is a larger insight, that there is a time-warp by which the future too can impose its prejudices.

> And right action is freedom
> From past and future also.

('The Dry Salvages')

This is the use of memory, and of Eliot's return upon prejudice: that it can bring

> liberation
> From the future as well as the past.

Disowning the past is one way of failing to be liberated from it. Moreover, Eliot knew that there were things that had been well done, and done to others' good, which he had been right to take for exercise of virtue. Yet even these good things stood in need of some forgiveness, since, being human, they were not perfect.

> These things have served their purpose: let them be.
> So with your own, and pray they be forgiven
> By others, as I pray you to forgive
> Both bad and good.

('Little Gidding')

'Morning at the Window' (1916) was and is a good poem, never to be rendered obsolete by Eliot's development, yet two of its patternings, one metrical, the other syntactical, were to be made new by Eliot in acts of what was self-knowledge.

---

1 – *New Statesman*, 24 June 1916 (of Paul Elmer More). The point is one of many which distinguish intellectual conservatism from fascism.
2 – *Notes towards the Definition of Culture*, pp. 88–9.

Morning at the Window

They are rattling breakfast plates in basement kitchens,
And along the trampled edges of the street
I am aware of the damp souls of housemaids
Sprouting despondently at area gates.

The brown waves of fog toss up to me
Twisted faces from the bottom of the street,
And tear from a passer-by with muddy skirts
An aimless smile that hovers in the air
And vanishes along the level of the roofs.

The poem's awareness, as clear as mud, is of potentialities (human, social, and rhythmical) sprouting despondently and then being nipped, even as the potentiality for a relationship between the glazed observer at the window and the violated passer-by from the street is nipped. We cannot tell the sex of the passer-by, for 'muddy skirts' is foggily suggestive and indeterminate (the long coat trailing in the mud, as much men's wear as women's). We cannot tell that an aimless smile is not to be preferred to an aimed or aimful one. But the dampness is not visited upon the housemaids only. The poem, nine lines ending with an alexandrine (complete with the alexandrine's Popeian word 'along'), is a twisted sprouting of a Spenserian stanza, a morning's moment from a day which will never be narrated.

The metrical pattern is set by the first quatrain as a cold friction of alternate feminine endings and masculine endings. And then for the second half of the poem this pattern is itself nipped, in a way that is both unsettling and relieved; masculine endings prevail.

Eliot was aware of the use of memory when in 'Little Gidding' he returned to an urban encounter between strangers at earliest morning. Here, though, Eliot chose to sustain the alternating metrical impulse throughout, yet with an utterly different spirit. The rhythmical and metrical form for the Dantesque section is this alternation of feminine and masculine endings, an inspiration of simple genius:

In the uncertain hour before the morning
  Near the ending of interminable night

263

At the recurrent end of the unending
After the dark dove with the flickering tongue
Had passed below the horizon of his homing
While the dead leaves still rattled on like tin
Over the asphalt where no other sound was
Between three districts whence the smoke arose
I met one walking, loitering and hurried
As if blown towards me like the metal leaves
Before the urban dawn wind unresisting.

Instead of the basement damp, there is an apocalyptic fire-watching. The lines admit the supreme animosities (the dark dove is a bomber, after all, and is both a dove and serpent with its flickering tongue) but they decline to play animosity's war-game.

Eliot felt hard to create this. The Dantesque section – which is the most passionately chastened sequence Eliot ever wrote – is without parallel as an instance of the revelatory power of the manuscripts of *Four Quartets*, revealing not something other than the poem (some sort of secret) but rather how it was that the poem perfected its manifest art. This section, of seventy-two lines, occupies twenty-six pages of Helen Gardner's book on *The Composition of Four Quartets*, and might occupy patient attention for years. The first of the typed drafts of the opening sentence had been:

At the uncertain hour before daybreak
Toward the ending of interminable night
At the incredible end of the unending
After the dark dove with the flickering tongue
Had made his incomprehensible descension
While the dead leaves still rattled on like tin
Over the asphalte where no other sound was
Between three angles whence the smoke arose
I met one walking, loitering and hurried
As if blown towards me like the metal leaves
Before the urban dawn wind unresisting.[1]

1 – *The Composition of Four Quartets*, p. 172.

One interest here is the evidence of how it was that Eliot hoped to let his alternating rhythm (a swell and a forbearance) be felt. For one striking thing about the draft is that here only the third and the last line end with what is our most common, the most naturally impinging, feminine ending: *-ing*.[1] Eliot's achievement is to incorporate immediately an undidactic and tacit assistance as to how we should hear his lines, and one crucial thing about the final text is the way, at once discreet and unignorable, in which the first, third and fifth of the opening lines now all end in *-ing*. But Eliot does not have all three of the endings be the easy participial *-ing*. Nor does he let the odd lines monopolize the *-ing*: the even lines, the second and fourth, have their *-ing* endings too, but not as endings ('ending' is not an ending but is within the second line, and 'flickering' is a flickering within the fourth). So it is not an external assignment of *-ing* to the odd lines, but a plaiting, a moving in and out. And it is this plaiting which is completed at the end of this eerie sentence – a sentence itself both 'loitering and hurried' – when the final word which rounds the sentence is found to be 'unresisting':

Before the urban dawn wind unresisting.

Eliot, who believed in self-surrender, was not unresisting. *Four Quartets* puts up a resistance to one propensity of 'Morning at the Window', in what constitutes another re-appraisal of a pattern in the earlier poem. 'Morning at the Window' had achieved its visionary dreariness through the unflinching monotony of its line-endings, their syntax a grim form of rhyme. The sequence is of prepositional phrases, and the level dismay of the poem is this story told conclusively:

1 – Praising Swinburne's 'mastery of feminine rhymes', A. E. Housman said: 'I will mention one significant detail. The ordinary versifier, if he employs feminine rhymes, makes great use of words ending with *ing*: they are the largest class of these rhymes, and they form his mainstay. Swinburne, so plentiful and ready to hand were his stores, almost disdains this expedient: in all the four hundred and forty lines of *Dolores*, for example, he only twice resorts to it' (*Collected Poems and Selected Prose*, edited by Christopher Ricks, 1988, pp. 286–7).

> in basement kitchens,
> of the street
> of housemaids
> at area gates.
>
> to me
> of the street,
> with muddy skirts
> in the air
> of the roofs.

'Morning at the Window' courts the accusation of prejudice: who is this brooder, to posit 'the damp souls of housemaids'? — and yet could such working living conditions *not* be bad for the soul? And then, twenty-five years later, Eliot re-imagined this same prepositional rhyming in the interests not of one season, of street-strangers and of 'brown waves', but of all four seasons brought home by 'the brown god' who is a river, too, of memory:

> His rhythm was present in the nursery bedroom,
> In the rank ailanthus of the April dooryard,
> In the smell of grapes on the autumn table,
> And the evening circle in the winter gaslight.
>
> ('The Dry Salvages')

The fact that in the earliest manuscript 'rank ailanthus' had at first been 'efflorescence' would suggest that part of Eliot's enterprise here is the redeeming of his prejudicial predation in 'Whispers of Immortality':

> The couched Brazilian jaguar
> Compels the scampering marmoset
> With subtle effluence of cat;
> Grishkin has a maisonnette;
>
> The sleek Brazilian jaguar
> Does not in its arboreal gloom
> Distil so rank a feline smell
> As Grishkin in a drawing-room.

266

'Effluence', 'rank', 'smell', and 'drawing-room' have come (via 'efflorescence') to be recollected, in tranquillity this time, as 'the rank ailanthus', 'the smell of grapes' and 'the nursery bedroom'.

The vulgarized foreign ('Grishkin has a maisonnette') had been, as it always will be, a focus for prejudice. In early Eliot, there is a persistent crackle and static of the exasperatedly foreign, whether in names or in words and phrases. But in *Four Quartets* there are only three occurrences of a foreign language and none of them is an irruption. There are the Greek epigraphs to 'Burnt Norton', where Herakleitos presides over the flux with a dignity which might be contrasted with the sardonic Greek within 'Mr. Eliot's Sunday Morning Service'. There is the German word *Erhebung* in 'Burnt Norton' II:

> *Erhebung* without motion, concentration
> Without elimination, both a new world
> And the old made explicit,

There is no English equivalent to *Erhebung* that one could substitute 'without prejudice' (to use a favourite term of Eliot's prose). 'Elevation of mind or soul': *Erhebung* is not at the expense of Germany in 1936 or then in 1942. Finally, there is a French phrase in 'East Coker' V:

> So here I am, in the middle way, having had twenty years –
> Twenty years largely wasted, the years of *l'entre deux guerres* –
> Trying to learn to use words, and every attempt
> Is a wholly new start, and a different kind of failure
> Because one has only learnt to get the better of words
> For the thing one no longer has to say, or the way in which
> One is no longer disposed to say it.

Needless to say, it is not only words that Eliot has learnt to get the better of, but animus, with the phrase 'get the better of' being itself less aggressive than usual, since words – at their best – will furnish something better than the animus or consciousness of their creator. In *The Waste Land*, 'He promised "a new start" ': this promise was heard with sardonic suspicion. In 'East Coker' the poet marks a new start with the old phrase, 'a wholly new start'. Likewise, the French of *l'entre deux guerres* here is entirely without hostility, this being both appropriate to and at odds with the meaning of the phrase. Such a foreign moment asks to be contrasted with the animus once excited by a French word in the mouth of one suspected of pretentiousness: 'Without these friendships – life, what *cauchemar!*' The French there in 'Portrait of a Lady' had been an act not of friendship but of the war between the sexes. It is a way in which the Eliot of *Four Quartets* is no longer disposed to say things.

But the phrase *l'entre deux guerres* is a reminder that if 'between' is of the greatest consequence to Eliot in the 1920s and 1930s, this is not only because of the graph of his poetic or spiritual progress. The sense of being *entre deux guerres* was a political nightmare and a political reality. William Empson's poem 'Just a Smack at Auden' caught this, as did his volume title, *The Gathering Storm* (a title which commended itself to Winston Churchill).

The Waste Land was a poem of the Great War and of its aftermath, that reaping which was also a sowing which would itself reap the whirlwind. 'Gerontion' and 'Coriolan' had not put their faith in the Treaty of Versailles. The phrase *l'entre deux guerres* catches the foreboding of the era, and does so in the language of England's traditional enemy. France, though, is no longer the enemy but the ally, the animosities known to be forgotten though France itself be unforgettable – *Inoubliable France*, in the title of the volume of 1944 for which Eliot provided an introduction. Of these photographs, Eliot wrote:

They will, I hope, help to span the gulf between the France you knew and the France you look forward to knowing, between the thoughts and sentiments and experience of the past and those of the future. So, when we receive a recent photograph, of a friend who has passed through agonies since our last meeting, we may say first "how little changed!" and presently, "Yes, changed, certainly, and I am glad to think that I have changed too; for unless we both change, and change in harmony, how can our affection survive?"

The change within Eliot and within such *betweens* is the redemption of the uneasy interim, the corrupt vacuum, of *l'entre deux guerres*.

Eleven days after the declaration of war in 1939, Eliot had published a letter in the *New English Weekly* on truth and propaganda.[1] He used the phrase *entre deux guerres*, in relation to self-criticism, individual and national. 'We cannot effectively denounce the enemy without understanding him; we cannot understand him unless we understand ourselves, and our own weaknesses and sins.' This entails transcending prejudice and hostility even at the height of hostilities.

The clear formulation of our own aims cannot be arrived at without a deal of hard thinking by our best minds over a considerable period of time. There must be many of our own folk (to say nothing of neutrals) who are visited by the suspicion that this expense of spirit, body and natural resources may only lead to another uneasy interim *entre deux guerres*; there may be many amongst the enemy who are inspired by no worthier ambition than that of reversing the situation of 1918. We have the obligation to reassure the one group, and to undeceive the other.

Those who run the Bureaux of Propaganda necessarily 'have as their job rather the propagation of existing views, than the creation of the valuable views of the future'. Existing views can all too easily be mere prejudices, but the future too, we may remember, can prejudice our thinking. Which means that 'the creation of the valuable views of the future' is the opposite of succumbing to what Eliot had called 'the dominant prejudices and tendencies of the coming time'.[2]

In October 1942, two months before the publication of the last of the *Four Quartets*, Eliot published some reflections on 'Poetry in Wartime':

I am impressed by the number of young British poets whose work has begun to appear during the war; and I am glad that so little of what they write gives an answer to satisfy the sort of people who ask 'where are our war poets?' Some of them, I believe, will turn out – if they survive – to be not poets but prose writers: a short poem is about the only form in which a man on active service has time to express himself. When these poets write about the war, it is mostly about some limited experience, even trivial experience, such as cold, discomfort, or the boredom of waiting at an isolated post. And this is a good thing too, for the bigger experiences need

1 – 14 September 1939.
2 – *The Criterion*, xii (1933), 248.

time, perhaps a long time, before we can make poetry of them. You cannot understand war – with the kind of understanding needed for writing poetry – or any other great experience while you are in the midst of it; you can only record small immediate observations. And when, after the war, the experience has become a part of a man's whole past, it is likely to bear fruit in something very different from what, during time of war, people call 'war poetry'.[1]

Four Quartets is not so much war poetry as between-wars poetry. The experience of living *entre deux guerres* had become a part of this man's whole past, and his whole past had become part of the experience of the war. The month after Eliot published the last of the Quartets, 'Little Gidding', he published 'A Note on War Poetry'. It begins:

> Not the expression of collective emotion
> Imperfectly reflected in the daily papers.

This full stop of Eliot's, two lines into his poem, is final and obdurate; in its repudiation it declines even to perfect a sentence. Eliot wrote letters to the newspapers, and he wrote for the newspapers; nevertheless, they are the one enemy towards which he never relented. *Four Quartets* is moved to no new valuation of them; they could not be devalued further than they had been in the earlier poems, and Eliot was not disposed to speak differently about them. *Prufrock and Other Observations* had allowed newspapers to make appearances in various discreditable lights. As squalid sensationalism:

> Particularly I remark
> An English countess goes upon the stage.
> A Greek was murdered at a Polish dance,
> Another bank defaulter has confessed.
>
> ('Portrait of a Lady')

As literal squalor:

> And now a gusty shower wraps
> The grimy scraps
> Of withered leaves about your feet

1 – *Common Sense*, October 1942, from a radio talk to a Swedish audience.

> And newspapers from vacant lots;
>> ('Preludes')

As ministering to squat complacencies:

> And short square fingers stuffing pipes,
> And evening newspapers, and eyes
> Assured of certain certainties,
>> ('Preludes')

And as genteel beyond words:

> The readers of the *Boston Evening Transcript*
> Sway in the wind like a field of ripe corn.
>> ('The "Boston Evening Transcript" ')

Early Eliot is fed by and feeds this animus; and likewise middle Eliot. The author of *The Waste Land*, for all his initial pleasure in a Dickensian epigraph or title ('He do the Police in different voices'), was not at one with Betty Higden and with Sloppy:

'For I ain't, you must know', said Betty, 'much of a hand at reading writing-hand, though I can read my Bible and most print. And I do love a newspaper. You mightn't think it, but Sloppy is a beautiful reader of a newspaper. He do the Police in different voices.'
>> (*Our Mutual Friend*, Book I, Chapter xvi)

He do loathe a newspaper. Contempt for 'the papers' ('You seen it in the papers'), and for what they inculcate, is lively in *Sweeney Agonistes*, as it had been in the poems accompanying *The Waste Land*:

> They know what they are to feel and what to think,
> They know it with the morning printer's ink
>> ('The Death of the Duchess')[1]

Here nothing was to change: *Four Quartets* reconsidered no previous judgement of Eliot's here, and this is not because the poet had expended all his charity but because newspapers

1 – *The Waste Land: A Facsimile and Transcript*, p. 105.

deserved none. 'Pastimes and drugs, and features of the press' ('The Dry Salvages'): *features* refuses to be mollified there.

The grounds for Eliot's animus are not unexpected or unpersuasive:

It is true that the common newspaper reader no longer consciously asks his paper to provide his opinions for him; but that would be a superior state of consciousness to what actually exists. What the reader allows his paper to do for him is to select what is important and to suppress what is unimportant, to divert his mind with shallow discussions of serious topics, to destroy his wits with murders and weddings and curates' confessions, and to reduce him to a condition in which he is less capable of voting with any discrimination at the smallest municipal election, than if he could neither read nor write.[1]

For the reason why Eliot, when he came to think again about the presence of prejudice in his work, was not moved to think again about the judgement on newspapers is this: that newspapers themselves are the most powerful colluders with prejudice. These manipulations of a reader's unconsciousness constitute another aspect of the pathology of rhetoric, one which regularly prompted Eliot to the word *prejudice*:

It seems doubtful whether a daily or Sunday newspaper, even if it merely *takes the place* of a paper of political opinion, is wholly without influence upon the political behaviour of its readers. It helps, surely, to affirm them as a complacent, prejudiced and unthinking mass, suggestible to head-lines and photographs, ready to be inflamed to enthusiasm or soothed to passivity, perhaps more easily bamboozled than any previous generation upon earth.[2]

Instead of political composure and composition, Eliot was met by 'a compost of newspaper sensations and prejudice'.[3]

The residuum in the public mind is hardly likely to be a distillation of the best and wisest: it is more likely to represent the common prejudices of the majority of editors and reviewers.[4]

1 – *The Criterion*, ix (1930), 184.
2 – *The Criterion*, xvii (1938), 688.
3 – *The Idea of a Christian Society*, p. 19.
4 – *Notes towards the Definition of Culture*, p. 87.

The supreme newspaperly prejudice is the sketching of 'a Hell for the *other people*, the people we read about in the newspapers, not for oneself and one's friends'.[1] In *Four Quartets*, Eliot was able to make friends with many necessities, but he also knew his enemy. Appleplex had mused: 'What we grasp, in that moment of pure observation on which we pride ourselves, is not alien to the principle of classification, but deeper.'[2] The impure observation endemic to newspapers (which like to call themselves things like the *Observer*) is not alien to the principle of classification but shallower. It has no sense of, let alone stomach for, the difficulty of relating the individual to the typical, a task which is the nub of principled prejudication and which unprincipled prejudice neglects.

> Not the expression of collective emotion
> Imperfectly reflected in the daily papers.
> Where is the point at which the merely individual
> Explosion breaks
>
> In the path of an action merely typical
> To create the universal, originate a symbol
> Out of the impact?
>
> ('A Note on War Poetry')

When in 1937 Eliot conceded that 'an ideally unprejudiced person, with an intimate knowledge of Spain' might be able to support decisively one side or other in the civil war, he then incarnated the ideal in Arjuna – and concluded his sentence and his paragraph by personifying the far-from-ideal: 'That balance of mind which a few highly-civilized individuals, such as Arjuna, the hero of the *Bhagavad Gita*, can maintain in action, is difficult for most of us even as observers, and, as I say, is not encouraged by the greater part of the Press.'[3]

1 – *After Strange Gods*, p. 43.
2 – *Little Review*, May 1917.
3 – *The Criterion*, xvi (1937), 289–90. For a discussion of newspapers and periodicals in Eliot as texts and institutions, see Leonard Unger, 'Intertextual Eliot', *Southern Review*, xxi (1985), 1098–1105.

Our curiosity

The opening of 'The Dry Salvages' is foremost an evocation of the river. The otherness of the great river, its being essentially 'untamed' in its alienness from the human, is the tribute which the poem must convincingly pay to a force of nature. 'I do not know much about gods; but I think that the river . . .': whereupon, unexpectedly, the word 'I', which had looked set to practise its canny prosiness for a while yet, altogether disappears from Eliot's sequence of lines. Which is one thing you might know about gods, their power to see that 'I' will be left behind. When, in 'The Aims of Education' (1950), Eliot writes: 'I do not know much about Man, but I am sure that . . .', he proceeds differently, to a paragraph which is properly happy to use the words 'we' and 'I'.[1]

But the force of nature, the river, is a form. So Eliot's lines insinuate a form, perhaps the only poetic one which is widely recognized, one which has long had a way of seeming a form of the past but which unexpectedly bides.

'The Dry Salvages' begins with a sonnet to the river. Rather, with fourteen lines, set apart by a white space though set to flow into where all rivers flow, the ensuing sea. Here are fourteen lines about an enduring power which (like the sonnet itself within literary tradition) can be 'almost forgotten' in the modern world but which can be felt 'waiting, watching and waiting', a 'reminder'. The lines themselves have their reminder of the sonnet (itself 'Useful, untrustworthy, as a conveyor'), there in the off-rhymes which hint an off-form:

> I do not know much about gods; but I think that the river
> Is a strong brown god – sullen, untamed and intractable,
> Patient to some degree, at first recognised as a frontier;

There 'river' sounds as if it may be striking up a relation with 'frontier', sonnet-wise; and 'intractable' will placate 'implacable' at the line-ending five lines later, with 'reminder' following

---

1 – *To Criticize the Critic*, p. 76.

at the end of the next line, itself a reminder of a submerged rhymery with 'river' and 'frontier'. The overt effect owes something to Hopkins's extraordinary distendings of the sonnet form; in due course, Robert Lowell was in turn to owe a debt to Eliot, in the elaborated teasing restlessness of the unrhymed sonnet (Lowell's form in *History*, *For Lizzie and Harriet*, and *The Dolphin*), the unrhymed sonnet which yet plants the occasional inciting rhyme, so that the sonnet becomes positively unrhymed, rhyme-less and rhyme-craving.

After its reminder of the sonnet, 'The Dry Salvages' follows the river down to the sea, with a geological gravity which hints too at the earlier and other creation of Tennyson's re-imagining of the sonnet sequence, *In Memoriam*.

> The river is within us, the sea is all about us;
> The sea is the land's edge also, the granite
> Into which it reaches, the beaches where it tosses
> Its hints of earlier and other creation:
> The starfish, the horseshoe crab, the whale's backbone;
> The pools where it offers to our curiosity
> The more delicate algae and the sea anemone.
> It tosses up our losses, the torn seine,
> The shattered lobsterpot, the broken oar
> And the gear of foreign dead men.

The couplet that culminates in the sea anemone is offered differently to our curiosity, is offered differently in that it is especially our curiosity to which it is offered. For it is a couplet, the first such in 'The Dry Salvages', with 'curiosity' rhyming strongly, albeit curiously, with 'anemone'. The rhyme wavers tentacularly. The couplet possesses, and offers, a transitory self-containedness. Yet the continuity of the pool of the couplet with the larger element which enfolds it ('the sea is all about us') is suggested by the amniotic ambience of the strong internal rhymes, of 'reaches' reaching into 'beaches' and of 'tosses' precipitating 'losses'; so that 'curiosity' and 'anemone' are not cut off from the currents of feeling in the shorescape.

The elemental continuity is brought home, with inching tidal unmistakability, in the further internal rhyming of the second line of the couplet itself, where it is not only that 'anemone' has 'sea' flowing directly into it, but that 'algae', a word which offers to our curiosity many a possibility as to its pronunciation (the sense of sound), is to be pronounced not al/jie but al/ghee. Eliot's voice in the reading is indubitable.

The couplet is not allowed to settle into sub-Augustan fixity or symmetry, since its rhymes are at once binary: 'curiosity' / 'anemone'; and triangulated: 'curiosity' extending to the two half-lines, 'algae' and 'sea anemone'. The couplet is itself like a rock-pool, distinguishable from but not distinct from the encompassing fluidity, its water transitorily independent of and yet enduringly dependent upon the larger waters:

> The pools where it offers to our curiosity
> The more delicate algae and the sea anemone.

The calm seclusion of the pools is won not only by the rhyme but by the syntax, arriving at the more expansive and yet the happily encompassed movement − after 'the granite / Into which it reaches' and 'the beaches where it tosses' − of 'The pools where it offers . . .', two complete lines with a consummated syntax to themselves, independent in punctuation and timing, and yet interdependent with the syntax that issues in them.

It is a cool relief that such a pool is so unNarcissistic; it offers us not ourselves but 'earlier and other creation'. Pure pleasure, this, for the child, and saltily salutary for the adult; a threat to Narcissus only, the non-Saint and the would-be Saint who fascinated Eliot early and late.[1] Of Valéry and what he offers to our curiosity, Eliot wrote: 'It would almost seem that the one object of his curiosity was − himself. He reminds us of Narcissus gazing into the pool, and partakes of the attraction and the mystery of Narcissus, the aloofness and frigidity of that spiritual celibate.'[2]

---

1 − See 'The Death of Saint Narcissus', *Poems Written in Early Youth*, and *The Waste Land: A Facsimile and Transcript*. On Narcissus, Bishop of Jerusalem, see Lyndall Gordon, *Eliot's Early Years*, p. 91. Maud Ellmann analyses the poem as 'Eliot's most fierce yet most ambivalent attack on personality' (*The Poetics of Impersonality*, pp. 62–8).

2 − Introduction to Paul Valéry, *The Art of Poetry* (1958), p. xxiii. Eliot's two preceding sentences are: 'Yet, when we peruse the list of titles of his essays, we find

Six years earlier than 'The Dry Salvages' (1941), Eliot had invoked the sea anemone for *Murder in the Cathedral* (Part II), setting it near the 'ingurgitation' which imagination – whatever else it may live on – lives by. 'I have lain on the floor of the sea and breathed with the breathing of the sea-anemone, swallowed with ingurgitation of the sponge.'

Two years earlier than that, in *The Use of Poetry and the Use of Criticism* (1933), Eliot had brought together the energies of digestion, of reading (read, mark, learn and inwardly digest), and of childhood memory. Marvelling at how much John Livingston Lowes had been able to call up of and from Coleridge's reading, Eliot yet marvelled at there being so much else:

But how much more of memory enters into creation than only our reading! Mr. Lowes has, I think, demonstrated the importance of instinctive and unconscious, as well as deliberate selection. Coleridge's taste, at one period of life, led him first to read voraciously in a certain type of book, and then to select and store up certain kinds of imagery from those books. And I should say that the mind of any poet would be magnetised in its own way, to select automatically, in his reading (from picture papers and cheap novels, indeed, as well as serious books, and least likely from works of an abstract nature, though even these are aliment for some poetic minds) the material – an image, a phrase, a word – which may be of use to him later. And this selection probably runs through the whole of his sensitive life. There might be the experience of a child of ten, a small boy peering through sea-water in a rock-pool, and finding a sea-anemone for the first time: the simple experience (not so simple, for an exceptional child, as it looks) might lie dormant in his mind for twenty years, and re-appear transformed in some verse-context charged with great imaginative pressure.[1]

Imagination and education as digestion: Coleridge's taste is voracious in its search for aliment.

———

a remarkably limited subject matter, with no evidence of omnivorous reading, or of the varied interests of a Coleridge or a Goethe. He returns perpetually to the same insoluble problems.' This makes a further link with the sea anemone couplet; see the quotation from *The Use of Poetry and the Use of Criticism* which follows here on Coleridge, omnivorous reading and digestion, and for Goethe's mind, see *The Athenaeum*, 18 July 1919: 'there was no influence throughout those years which it did not register and absorb. Perhaps minds like his, because of their omnivorous digestion, lack something of intensity and fineness.'

1 – *The Use of Poetry and the Use of Criticism*, pp. 78–9.

Eliot's personal reminiscence of 1933 is quietly astonishing in its nature. For this very instance of the imagination's mysterious power to digest memory is itself evidence of how unexpected, indeed counter to expectation, are the ways of the imagination with memory. The one thing of which Eliot must have felt sure in 1933 will have been that his imagination would never now digest into art this particular memory of the sea anemone, a memory which had been lying dormant in his mind for thirty-five years (he was a man of forty-five, recalling a child of ten) and which was never going to awaken into transformation. 'For twenty years': twenty years had come and long gone. He must have chosen this example because he now knew that it had been not accepted but rejected by his digesting imagination, despite all the unforgettability with which the child of ten had imaginatively digested the sea anemone, itself a haunting image of non-human digestive power. Eliot in 1933 could proffer the example because it was shelved, having never become aliment for poetry, having never reappeared.

For how otherwise would he have been able to say such a thing as '(not so simple, for an exceptional child, as it looks)', or 'charged with great imaginative pressure'? We have only to entertain the idea that this critical reminiscence was uttered eight years *after* rather than eight years before the poem, to see how unspeakable the self-congratulation of the man of letters would be.[1]

The imagination moves in a mysterious way, and eight years after Eliot offered this critical example (which was understood to be personal, indeed, but was free from purring, since Eliot had written no such lines – must have had no intention now of ever writing any such lines), the very process of digestion which he had not anticipated had been brought to pass. For the surrender to prose of the childhood memory proved to be its recovery for poetry. Floating free because of Eliot's having

---

1 – Eliot was risking being too late with the words which he delivered in February 1942: 'there are possibilities of transitions in a poem comparable to the different movements of a symphony or a quartet' ('The Music of Poetry', *On Poetry and Poets*, p. 38); but these words say nothing about 'great imaginative pressure'. *Four Quartets* was not published until 1943 in the US A and 1944 in England.

jettisoned it (the sea 'tosses up our losses'), the experience of a child of ten became the landfall of poetry.[1]

From the poem of 1941 to the criticism of 1933: and then, far nearer the original exceptional child of ten, there is the philosophy student of 1911–16. It was the sea anemone's own intuition of digestion which tentacularly caught Eliot in 1933, gathering to itself Coleridge's 'taste', his reading 'voraciously', his 'aliment'. The sea anemone could reconcile – within that depth of prejudice which is instinct ('instinctive and unconscious') – a power 'to select automatically' with something not at all suggested by the word 'automatically': 'the whole of his sensitive life'. The whole of Eliot's sensitive life, both in the variety of his interests and in the longevity of his convictions, was sustained by such an experience as that of the contemplated sea anemone. The sea anemone is entirely without animosity, and yet is instinctually as much a predator as the tiger who springs in the new year: 'Us he devours'. We can be devoured by curiosity too.

It had been the young philosopher Eliot who, in the Harvard thesis on F. H. Bradley which he completed in 1916, had originally found aliment in the sea anemone for his arguments and his aphorisms:

The idea, and the predication of reality, may exist previous to the articulation of language. It is not true that language is simply a development of our ideas; it is a development of reality as well. The idea is developed from within, as language shows a richness of content and intricacy of connections which it assumes to have been really there, but which are as well an enrichment of the reality grasped. Wherever there is an appreciation of a presentation and a relating of it to the subject's world there is an idea and a judgment: and this is practically universal. The sea-anemone which accepts or rejects a proffered morsel is thereby relating an idea to the sea-anemone's world.[2]

1 – Joan Rutter has pointed out to me that John Livingston Lowes had offered to Eliot's curiosity images which played their part in prompting Eliot's sea anemone memory, for in Book I, Chapter III of *The Road to Xanadu*, Lowes writes of imagination and a memory: 'What I recalled (or thought I had recalled) had been cast in a vividly figurative form – the figure of something germinating and expanding, dimly and occultly, with white and spreading tentacles, like the plant life which sprouts beneath a stone, or burgeons in the obscure depths of a pool.'

2 – *Knowledge and Experience in the Philosophy of F. H. Bradley*, p. 44.

A non-philosopher may wonder whether a budding philosopher is well advised to speak so, but there can be no doubt of the poetic tissue of this, alive to language in relation to thought, and to language as at its finest within literature. 'The idea is developed from within, as language shows a richness of content and intricacy of connections which it assumes to have been really there, but which are as well an enrichment of the reality grasped.' The richness of content here, like the promise of the poetry to come, burgeons from one particular intricacy of connections: to predications and to judgements. This is why the sea anemone, alive with and because of the highest and deepest form of prejudice – instinct or reflex – is so naturally the climax, something more than an image, an instance altogether unforeseen and yet altogether an enrichment of the reality grasped.

'The sea-anemone which accepts or rejects a proffered morsel is thereby relating an idea to the sea-anemone's world': the central terms, *accept or reject*, are crucial to the account which Eliot was to give of the 'unconscious assumptions' which constitute both prejudices and convictions:

'What is Man for?' We may not know what our own answer is, because it may not be fully conscious, and may be wholly unconscious; our answer is not always in our minds, but in the unconscious assumptions upon which we conduct the whole of our lives. The man who has made the definition which you accept or reject, wholly or in part, may be more aware or less aware of the implication of his definition than you are: at the moment when he makes the definition, and at the moment of your reaction to it, probably neither of you is aware of all that is beyond the margin of the field of discourse.[1]

'The sea-anemone which accepts or rejects a proffered morsel is thereby relating an idea to the sea-anemone's world': 'proffered' was to suffer a sea-change into 'offers', with the sea anemone itself becoming the proffered morsel and with our curiosity mirroring in the pools the mysterious stirring of a digestive apprehension:

> The pools where it offers to our curiosity
> The more delicate algae and the sea anemone.

1 – 'The Aims of Education', *To Criticize the Critic*, p. 76.

The relation of the poet's ultimate wording, 'offers', to the philosopher's early 'proffers' incarnates the rebuke which the young philosopher had mildly offered to human hubris: our idea of an *idea* had better recognize that the sea anemone is engaged in a judgement, and that when it accept or rejects a proffered morsel, it 'is thereby relating an idea to the sea-anemone's world'. Again the non-philosopher may be retrospectively anxious for the young Harvard man's career. Eliot's sentences do not appear to be using the word 'idea' as philosophers might be expected to. So much the worse, perhaps, for philosophers. Or perhaps Eliot was thereby relating an idea to his world, and already was aware that the poet is obliged in some ways to be not only non-philosophical but anti-philosophical. 'I believe that for a poet to be also a philosopher he would have to be virtually two men; I cannot think of any example of this thorough schizophrenia, nor can I see anything to be gained by it: the work is better performed inside two skulls than one.'[1]

The genius for conceptual formulation and abstraction, which the greatest philosophers possess, and the genius for transmuting a philosophy into poetry, were in my opinion quite distinct: it would be a miracle, and almost a monstrosity, for the two gifts, to the point of genius, to co-exist within the same mind.[2]

So in due course to our curiosity there was offered this delectable couplet, a proffered morsel which sea anemone readers have related to their world. And been nourished by. Eliot's original attempt at 'The pools where it offers to our curiosity . . .' had been 'The pools where it nourishes for our curiosity . . .' Curiosity is the nub, for curiosity is the creative adversary of prejudice, and when Eliot deprecated the death of curiosity in the novelist Paul Bourget he was moved to speak at once of tolerance, of bias and of judgement:

1 – *The Use of Poetry and the Use of Criticism*, pp. 98–9.
2 – 'Scylla and Charybdis', *Agenda*, xxiii (1985), 13. Also *The Sacred Wood*, p. 162: 'Without doubt, the effort of the philosopher proper, the man who is trying to deal with ideas in themselves, and the effort of the poet, who may be trying to *realize* ideas, cannot be carried on at the same time.'

What has since happened to M. Bourget, in fact, has been the disappearance of the sense of curiosity. Curiosity is suppleness, it is tolerance, it is the source of unbiased judgment as well as of enthusiasm and feeling.[1]

The philosophical account which the young Eliot gave of development is one which he himself lived in his own poetic development; and what he said of the character of a science, and of its likeness to the character of a man, should be said too of a poem and of a lifetime's body of poetry:

Facts are not merely found in the world and laid together like bricks, but every fact has in a sense its place prepared for it before it arrives, and without the implication of a system in which it belongs the fact is not a fact at all. The ideality essential to fact means a particular point of view, and means the exclusion of other aspects of the same point of attention. There is a sense, then, in which any science – natural or social – is *a priori*: in that it satisfies the needs of a particular point of view, a point of view which may be said to be more original than any of the facts that are referred to that science. The development of a science would thus be rather organic than mechanical; there is a fitness of the various facts for each other, with that instinctive selection and exclusion which is a characteristic of human personality at its highest. Thus the character of a science, like the character of a man, may be said to be both already present at the moment of conception, and on the other hand to develop at every moment into something new and unforeseen.[2]

Eliot spent his life in the contemplation of these things and in the making of art from their contemplation. To what end? To give pause. Those who believe that poetry makes nothing happen must concede that giving pause is not nothing. 'It isn't that I need time to make up my mind: I need time in order to know what I really felt at the moment.'[3] This self-understanding is continuous with Eliot's understanding of art and of the nature of intelligence within art, 'intelligence, of which an important function is the discernment of exactly what, and how much, we feel in any given situation'.[4] Much of Eliot's discernment as a poet went to considering not only 'that instinctive

1 – *New Statesman*, 25 August 1917.
2 – *Knowledge and Experience in the Philosophy of F. H. Bradley*, pp. 60–1.
3 – 'What is Minor Poetry?', *On Poetry and Poets*, p. 52.
4 – *The Egoist*, November 1917.

selection and exclusion which is a characteristic of human personality at its highest' but also such instinctive selection and exclusion as is a characteristic of human personality at its lowest.

The worth of poetry is not limited to the imaginative intelligence of such engagements, but Eliot was no aesthete. His poems invite us to judge exactly how much easier it is to attack the prejudices of other people than our own, for the edged reason that 'prejudices are attacked, not with arguments, but with *convictions*'.[1]

Does 'culture' require that we make (what Lawrence never did, and I respect him for it) a deliberate effort to put out of mind all our convictions and passionate beliefs about life when we sit down to read poetry? If so, so much the worse for culture.[2]

1 – *English Review*, liii (1931), 245.
2 – *The Use of Poetry and the Use of Criticism*, p. 97.

ACKNOWLEDGEMENTS

The T. S. Eliot Memorial Lectures (1987) at the University of Kent form part of this book; I am very grateful to Dr Shirley Barlow, Master of Eliot College, and to Faber and Faber. Quotations from letters of T. S. Eliot to J. V. Healy dated 1940 are reprinted with the kind permission of Mrs Valerie Eliot. Extracts from previously unpublished and uncollected sources are reprinted by permission of Mrs Valerie Eliot and Faber and Faber Ltd. © Set Copyrights Ltd 1988. Extracts from *Collected Poems 1909–1962, Selected Essays, After Strange Gods, Notes towards the Definition of Culture, The Idea of a Christian Society, For Lancelot Andrewes, Knowledge and Experience in the Philosophy of F. H. Bradley, On Poetry and Poets, To Criticize the Critic* and *The Use of Poetry and the Use of Criticism* by T. S. Eliot are reprinted with the permission of Faber and Faber Ltd. For permission to include Robert Frost's 'Never Again Would Birds' Song Be The Same', from *The Poetry of Robert Frost* edited by Edward Connery Lathem, I am indebted to Jonathan Cape Ltd and The Estate of Robert Frost; for Roy Fuller's 'Outside the Supermarket', from *New and Collected Poems 1934–1984*, to Secker and Warburg Ltd; C. S. Lewis's letter to Paul Elmer More Copyright © 1988 C. S. Lewis Pte Ltd., reproduced by kind permission of Curtis Brown, London; Peter Viereck's poem (copyright retained by author) first appeared in his poetry book *The First Morning*, NY, Scribners, 1950, out of print, reprinted 1972 by Greenwood Press, 88 Post Rd West, Westport, Conn., 06881, and reprinted with further criticism of Eliot and Pound in Peter Viereck's book *Archer in the Marrow*, W. W. Norton Co., 500 5th Ave, NY NY 10110, 1987. I am grateful to the Harry Ransom Humanities Research Center, at the University of Texas at Austin, and to Princeton University Library.

Faber and Faber Ltd apologize for any errors or omissions in the above list and would be grateful to be notified of any corrections that should be incorporated in the next edition of this volume.

INDEX

The T. S. Eliot Memorial Lectures